writings

electronic mediations

Katherine Hayles
Mark Poster
Samuel Weber
Series Editors

writings

Vilém Flusser

Andreas Ströhl, Editor   **Translated by Erik Eisel**

electronic mediations, volume 6

University of Minnesota Press   Minneapolis / London

The publication of this work was subsidized by a grant from INTER NATIONES, Bonn.

See pages 219–22 for copyright and previous publication information for specific works.

Published by the University of Minnesota Press
111 Third Avenue South, Suite 290
Minneapolis, MN 55401-2520
http://www.upress.umn.edu

Library of Congress Cataloging-in-Publication Data

Flusser, Vilém, 1920–1991
    [Selections. English. 2002]
    Writings / Vilém Flusser ; Andreas Ströhl, editor ; translated by Erik Eisel.
        p.   cm. — (Electronic mediations ; v. 6)
    Includes bibliographical references and index.
    1. Philosophy.   2. Communication—Philosophy.   I. Ströhl, Andreas.
    II. Title.   III. Series.
    B1044.F572 E5 2002
    193—dc21

                                            2001005960

Printed in the United States of America on acid-free paper

The University of Minnesota is an equal-opportunity educator and employer.

12 11 10 09 08 07 06 05 04 03 02   10 9 8 7 6 5 4 3 2 1

Contents

Acknowledgments

Vilém Flusser´s widow Edith Flusser encouraged me to edit this book, and I thank her most of all. I would also like to thank Andreas Müller-Pohle, William Murphy, Mark Poster, Silvia Wagnermaier, Michael Wutz, Siegfried Zielinski, and Jana Vymazalová.

Andreas Ströhl
June 2001

Introduction

Andreas Ströhl

The new is terrifying. Not because it is this way and not another way, but because it is new.[1]

Perhaps we are about to remember again the forgotten celebrating. Perhaps we
are about to find our way back through the strange detour through telematics to
"authentic" being human, which is to say, to celebratory existence for the other,
to purposeless play with others and for others.[2]

Vilém Flusser (1920–91) was a philosopher and writer born in Prague.
He held Brazilian citizenship and wrote most of his work in German.
This volume of essays makes his work available to an American audience for the first time. With one exception, all the essays and lectures are
brief and complete in themselves. Much care went into the selection of
these texts and I feel a great sense of responsibility in writing this Introduction. It is important to present this philosopher in the proper light,
to present as true a picture of him as possible, and to promote genuine
interest in his work. Flusser has already generated considerable interest
in the German-speaking world, and this volume will introduce the wide-
ranging yet subtle oeuvre of this extraordinary, unconventional author
to a wider audience. The University of Minnesota Press is the first American publisher to honor this inspiring thinker with a comprehensive
anthology.

Vilém Flusser divides European intellectuals into two camps. One person sees in him a pessimistic, cynical prognosticator of the decline of our
writing-based culture and, with it, Western civilization as we know it.

Another sees in him the prophet of a new, posthistorical humanism that will rise up from the present environment of media and communication structures.

Flusser himself encouraged both of these views. As a philosopher, media theorist, writer, and journalist, he never wrote in the "academic style" that many might have expected of him. Provocative wordplay, linguistic games using etymology, a language colored by existentialist brushstrokes, and his phenomenological method of questioning both annoyed and confused the academic world.

In addition, Flusser reworded his most important issues in unique ways, producing countless variations of the same arguments. He developed ideas through repetition and, for the most part, with essays in different languages. The concentrated yet often laconic sentences represent new ideas that he himself, as much as his reader or his audience, wanted to hear. Each essay is literally an attempt to philosophize ex nihilo. One thus observes a philosopher thinking, the disadvantage of this method being that Flusser's lectures and writings contain themes that intersect with each other in a more consequential way than is usually the case for other thinkers.

Flusser saw himself as an Old European, especially when he was in Brazil. He often suffered at the hands of academic circles that dismissed him. On a personal level, his success in the 1980s was therefore all the more overwhelming for him. It did not matter that success was at first limited to a relatively small circle of intellectuals, most of whom were artists. Tragically, it would not be until his death in 1991 that a larger audience would know this unconventional thinker. Today, his extraordinary influence on developments in the arts and European media studies is unquestioned. His relevance as a European philosopher is just now being discovered.

For a number of reasons, reaction to Flusser has been ambivalent. Whereas his later work is available only in German—if at all—his early work was published in Portuguese only. Moreover, Flusser's characteristically equivocal means of expression literally fosters misunderstandings. It is not easy to catalogue Flusser within the canon of contemporary media theorists and philosophers. Except for rare points of contact, his texts have less in common with those of Marshall McLuhan or Jean Baudrillard than with those of Edmund Husserl or Martin Buber. Flusser remained an outsider, never becoming part of an accepted history of philosophy.[3] In addition, he never created a complete philosophical system. Instead, he preferred mastering the small form. His essays formulated the same questions in continually new variations. His thematic concerns are woven together like threads, which in the end form a complete network of texts. This method of hesitant questionings and playful appropriations is clearly dialogic. It shapes Flusser's texts to such a degree that it is possible, while reading his work, to believe that one actually hears Flusser's voice or that one is carrying on a conversation with him.

From Old Central Europe to Cyberspace

Vilém Flusser was born May 12, 1920, in Prague, the capital of Czechoslovakia. The unique dynamics of Prague's cultural and intellectual life in the 1920s and 1930s was a result of the productive yet competitive interaction of the three cultures that shaped it: Czech, Jewish, and German. Like the other sons of assimilated Jewish intellectuals, Flusser grew up with Czech and German, becoming equally proficient in both. He acquired a comprehensive humanistic education, which included Latin and Greek as well as a complete introduction to philosophy. The fertile intellectual ground of this unique Central European and Jewish cultural environment would shape his thinking and his personality till the end of his life. When he first emigrated to Brazil, it was a strange and exotic world that presented itself as a vision of the New World. Flusser would remain an Old European in the best sense of the word, despite the strong cultural influences of Brazil.[4]

Flusser hardly ever mentions other thinkers explicitly. Every once in a while, however, we find references to Hannah Arendt, Martin Buber, Edmund Husserl, Franz Kafka, Franz Werfel, and Ludwig Wittgenstein.[5] We occasionally find traces of Thomas Kuhn and Marshall McLuhan. Beyond this, the influence of Albert Einstein and Werner Heisenberg is perceptible.

The greatest influence on his philosophical temperament is his compatriot Edmund Husserl, who was born in 1859 in the Moravian city of Prossnitz (Prostějov) and died in 1938. Like Flusser, he was a German-speaking Czechoslovak Jew. As a philosopher, Husserl is considered the father of phenomenology, which still dominates Central European philosophical thought. Flusser made Husserl's method of phenomenological reduction, which depended on the bracketing of prejudices from reflection on the life-world, into an analytic instrument of his own making. His intellectual debt to Husserl's phenomenology gave Flusser privileged insights and points of view. These, in turn, made him radically different from the popular media theorists of the 1970s and 1980s, who were more oriented toward poststructuralism and Marxism. The phenomenological method enabled Flusser to recognize a certain "apparatus-operator complex" *(Apparat-Operator Komplex)* as the motivating force *(movens)* behind all contemporary social and technological change.

In his *Kommunikologie* (Communicology), Flusser demonstrates the manner in which "the apparatus-operator complex devours texts, to spit them out again as techno-images."[6] Flusser asks how this complex changes our interaction with the world when it transforms texts, such as history, into techno-images, such as television programs, and thus impedes our perception of texts: "If, however, every historical action feeds the apparatus-operator complex, then history literally proceeds toward its end."[7]

"Complex" signifies in this instance that there is no substantial reason for differentiating between the apparatus and the operator of the apparatus. This interpretive position comes from a phenomenological perspective:[8] the apparatus functions only in terms of the function of the operator, just as the operator functions only in terms of the function of the apparatus. Both exist only through their relationship to each other. Each makes the other's existence possible, and each defines the other. Flusser treated this "indivisible oneness"[9] as a "black box":

> It's a matter of drawing up theories and explanations, ideologies and dogmas as images, and that means, not being *procedural,* one-dimensional, linear, but rather wanting to grasp things as *structure,* multidimensional, pictorial; not being *history-minded* about scenes, but rather reflecting about processes in a *phenomenological* manner; not seeing a method in history, to see how scenes could be changed, but rather seeing how a process can be changed, from the outside, from below, from above, which is to say from an extrahistorical perspective. Fundamentally, it's an attempt to codify the world in such a manner that it can be described *cybernetically* in all of its inexplicable complexity and is thus given meaning.[10]

The phenomenological character of Marshall McLuhan's conception of media has perhaps been given too little attention. In this approach, the media become an extension of the body's organs and, thus, a sort of irreplaceable prosthesis.[11] This way of thinking is comparable to Flusser's, in that it bases itself in a reductive method that brackets off all contingencies. In addition, the phenomenological influence is operative in Paul Virilio's thought.[12] Still, McLuhan did not influence Flusser directly. There is no evidence in Flusser's work that other contemporary media theorists influenced him. Perhaps it is an idle question to ask about any evidence of influence. McLuhan and Flusser could have just as simply been led to the same conclusions by following similar logical steps. It is important to recognize, however, that this is Flusser's only point of contact with contemporary media theory. And, even in this case, we can observe Flusser develop his ideas by following the strictest phenomenological methods.[13]

Works in the natural sciences always were at the top of Flusser's extensive reading list, and he was well informed about contemporary developments. A number of hypotheses borrowed from the sphere of natural history are recognizable in his philosophical texts. For instance, he constantly returns to the second law of thermodynamics, according to which the universe tends toward entropy and the unimpeded loss of information. More important, Werner Heisenberg's quantum theories left their imprint on Flusser's pattern of thought, for they are also the basis for Thomas Kuhn's reflections on the paradigm shift in the natural sciences.[14]

Thomas Kuhn's hypothesis of the paradigm shift describes a process in which a quantity of existing problems within one discursive model turns into a qualitatively new model. This hypothesis served repeatedly as a metaphor for Flusser's description of technological revolutions. These revolutions led to new forms of consciousness through the creation of new codes and thus had an immediate impact on the agenda and content of human history:[15]

> In the same manner that the alphabet was directed against pictograms, so digital codes currently direct themselves against letters, to overtake them. In the same manner that a form of thinking based on writing opposed itself to magic and myth (pictorial thinking), so a new form of thinking based on digital codes directs itself against procedural, "progressive" ideologies, to replace them with structural, systems-based, cybernetic modes of thought. . . . This can no longer be thought dialectically, but rather through Kuhn's notion of "paradigm": no more a synthesis of opposites, but rather a sudden, almost incomprehensible leap from one level to another.[16]

Cybernetic thinking links Flusser in a characteristic way to Ludwig Wittgenstein's philosophy in *Tractatus Logico-philosophicus*: "The world is the totality of the facts, not of things. . . . What is the case—a fact—is the existence of states of affairs. A state of affairs (a state of things) is a combination of objects (things)."[17] Relations, not things, are real; dialogues, not the men themselves, are relevant; the Self is a node in an entire network of connections. Flusser juxtaposes the traditional notion of a world that contains "hard" objects and subjects to his own concept in which only the relations between subjects and other subjects are concrete. Man is an interpolation, something like a node in a network of interactions and possibilities.

In a syncretic yet original manner, Flusser relates Husserl, Buber, and Wittgenstein to contemporary theories in the natural sciences to build a unique, posthistorical communications philosophy. Flusser's view of communications and its parameters might at first glance seem scientific and unemotional. However, his analysis of radical cultural changes shows his deep passion for what he called the "project for humanization." In his eyes, Homo sapiens sapiens is far from being perfect, or at the end of his biological, spiritual, cultural, or social development. The final purpose of the human race is a leisurely life of contemplation and celebration, in a society that delegates work to machines and enables its members to live a cheerful life of playful and creative communication. Flusser was interested in the creation of specific communicative and technological conditions for a society of free, independent, and responsible citizens.

In light of Husserl's notion of the life-world as a network of concrete intentionalities, Flusser foresees the coming technological implementation of a telematic culture that will establish a "relationship of mutual respect" *(Anerkennungsverhältnis)* among individuals. In many ways, Flusser radicalized Daniel Bell's thesis concerning the creation of a postindustrial society, but at the same time he removed many of its ideological tendencies.[18] He brings the techniques of phenomenological reduction to bear on the human situation, which, he believes, is in need of technological progress. The "Enlightenment project," aiming for the human emancipation from restrictions of all kinds, begun in the eighteenth century by philosophers such as Locke, Hume, Rousseau, and Kant and an unfinished project to this very day, runs parallel to developments in technology, for all revolutions are technological revolutions, and they help realize the project for humanization:

> A telematized society will be exactly that network of pure relationships that Husserl defines as the concrete structure of the social phenomenon. . . . We can see, then, in what sense it may be said that Husserl has done away with humanism. Instead of the individual man being the supreme value, it is now the dialogue between men that becomes the supreme value, or what Martin Buber, whose thought was profoundly influenced by Husserl, called the "dialogical life" *(das dialogische Leben).*[19]

Martin Buber, a religious scholar and Jewish ethicist, was born in 1878 in Vienna and died in 1965 in Jerusalem. He developed a concept of human existence based on dialogue: "Man becomes I through Thou."[20] The dialogue between men, the "medium of the Thou for all beings," was for Buber a metaphor for the relationship between God and man: "The extended lines of this relationship cut through the eternal Thou. Every individual Thou is a window to Him. . . . The worldly Thou . . . completes itself finally in the direct relationship with the Thou that cannot become It due to its very existence."[21]

Only by carefully reading between the lines does it become clear how Flusser, despite being in complete agreement with Buber, subtly secularizes the transcendental teleology of Buber's thought and unobtrusively empties it of all metaphoricalness:

> I believe that what differentiates our culture from others is the experience of the sacred in man. We can express this in at least two different ways. Either God is experienceable as man, as an Other, who says "Thou" to us and whom we also address in this manner, or man is the only image of God that we possess.[22]

Flusser ostensibly agrees with Buber's existential interpretation of dialogue, and he makes a direct appeal to the Jewish tradition and Buber's transcendental intentions. Meanwhile, he introduces his own subtle reinterpretation:

> Naturally, Buber's book A Dialogical Life should be considered a theological work; it does not speak "of" God, but rather "to" God, and it does this in that it speaks to us. It therefore can be said that the Judeo-Christian tradition breaks through to our present time not as theology, but rather as a search for intrahuman relationships. In this sense, every attempt at defying the loss of one's identity in the massification through discourse should be considered evidence of the Judeo-Christian tradition breaking through the technological surface.[23]

Buber considers all human communication to be always already imperfect. It is only a metaphor for a final communicative act in which God is a partner in dialogue. Flusser, on the other hand, uses the concept "God" as a metaphor for the sacred "in" man communicating with other men, "with the intention of forgetting the meaninglessness and loneliness of a life unto death and, in this manner, making life livable."[24]

In this context, we see Flusser's connection to Franz Kafka:[25]

In my opinion, this is Kafka's message *in nuce*: The pedantic, over-organized, ridiculously incompetent God sick and tired of himself is nothing other than the increasing accumulation of man's reflection on nothingness. The progress of thought, the progress of human existence, is progress in the direction of nothingness. It leads through a hierarchically organized range of experiences of nothingness.[26]

Kafka, the plaintiff who pleaded emotionally in his case against the status quo, was at the same time a prophet who recognized the absurdity of his own undertakings. For these reasons, Flusser recognized in Kafka the threatening older brother. Almost contemporaries, they were both bilingual; they were intellectual, Jewish citizens of Prague; and they were connected by common existential questions that both spent their entire lives writing about. Flusser always speaks of Kafka in emphatic tones, as the

> highly polished but broken crystal of Kafka. In it, the light of Europe is refracted into its Prague spectrum. That is to say, faith and the creative impulse appear with a rationalist aura and thus acquire a devilish glimmer. Or, put differently, the mystically mysterious becomes clear and banal and the quotidian and the taken-for-granted become opaque.[27]

Flusser's media theory is characterized by its soundness and independence, and by the originality with which he uses Husserl's phenomenology. As a technique for analyzing the communication structures that shape society, Husserl's hermeneutic leads to ominous results. This menace is then tied to the hope Buber puts in dialogue. The ambivalence of Flusser's theses is disorienting, and his seeming hesitation between pessimism and optimism is sometimes unsettling to the reader. However, if one puts them in the context of intellectual history, one also sees in them the thoroughness and profundity of his thought.

Flusser became famous because of his speculations concerning a future telematic society. However, the focus of his thought was on a possible dialogue among men and on his analysis of bottomlessness. He posits that existential "uprooting" is a condition of freedom. In comparison to his existential thought, his work in media theory is almost secondary, as though it were nothing more than a discrete insight into the "spiritual condition of the time." Despite Flusser's undeniable contribution to media theory in the second half of the twentieth century, he became a media theorist almost by accident. He developed his original distinction between dialogue and discourse into a communications theory. The application of this theory to society made him seem like a media theorist in most people's eyes: "Communication is possible only when dialogue and discourse balance each other out. If, as we see today, a discursive form dominates, which prevents dialogues from taking place, then society is dangerously close to decomposing into an amorphous crowd."[28] Preventing dialogue more than fostering it, this contemporary imbalance was the result of the overbearing "amphitheatrical" (that is, fascist) structure of discursive mass media and of the equally discursive, pyramidal modern institutions in the public sphere, such as political parties, churches, and bureaucracies. In an amphitheatrical structure, one sender transmits the same message to many addressees.

The basic existential experience of bottomlessness reaffirmed Flusser's belief in dialogue as a possible escape. After analyzing the differences between dialogue and discourse, he developed a system of communication structures, which he called "communicology."[29] Using Husserl's method of phenomenological reduction, he analyzed communication structures that are constitutive of—or have influenced—present society. Moreover, he introduced his own "communicological" analysis of communication structures and everything this analysis implies into his overarching social critique. The principle of "dialogical life," together with the analysis of communication structures and current technological developments, led Flusser to the idea of a utopian, liberated society. In this society to come, humans communicate and philosophize freely in a network that allows communication between all members of that society. This communication structure, called "net dialogue" by Flusser, carries its purpose within itself and is technologically supported by communication channels.

Flusser saw that the discursive forms programming behavior are doing so disproportionately. An anonymous apparatus-operator complex produces these discourses. With the technological support of communication channels that send messages but do not receive them, they rain down on us continually. Dialogues threaten to take on the limited function of synchronization. They now only fine-tune and align information directed from above among its addressees:[30] "The crowd does not dialogue with itself in the classical Greek sense, because it is continually exposed to discourses and therefore it only has control of information which is sent to everyone and everyone receives."[31]

In his book *The Structural Transformation of the Public Sphere,* the influential German sociologist Jürgen Habermas describes the evolution of a "type of opinion that originates . . . from relationships within the group, completely preformulated, flexible in its transmission. . . . The communication processes within this group are under the influence of the mass media, either directly or, which is often the case, relayed by 'opinion leaders.'"[32]

Like Flusser, Habermas is appealing to Hannah Arendt when he describes the ideal form of the communicative act as a "discourse without coercion." Instead of taking this sociological perspective, Flusser takes the tack of an actively engaged participant and thus speaks of "dialogue as a noncoercive relationship of mutual respect." The difference between these two views is not the result of an "unpolitical" stance, which Flusser is sometimes accused of in an effort to contrast him with Habermas's more public "political" stance. Instead, Habermas is simply limiting himself to a linear, more strategic method of argumentation that he inherited from the philosophical tradition of the Enlightenment project. As an outsider, Flusser relegates this Enlightenment "way of thinking" to a paradigm of historical thinking that is on the wane. Of course, both of these thinkers are interested in the function of communication in society. Yet, Habermas is more interested in learning how public opinion came into being, and thus how the public sphere developed. He believes that controversial speech—in his terminology, "discourse"—is the one possible battlefield and legitimate means of redress for potentially conflicting interests in society. In his view, communication means the same thing as reason.

Flusser, on the other hand, believes that dialogue is the purpose of existence. The sense of responsibility inherent in the dialogic relationship between speaker and addressee offers the speaker an opportunity to give his or her own life meaning in the face of entropy and death. For Flusser, dialogue has more a synthetic connotation than a normalizing one. In dialogue, information stored in memory is processed and recalculated into new information. A society of individuals responsible for one another is fashioned out of a net dialogue.

In his *Kommunikologie*, Flusser describes in detail what Habermas only gestures toward, namely, the "spontaneous, unlegislated channels of communication of a public sphere not yet closed off, but rather an 'unorganized' public sphere programmed for discovery and solution providing."[33] Still, both approaches offer a comparable analysis of the status quo: "The communication network between a reasoning public of private lives is torn apart; the public opinion that once came of it has been partly deconstructed within the informal opinions of private lives without public impact and partly concentrated within the formal opinions of the more effective institutions of publicity."[34]

According to Flusser, a meaningless historical rebellion against the supposed motivations of an intentionless machine cannot change this situation. It can only be changed by means of a complete transformation of the technical and material forms of discursive structures into dialogical forms:

> Our dialogues are handled today in such an archaic manner, as before the industrial revolution. Actually, with the exception of the telephone, we dialogue with each other in the same way as those who lived during the Roman age. At the same time, the discourses raining down on us avail themselves of the most recent scientific advances. However, if there is hope in preventing the totalitarian danger of massification through programming discourses, it lies in the possibility of opening up the technological media to dialogue.[35]

Prague Roots

It was not until German National Socialism threatened a young Vilém Flusser that he began seriously asking questions about his own Jewish roots. Despite his interest in the religious and intellectual traditions of Judaism, Flusser dismissed the Zionist movement as well as any movement he considered nationalistic, and he continued to do so later in life. Like his friends, he believed in internationalism. At that time, one was "of course" a Marxist, even if one always knew "that one was a bad Marxist."[36]

In March 1939, German troops occupied Bohemia. Nevertheless, Flusser began studying philosophy at Charles University in Prague. But, that same year, he flew with his future wife, Edith Barth, to London, where he continued his studies. They both emigrated to São Paulo the following year.

Bottomless

Vilém Flusser experienced the collapse of his world as if it were a catastrophe that tore him out of history. This feeling of vertigo and of a complete loss of orientation was not only the key experience of his life, but also the starting point of all his future thoughts and feelings. It became his essence.

The Hitler–Stalin pact of 1939 led to Flusser's complete break with Marxism. After having landed in the completely strange world of Brazil,

Flusser received word of the murder of his parents, his grandparents, and his sister in concentration camps. The world of Prague had died, and his friends were dead: "All of the people to whom I was mysteriously bound in Prague were murdered. All of them. The Jews in gas chambers, the Czechs in the Resistance, the Germans on the Russian front."[37] Flusser experienced the forced separation from his home as a feeling of "bottomlessness," which he describes in his autobiography, *Bodenlos* (Bottomless):

> Even reason forever lost its bottom. One could never rid oneself of the conviction—totally irrational, but appropriate for the times—that "actually" one should have perished in the gas ovens; that from this point on one is leading an "unforeseen" existence; that through emigration one is responsible for separating oneself from one's home, to throw oneself into the yawning abyss of meaninglessness. . . . From this point on one is consuming one's own energy, not the energy that comes from the nurturing earth. . . . A life in bottomlessness had begun.[38]

Prague, a spiritual and physical homeland now lost, was not to be replaced by another. Generally speaking, Flusser turned his back on the notion of homeland:

> Thus the man who analyzes himself recognizes the degree to which his secret rootedness in home has obscured his clear view of the scene. He recognizes not only that every home blinds those involved in its own way, but also that in this sense all homes are equal. Most of all, noncoercive judgments, decisions, and actions become possible only after overcoming this involvement in home.[39]

Later, Flusser accepted bottomlessness as the existential condition and as his existential agenda. His inescapable despair gave rein to an intoxicating sense of freedom: "The changing of the question 'freedom from what?' into the question 'freedom for what?'—this turning of one thing into another, which is characteristic of hard-won freedom—followed me like a *basso continuo* through all my future migrations."[40]

For Flusser "humanization" means overcoming one's own "thrownness" *(Geworfensein)*. It means release from the burdensome ties that bind oneself since birth (family, nation, earth, blood, and soil), to develop through self-determination. It means a conscious choice to enter into new relationships with deliberateness and a sense of duty. Physical distance does not play a role in this process. Telematic techniques, which Flusser calls "proxemics," should make an essentially new intimacy possible:

> It was my birth that threw me into my first homeland, without anyone asking me if this was something I wanted. The chains that bound me there to my neighbors were, for the most part, placed on me. In my now hard-won freedom, it is I who ties the binds that connect me to my neighbors, in cooperation with them. . . . Unlike the one who is left behind and who remains mysteriously chained to his neighbors, I am instead bound to them by my own free will. These ties are not less emotionally and sentimentally charged than his chains, but rather just as strong and more independent.
>
> This, I believe, demonstrates what freedom means.[41]

Project for Brazil

In São Paulo, Flusser continued his study of philosophy in private. He worked mostly in a radio factory, in order to feed the five members of his family, who included one daughter and two sons. He devoted himself fervently to learning Portuguese, to studying the philosophy of language, and the phenomenology of Edmund Husserl. During this time, he was continually plagued by thoughts of suicide.

Flusser was driven by the idea of becoming a Brazilian citizen and of working toward developing Brazilian culture. At the same time, his experience of bottomlessness taught him that an exile existence provided a more human and existential perspective. This tension allowed him to contribute substantially to an ongoing debate concerning speech and reality, on the one hand, and the possibility of creating a Brazilian civilization that would, on the other hand, be based on the idea of nature as a resource to be transformed and informed. This dichotomy showed itself later to be insoluble. It reappeared again and again during Flusser's thirty-year residence in Brazil. In the end, it was the final straw that forced him to make a decision to return to Europe. The "ungrounded," bottomless Brazilian had remained an Old European.

Having been yanked from Prague, burdened as it was by its history, Flusser compared Brazil in the 1940s and 1950s to a blank, unmarked page. The vastness of the page guaranteed the fulfillment of a utopian project for a society both humane and cultured. With a great amount of enthusiasm, as well as a healthy dose of skepticism, Flusser became involved in a project he called "Brazil or the Search for the New Man":[42]

We should formulate a cognitive science of reality and values that unifies all of the physical elements. Otherwise, we will perish in a chaos of incommunicability, of misunderstandings, and of incongruent values. And we should do it because that way it may be possible to discover a more dignified way of life, giving meaning to absurdity while the traditional institutions surrounding us continue their obvious decline. Whipped up by vital necessity, we try to overhaul this legacy regardless of whether it is inside us or outside us. Essentially, we are being challenged to set up a new philosophy. It will be new not because of the questions it asks, but because of its contexts. . . . Would this not be an incomparable achievement in the history of the West? A new culture at the West's horizon, which at the same time synthesizes the West and is the embodiment of Middle Eastern and Far Eastern elements, and everything tempered by an African mood? Wouldn't this kind of achievement be a pivotal moment for the entire West? Wouldn't it be true that the bankrupt West had saved itself at its horizon, where it blossomed once more?[43]

In order to help make this utopian vision come true, to become completely involved in what he referred to as the "project for Brazil," Flusser needed time for reflection as much as he needed an audience. Philosophizing, writing, and publishing would be the means to get it. In 1959, Flusser became a lecturer in philosophy at the University of São Paulo. In the following year, he began publishing regularly in the *Revista Brasiliera de Filosofia*. In the 1960s, he became a columnist for news and culture magazines. In the early 1970s, he published a philosophical essay on a daily basis for the most important newspaper in São Paulo, *Folha de São Paulo,* which played an important role as an opposition newspaper during the military dictatorship.

In 1963, Flusser was named professor of communications studies at the College of Communications and Human Sciences in São Paulo. That same year, his first book appeared. Written in Portuguese, *Lingua e realidade* was the result of a lengthy preoccupation with questions concerning the philosophy of language. The book achieved widespread acclaim and led Miguel Reale to nominate Flusser to the Instituto Brasileira de Filosofia in São Paulo. *Lingua e realidade* gained him the rank of full professor. His next book, *A história do diabo* (The history of the devil), was written in German and published in Portuguese.[44] This book is fascinating, exquisitely written cultural criticism. It attempts to look at the human situation from a fresh, unselfconscious perspective that brackets off all prejudices. This attitude characterizes all of Flusser's writing and casts a new light on the contemporary situation:

> The history of the devil is the history of progress. We could have just as well named our book *Evolution.* Naturally, progress and history are identical: The things that develop are the things that have history. Thus, we see that the devil and progress and history are synonyms. We could also have named our book *The History of History* or *The Devil of the Devil.*[45]

In 1964, the Brazilian army's coup d'état under General Castello Branco was a turning point for Flusser's involvement in the Brazil project. Where once enthusiasm reigned, because everything seemed possible, now his spirits were dampened. From this point on, Flusser mostly dedicated himself to his teaching duties at the philosophy institute of the University of São Paulo, at the Escola de Artes Dramática (dramatic arts school), later at the polytechnic school of the University of São Paulo, and at the new department of communications of the Armando Àlvarez Foundation (FAAP). In response to the increasingly dangerous political situation, Flusser looked to his young students for a sense of hope. During this time, the terrace at Flusser's house became a weekly meeting place for São Paulo's intellectual elite and a sanctuary for the free exchange of ideas during a time of limited freedom of the press and of brutal crackdowns on dissidents.

> I myself was unable ... to understand the state of affairs. For a number of years, I thought it was simply a passing phase and that a more robust culture would come from this transition. That is why in 1967 I accepted a foreign service mission to Europe and America. Because of my own deception about the seriousness of the situation, I hoped to temper the young people's anger by appealing to reason and urging an objective analysis of the state of things. ... It was one of my darkest periods, because I saw that I was being forced to teach something that I considered false.[46]

Slowly, Flusser began leaving his Brazil project behind. Although it was close to his heart, he also knew that it would soon be a failure. He set his sights toward Europe. He started publishing essays in Germany, especially in the journal *Merkur.* Increasingly, Flusser published essays in the influential *Frankfurter Allgemeine Zeitung,* and he undertook lecture tours that brought him to Europe and the United States. After a series of extended vacations in Italy and France, Edith and Vilém Flusser decided in 1972 to establish themselves in southern France. The city of Robion was also in close proximity to Flusser's friend Louis Bec.[47]

The Traveler from Robion

Robion is located near Aix-en-Provence, more than three hundred miles from Paris and equally as far from Germany. Clearly, it was Flusser's intention to seek out a life of contemplation when he moved there in 1973. Removed from the world, the idyllic life of Provence gave him the opportunity to dedicate himself to philosophical research. Both the impression that Brazil left upon him and the influence of his friend Abraham Moles convinced him that an intellectual must take a "disengaged" attitude and remove himself from contemporary history.[48] In fact, he seldom appeared in public and rarely published during the first ten years after his return to Europe. During this period of rest, he was preoccupied with issues concerning migration and the loss of one's homeland. Spurred on by Louis Bec, Flusser became interested in the numerous possibilities and hidden dangers presented by communication technologies, such as the computer and video. His conversations with Bec resulted in a book that was a true collaborative effort.[49] In the meantime, Flusser's instinctual distrust of new technology evolved into what might be called "skeptical euphoria." New media and communication technologies, which were just then making their appearance, promised to free people from their duties to an objective world. Finally, Flusser had found the topic that would later make him famous in the German-speaking world.

In 1983, Andreas Müller-Pohle published an inconspicuous little volume by Flusser titled *Für eine Philosophie der Fotographie (Towards a Philosophy of Photography)* in a small Göttingen press. This would turn out to be Flusser's breakthrough moment.[50] Starting with a philosophical consideration of photography, Flusser goes on to propose a completely new systematization of cultural techniques. The contemporary cultural crisis is analyzed from the various perspectives offered by the technical image—of which photography is representative. First, Flusser describes a paradigm shift in which a two-dimensional, magic-based pictorial culture evolves into a linear, text-based alphabetic culture. Then he demonstrates how the technical images of the posthistorical age truly represent another radical change:

> A philosophy of photography is necessary if we are to lift photography into full consciousness. It is necessary to do this, because photography may then serve as a model for freedom in a post-industrial context. Thus, the task of a philosophy of photography is to show that there is

no room for human freedom in the realm of automated, programmed and programming apparatus; and having shown this, to argue how, despite apparatus, it is possible to create room for freedom. The task of a philosophy of photography is to analyze the possibility of freedom in a world dominated by apparatus; to think about how it is possible to give meaning to human life in the face of the accidental necessity of death. We need such a philosophy because it is the last form of revolution that is still accessible for us.[51]

The success of *Towards a Philosophy of Photography* was immediate. The public recognition that greeted the book in Germany was a surprise to both author and publisher. It would be translated into ten languages during Flusser's lifetime.[52] The German text alone had nine editions. To this day, *Towards a Philosophy of Photography* is Flusser's most read and most influential book. Unfortunately, contemporary reception of the book has missed the mark, owing to its misleading title. The Flusser Archive in Cologne has seventeen reviews, and all of them appeared in photography magazines. In these reviews, Flusser is compared to Walter Benjamin, Marshall McLuhan, Roland Barthes, Pierre Bourdieu, and Susan Sontag. Although all of these theorists of the technical image are investigators of its documentary essence—that is, they question the relationship between the object and its representation—Flusser's mode of questioning begins with a completely different approach. For him, photography is an overcoming of the artificial separation of culture into science, technology, and art. Because photography is founded on the laws of natural science and technical innovations, it successfully reintegrates the image into a linear unfolding of events and narrative of history. Thus, this flood of events can be pushed back. Photography becomes the damming up of history. Technical images freeze events into scenes. Therefore, the photograph counts as the first posthistorical image, especially because of its origins in formal, calculated, unhistorical thought. From the perspective of formal consciousness, the photograph is information selected from a field of virtual pixels with a specific purpose. Photographs are posthistorical because they do not find their origin in a process of abstraction, but go through a process of concretization. They have been studied falsely in terms of techniques of representation. In fact, their structure is one of projection.

Flusser's theory takes up the notion of calculation, of computation, and of projection, whereas theorists of photography have traditionally asked about the "realistic" quality of the photograph, or if there is a universal language of photography.

Nearly every European trade publication for photography has discussed this work. Despite the success of *Towards a Philosophy of Photography*, critics have overlooked the fact that it represents a general analysis of cultural and media techniques, or even that it is a work of cultural anthropology.

The radical manner in which Flusser sets his sights on the structures of communication—instead of on the content of communication, the so-called messages—goes way beyond Marshall McLuhan's differentiation between "hot" and "cold" media. Flusser extracts an entire universe of political and cultural phenomena out of a handful of fundamental communication structures. The most notable example of Flusser's ability to reduce the most complex process to its simplest structure is his historical outline of the evolution of codes inherent in the most important cultural techniques. Starting with the four-dimensional time-space continuum of our life-world, Flusser leads us from the world of three-dimensional sculpture to that of the two-dimensional image and one-dimensional writing, ending with zero-dimensional binary code and its representational form, the pixel. Human communication is a sleight of hand; it is an attempt to overcome the loneliness and meaninglessness of existence in the face of death. In comparison to other natural processes, it is directed against their entropic tendencies.

Two years after the first German edition of *Towards a Philosophy of Photography* in 1983, a sequel appeared. *Ins Universum der technischen Bilder* (Into the universe of technical images) was also published by Müller-Pohle's European Photography. This book reaches beyond the preceding one in three important aspects.

First, Flusser now speaks of "technical images" in general, whereas before he focused on the example of photography alone, causing some misunderstandings. Technical images are meaningful surfaces. Created by programs, they are dependent on the laws of technology and the natural sciences. They do not represent objects; instead, they represent texts, such as ideologies or scientific laws. In the category of technical images, we find photography, film, video, computer graphics, holography, and virtual reality.

Second, the new book sees itself as a predictor of the future to a much greater extent. While discovering futuristic trends already present in contemporary society and interpreting their mostly ambiguous explosive power, the book outlines a utopian society based on telematics and information.

Third, this work gives Flusser an opportunity to concentrate on a thematic problem that truly motivates him. Under the pretext that he is doing media studies, he explores the meaninglessness of human existence in the face of death, as well as the individual activity of creating meaning through dialogue with the Other, supported by the technical implementation of communication structures that allow a net dialogue. The individual can establish a noncoercive relationship of mutual respect. No longer treated as a means to an end, the individual is called to lead a life of self-determination, and in this sacred existence dedicates himself or herself to contemplation, to theoretical reflection, to dialogue, games, and celebration. In a passage that is more transparent than any other in his oeuvre, chapter 18 offers the anthropological core, the summum bonum, of Flusser's philosophy. Titled "Celebrating," this chapter is the one exception to my editorial agenda. Whereas the other essays chosen for this anthology are concise and complete in themselves, this "selected writing" is taken from a rather extended text.

Flusser eventually took on an active traveling schedule. His books and essays made him increasingly famous in the German-speaking world. Slowly, the remoteness of his new home in Robion was becoming a disadvantage. Extended reading tours constantly brought Flusser and his wife to Germany. Numerous essays and reviews appeared in German, Austrian, and Swiss publications.

In 1987, another of Flusser's outstanding books was published. *Die Schrift* (Writing) is a sometimes melancholic, sometimes cheerful farewell to the dominant cultural technique of the historical age. "History" and "criticism" are phenomena that written codes have called into existence. Written letters represent sounds, which in turn represent things. This makes writing a rather complicated code. Now that images are calculable and computable, it is unlikely that writing will remain our paradigmatic cultural technique. It will be detached from the image. These images will be completely different from those that existed before the invention of writing. They represent texts—which in turn represent images and which in turn represent things. In comparison, pretechnical, prehistorical images are directly related to things.

An unmistakable cultural pessimism appears for the first time in Flusser's analysis:

> As we await the end of alphabetic writing as well as its most complete form, the thing that we fear is the decline of reading, that is, critical deciphering. We fear that in the future all communications, especially our models of perception and experience, will be accepted uncritically.

We fear that the information revolution could transform men into un-critical mutant addressees, which is to say robots.[53]

Grieving over the impending loss of humanity will not get us any-where. According to Flusser's way of arguing, we should not think that we could turn back the clock, nor should we want to. Seen from the per-spective of its decline, we might discover that writing was all along a cul-tural burden: "We like to say that once writing is lost, everything is lost for which we are grateful to Homer, to Aristotle, to Goethe. Not to men-tion the Holy Scriptures. Except, how do we actually know that these great writers (including the author of the Holy Scriptures) would not rather have spoken into a tape recorder or have been filmed?"[54]

The spontaneous irreverence with which Flusser attacks sacred cows lends the book an admittedly humorous tone. The freshness of his views functions as a counterbalance to his very serious plea that we incorporate the new into our lives proactively, instead of subjugating ourselves to it through our passivity. We should not waste our energy senselessly on res-cuing a sinking ship.

This book's difficulty—but also its appeal—lies in its self-referentiality. Using the code of writing, Flusser reflects on the material conditions of writing as well as the imminent death of writing that writing itself brings about. Added to this, he reflects on the self-referential character implied in a written analysis of writing:

> That it is indescribable is precisely what is novel in the new. Which is to say that the novelty of the new is precisely that it does not make sense to make sense of it. The Enlightenment has run its course, and there is nothing in the new left to explain. Nothing in the new is opaque. It is transparent like a network. There is nothing behind it. The Enlightenment has come full circle in the new, and it must now begin to enlighten itself. The alphabet is the Enlightenment's code. If we are going to continue writing, then only in order to enlighten the alphabet, to describe writing. Otherwise, there is nothing more to ex-plain or to describe.[55]

Discussions of *Die Schrift* drew parallels to Neil Postman, whose conserva-tive cultural pessimism also met with a receptive audience in the German-speaking world:

> In comparison to the American Neil Postman, Flusser's book does not try to gain any advantages through television-friendly sound bites in its criticism of the media. It testifies . . . to an unsentimental relation-

ship to writing. It is superior in its refusal to conjure up images of a supposed enemy. . . . Postman, on the other hand, resorts to a number of relevant insights concerning a media he reviles, to propagate restorative notions of education. Flusser is very practical in his treatment of the new media.[56]

Flusser's prediction concerning the decline and fall of writing made him famous. It was closely tied to the thesis on the "end of history." Unfortunately, the reviewers also misunderstood this slogan and the manner in which Flusser put it to use. Mostly, his book experienced a sweeping dismissal that was not even disguised as criticism. Nevertheless, he became a "prophet of information technology: . . . a cult figure for high-tech visionaries."[57]

It is perhaps necessary at this point to throw some light on the philosophical history of the expression "end of history." The philosopher who first coined the term, Georg Wilhelm Friedrich Hegel, associated it with the year 1806, during which Napoleon's armies were victorious in the Battle of Jena and Auerstedt. In Hegel's view, Napoleon personified the World Spirit. In his book *The End of History and The Last Man,* Francis Fukuyama alludes to this philosophical tradition when he celebrates the "end of history" as part of a continuous, dynamic process.[58] With the collapse of "real existing socialism," the dualistic world order that fueled this dynamic process has been negated. We have achieved a historic moment of equilibrium, which is the goal or "end" of all history. Liberal, market-oriented democracy has won out over communism.

Even before the publication of Fukuyama's book, Flusser's thesis had already been falsely understood as saying essentially the same thing. By no means did Flusser share the naive view that "nothing more will happen." He was concerned with the a priori of consciousness and the material technologies of culture that interpret every "event" in terms of a "*historical* event":

> It is not as if there were a historical consciousness that could express itself in different codes, writing being one of them. Writing, this linear organization of signs, is what makes historical consciousness possible in the first place. Only after one writes in a line or row is one able to think logically, to calculate, to critique, to do science, to philosophize— and to act accordingly. . . . And the longer one can write one's lines, the more one thinks and acts historically. The gesture of writing calls historical consciousness into the light. More writing strengthens it and makes it more profound. In turn, it makes writing become even

stronger and more entrenched. . . . It is therefore a mistake to believe that there has always been history, because something always took place. Or, to want to believe that writing only preserves what took place. Or, to equate the Historic Age with the period in history during which people preserved events in a written record. This is a mistake, because nothing took place before the invention of writing, everything simply happened. . . . In the Prehistoric Age—this term is significant—nothing could take place, because there was no consciousness that could perceive or interpret "events." . . . Only after the invention of writing and the surfacing of historical consciousness did events become possible. If we speak of prehistorical happenings, then we write history in an untimely fashion and open ourselves up to anachronisms. . . . History is a function of writing and of consciousness, which expresses itself in writing.[59]

Choosing the expression "end of history" was perhaps a misleading provocation on Flusser's part. It unintentionally brought him closer to postmodern thinkers such as Jean Baudrillard or Paul Virilio. What Flusser really intended by using this phrase was the "end of historical consciousness" or the "end of a dominant mode of thought, which is a prerequisite, that all events be interpreted historically."

Along with Jean Baudrillard but also throughout Europe, Flusser's name was associated with the word *posthistory*—or rather, *posthistoire*. Like Baudrillard and Virilio, Flusser tended to use scientific and technical terms in an equivocal manner, sometimes descriptively, often programmatically or provocatively. Whereas Baudrillard formulated the sentence "reality itself . . . has been confused with its own image,"[60] Flusser doubted this was a meaningful pronouncement. He objected that reality and fiction could not be distinguished from each other by a criterion of truth, but only by the criterion of higher or lower probability. Consequently, he dismissed Baudrillard's notion of "simulation." In his opinion, it implied a naive, positivistic notion of reality that was theoretically untenable.

Although Flusser came from a different tradition and point of departure, his books were welcomed in the German-speaking world, together with those of a handful of former structuralists and discourse analysts who worked in media studies and were largely influenced by Flusser's ideas. The most important of these was Friedrich Kittler, a literary theorist preoccupied with the a priori relationship between literature and the material history of writing. Along with Kittler, there were the Kant specialist Norbert Bolz and the sociologist Dietmar Kamper.

Toward the end of the 1980s, Flusser was invited to countless panel discussions, lectures, and think tanks devoted to futurist studies. He and his wife were constantly on the road, and drove their car all across Europe.

On November 25, 1991, Flusser gave a lecture in Prague at the invitation of the Goethe Institute. It would be his first public lecture in the city that he once called home and that he had fled some fifty-two years earlier. He spoke mostly in German and occasionally in Czech, a language he had not spoken for half a century. He surprised his audience with a breathtaking journey through his own philosophical theses as well as many found in the last few thousand years of philosophy. Not only did he quickly abandon his prepared lecture, titled "Change of Paradigms," but he also did not pay much attention to an audience clearly overwhelmed by a technological revolution that had passed them by. Recognizing that they had missed out on the technological progress of the West, the citizens of Prague made their anxiety felt with outbursts such as "We are just now getting used to the telephone!" Vilém Flusser passed his own judgment on a city that "does not kill its children, as Athens did Socrates, but . . . maims and abandons them."[61]

The next day Flusser held one more seminar, sort of a question-and-answer period, in the Goethe Institute in Prague. In the evening, the end of Flusser's stay in Prague was recognized with an opulent and joyful dinner in his honor at the home of the institute's director. The following day, November 27, 1991, Edith and Vilém Flusser set off at daybreak to travel back to Germany. Their sedan had not even reached the border when it hit a truck standing on a country road near Bor u Tachova. Owing to weather conditions, the stranded truck was almost invisible. Edith was barely hurt. Vilém Flusser was immediately killed.

Post Scriptum

Flusser was laid to rest in the New Jewish Cemetery in Prague na Olšanech, not far from the grave of Franz Kafka. Several obituaries appeared in Czechoslovakia, and especially in Germany. Flusser had finally reached a larger circle of readers. The two most important German news journals, *Der Spiegel* and *Die Zeit,* had already produced extensive, flattering portraits, ensuring Flusser a high degree of fame (Schmidt-Klingenberg 1989; Müller 1991, respectively). But, posthumously, Flusser became a guru for the postmodern zeitgeist. Journals dedicated special issues to him. The publisher Stefan Bollmann began an ambitious publication project. He planned on bringing out a fourteen-volume edition of collected writings.

Unfortunately, Bollmann went bankrupt under dubious circumstances, and only five volumes appeared. One year after Flusser's death, a series of International Flusser Symposia was established in Prague. Since then, they have taken place each year in a different city.

To this day, many Flusser texts remain unpublished. Those that have been published represent an oeuvre in splinters, spread across many different publishers. Many of these books are out of print. Meanwhile, translations of his work represent the largest deficit. The German texts have not appeared in Portuguese, and only a few of the Portuguese texts are now in German. Very little exists in French. The present volume is the first anthology in English. Nothing else has been published, except for a translation of *Towards a Philosophy of Photography* that appeared in Germany in 1984 and only in 2000 in England, and a few other scattered translations, such as *The Shape of Things: A Philosophy of Design*.[62] On top of this, the editorial policies of the Bollmann press have aggravated the distribution of Flusser texts by categorizing them as "media studies," without recognizing Flusser's stature as a philosopher. Apparently, the branding and marketing of Flusser as "prophet of the media world" increased name recognition, as well as sales, but it did little to present a truer image of him as a phenomenologically oriented media philosopher.

At the end of 1998, the renowned Academy of Media Arts in Cologne, under the directorship of a media historian, Siegfried Zielinski, took over the Flusser Archive from Edith Flusser, who had organized it up to that time. Now the archive categorizes and collects all of Flusser's unpublished works, manuscripts, correspondence, and books, as well as any secondary literature that has been published. The archive is involved in both editorial projects and philosophical research. Several dissertations and postdoctoral theses have already been or are at present being dedicated to Flusser's work.

The Text Selection in This Volume

The following essays and lectures by Vilém Flusser are from the years 1963 to 1991. Although a retrospective of works that spans nearly three decades should perhaps follow a certain chronology, I have decided to group these selections around specific motifs. I readily admit that the selection and arrangement of texts reflect a definite agenda. Still, in order to preserve the universality and originality of these texts, they have not been divided into chapters or grouped under thematic headings. This is done in deference to future readers and reviewers of Flusser's work, so that they might have the freedom to form their own opinions. The texts chosen for this anthology are compiled according to the following thematic concerns:

Communications Philosophy and Communicology: "What Is Communication?" "On the Theory of Communication," "Line and Surface," and "The Codified World."

Media Aesthetics and Cultural Techniques: "Criteria—Crisis—Criticism," "Habit: The True Aesthetic Criterion," "Betrayal," "The Future of Writing," and "Images in the New Media."

Paradigm Shift and Bottomlessness: "On the Crisis of Our Models," "Change of Paradigms," "Taking Up Residence in Homelessness," "Exile and Creativity," and "A New Imagination."

Posthistory and Programs: "Mythical, Historical, and Posthistorical Existence," "Photography and History," "A Historiography Revised," "The Vanity of History," and "On the End of History."

Humanism and Responsibility: "Waiting for Kafka," "Orders of Magnitude and Humanism," "Celebrating," "Designing Cities," and "Humanizations."

This anthology ends with two selections written in a self-reflective mode. In "Essays," Flusser justifies his decision to restrict the expression of his thought to the genre of the philosophical essay. "In Search of Meaning (Philosophical Self-portrait)" is the one brief autobiographical sketch that Flusser offers his readers.

Notes

1. Vilém Flusser, "Zurück," in Vilém Flusser, *Nachgeschichten: Essays, Vorträge, Glossen,* ed. Volker Rapsch (Düsseldorf: Bollmann, 1990), 168.

2. Vilém Flusser, *Ins Universum der technischen Bilder,* 3d ed. (Göttingen: European Photography, 1990), 132.

3. The same can be said for the very interesting, yet little-known philosopher and logician Gotthard Günther (1900–1984: *Das Bewußtsein der Maschinen: Eine Metaphysik der Kybernetik* [Baden-Baden und Krefeld: Agis-Verlag, 1957]; *Idee und Grundriß einer nicht aristotelischen Logik: Die Idee und ihre philosophischen Voraussetzungen* [Hamburg: Meiner, 1959]; *Beiträge zur Grundlegung einer operationsfähigen Dialektik,* 3 vols. [Hamburg: Meiner, 1976–80]). I owe the reference to Günther's philosophy of technology to Mario Limbach. Günther's work shows some parallels to Flusser's, especially concerning the overcoming of subject–object split, and the telematic

paradigm shift. The Web site http://www.techno.net/pkl/media/kurtk/ index.htm offers a good introduction into the thought of Günther.

4. See Friedrich Kittler's homage to Flusser as the "messenger from Old Europe, from Central Europe" in Friedrich Kittler, "Flusser zum Abschied," ed. Dieter Bechtloff, *Kunstforum International* 117 (1992): 99. Flusser's close friend, Professor Milton Vargas (b. 1915), would contradict this description. He represents the opposing view, arguing that Flusser was shaped completely by experiences gathered at the Instituto Brasiliera de Filosofia in São Paulo.

5. Hannah Arendt (1906–75), political scientist and philosopher, was a student of Edmund Husserl and Martin Heidegger and is known especially for her studies of totalitarianism. Franz Werfel (1890–1945), German-speaking Expressionist Prague author, was torn between Judaism and Catholicism for his entire life. Ludwig Wittgenstein (1889–1951), Austrian mathematician, logician, and philosopher, threw out the possibility of the construction of systems in favor of philosophy as critique of language.

6. Vilém Flusser, *Kommunikologie, Schriften* 4, ed. Vera Eckstein and Stefan Bollmann (Mannheim: Bollmann, 1996), 151.

7. Ibid., 153.

8. Flusser provides a different emphasis here than is usually the case for Heidegger and Jaspers, who also make use of the method of phenomenological reflection. It is not the relationship between mind and machine that interests him (nowhere does he postulate the existence of "mind"). His is a media-theoretical argument. It does not concern itself with the producing machine, but rather only with the information-processing apparatus. Despite its apparent threat to humanity, technology is mostly an aid to humanization.

9. Flusser, *Kommunikologie,* 150–51.

10. Ibid., 155.

11. Marshall McLuhan (1911–80), Canadian literary critic, was considered the most important representative of a media theory based on anthropology and sociology. His seminal work was *Understanding Media* (1964).

12. Virilio is a French architecture critic and media theorist, born in Paris in 1932. His notion that war is the motor of media and technological developments and the notion that there have been neurophysiological and epistemological effects of speed are some of the theses of his anthropological and philosophical reflections.

13. This can be seen, for example, in the chapter "The Gesture of Photography," in Vilém Flusser, *Gesten: Versuch einer Phänomenologie* (Gestures: toward a phenomenology) (Düsseldorf and Bensheim: Bollmann, 1991), 127–50.

14. Werner Heisenberg, German physicist (1901–76), formulated the famous Heisenberg uncertainty principle, which revolutionized the natural sciences, and eventually philosophical thought. Heisenberg is considered the father of quantum theory. Thomas Kuhn (1922–96), in his book *The Structure of Scientific Revolutions,* explains his scientific model for an explanation of the succession of scientific paradigms. His term *paradigm shift* has become part of everyday language.

15. For example: "The quantum character of the gesture of photography (the fact that it is a 'clara et distincta perceptio') makes its structure into a philosophical gesture, whereas the gesture of film dissolves this structure" (Flusser, *Gesten,* 140).

16. Vilém Flusser, *Die Schrift: Hat Schreiben Zukunft?* (Frankfut am Main: Fischer Taschenbuch Verlag, 1992), 129–32.

17. Ludwig Wittgenstein, *Tractatus Logico-philosophicus* (Frankfurt am Main: Suhrkamp, 1984), 11 (1.1–2.01).

18. Daniel Bell (b. 1919) is an American emeritus professor of sociology (Harvard, Columbia) and journalist. See Daniel Bell, *The Coming of Post-Industrial Society: A Venture in Social Forecasting* (London: Heinemann Educational Books, 1974).

19. Vilém Flusser, "On Edmund Husserl," ed. Lewis Weiner, *Review of the Society for the History of Czechoslovak Jews* 1 (1987): 98–99.

20. Martin Buber, *Ich und Du* (Stuttgart: Philipp Reclam, 1995), 28.

21. Ibid., 71.

22. Vilém Flusser, "Jude sein: Religiöser Aspekt," in *Jude sein: Essays, Briefe, Fiktionen,* ed. Stefan Bollmann and Edith Flusser (Mannheim: Bollmann, 1995), 86.

23. Vilém Flusser, "Dialogische Medien," in *Kommunikologie,* 295.

24. Vilém Flusser, *Kommunikologie,* 16.

25. Franz Kafka (born in Prague in 1883, died near Vienna in 1924) was one of the most important writers of the twentieth century. Like Flusser, he was a member of the German-speaking Jewish minority in Prague.

26. Vilém Flusser, "Warten auf Kafka," in *Jude sein,* 178.

27. Vilém Flusser, "The Glory That Touches the Stars," trans. Elizabeth Wilson and Andreas Ströhl, ed. Michael Wutz, *Wéber Studies: An Interdisciplinary Humanities Journal* 14:1 (winter 1997): 33.

28. Vilém Flusser, "Gespräch, Gerede, Kitsch: Zum Problem des unvollkommenen Informationskonsums," in *Nachgeschichte: Eine korrigierte Geschichtsschreibung,* ed. Stefan Bollmann and Edith Flusser (Bensheim and Düsseldorf: Bollman, 1993), 232.

29. Flusser, *Kommunikologie,* 16–34.

30. "The coimplication of dialogue and discourse in conversation is similar to the 'feedback' in everyday speech between public opinion and political program, such as marketing research, opinion polls, and governmental elections" (Flusser, "Gespräch, Gerede, Kitsch," 234–35).

31. Flusser, "Dialogische Medien," 292.

32. Jürgen Habermas, *Strukturwandel der Öffentlichkeit: Untersuchungen zu einer Kategorie der bürgerlichen Gesellschaft* (Frankfurt am Main: Suhrkamp, 1990), 355. Habermas, born 1929 in Düsseldorf, sociologist and philosopher, was a student of Max Horkheimer and Theodor Adorno (Frankfurt School). "His work in the theory of ethics and communications derives from Max Weber's fight against the worsening of human life through technological change, bureaucratization, and deindividualization. In his defense of the 'project of modernity,' he argues for the institution of noncoercive interactions between men" (*Der Knaur: Universallexikon* [Munich: Lexikographisches Institut, 1991]).

33. Habermas, *Strukturwandel der Öffentlichkeit,* 43.

34. Ibid., 39.

35. Flusser, "Dialogische Medien," 286–87.

36. Vilém Flusser, *Bodenlos: Eine philosophische Autobiographie* (Bensheim and Düsseldorf: Bollmann, 1992), 19.

37. Vilém Flusser, "Wohnung beziehen in der Heimatlosigkeit: Heimat und Heimatlosigkeit—Wohnung und Gewohnheit," in ibid., 252.

38. Flusser, *Bodenlos,* 28.

39. Flusser, "Wohnung beziehen in der Heimatlosigkeit," 251.

40. Ibid., 250.

41. Ibid., 252–53.

42. Thus, the title of an anthology posthumously compiled by Stefan Bollmann and Edith Flusser with Flusser's texts concerning Brazil: Vilém Flusser, *Brasilien oder die Suche nach dem neuen Menschen: Für eine Phänomenologie der Unterentwicklung,* ed. Stefan Bollmann and Edith Flusser (Mannheim: Bollmann, 1994).

43. Vilém Flusser, "Suche nach der neuen Kultur: Brasilien als Modell für die künftige menschliche Gesellschaft," in ibid., 223–28.

44. Vilém Flusser, *A história do diabo* (São Paulo: Livraria Martins Editoria, 1965).

45. Vilém Flusser, *Die Geschichte des Teufels,* ed. Andreas Müller-Pohle (Göttingen: European Photography, 1993), 10.

46. Flusser, *Bodenlos,* 212.

47. Born in 1936, Louis Bec, *zoosystémicien* and president of the Institut

Scientifique de Recherche Paranaturaliste in Marseilles, is a biologist and artist and lives in Sorgues near Avignon.

48. Abraham Moles, 1920–92, was professor of social psychology at the University of Strasbourg.

49. Vilém Flusser and Louis Bec, *Vampyroteuthis infernalis: Eine Abhandlung samt Befund des Institut Scientifique de Recherche Paranaturaliste* (Göttingen: Immatrix Publications, 1987).

50. Vilém Flusser, *Für eine Philosophie der Fotographie* (Göttingen: European Photography, 1983). This book has also been translated into English: *Towards a Philosophy of Photography*, ed. Derek Bennett (Göttingen: European Photography, 1984), republished, with an introduction by Hubertus von Amelunxen, by Reaktion Books (London, 2000). Born in 1951, Andreas Müller-Pohle, German photographer and publisher and editor of the journal *European Photography*, is the one who "discovered" Flusser for Europe and was his first German publisher. Through him, Flusser became well known in the photography trade.

51. Flusser, *Towards a Philosophy of Photography*, 59.

52. Today this work is available in nineteen languages.

53. Flusser, *Die Schrift*. All citations from this work will be from the Frankfurt edition (Frankfurt am Main: Fischer Taschenbuch Verlag, 1992), 70.

54. Ibid., 7.

55. Ibid., 133.

56. Wolfgang Preikschat, "Das Zeitalter der Buchstaben ist am Ende: Vilém Flusser, Prophet der Informationstechnologien," *PS* 256, 32.

57. Ibid., 30.

58. Francis Fukuyama, *The End of History and the Last Man* (New York and Don Mills: Free Press, 1992).

59. Flusser, *Die Schrift*, 11–12.

60. Jean Baudrillard, *Simulations*, trans. Paul Foss, Paul Patton, and Philip Beichtman (New York: Semiotext[e], 1983), 150. Baudrillard, born in 1929, French emeritus professor in sociology, media theorist, writer, and translator, developed an extremely influential theory of simulation in the 1980s.

61. Flusser, "The Glory That Touches the Stars," 33.

62. Vilém Flusser, *The Shape of Things: A Philosophy of Design*, introd. Martin Pawley (London: Reaktion Books, 1999).

writings

What Is Communication?

Human communication is an artificial process. It relies on artistic techniques, on inventions, on tools and instruments, that is, on symbols ordered into codes. People do not make themselves understood through "natural" means. When speaking, "natural" tones do not come out as in a bird's song, and writing is not a "natural" gesture like a dance of bees. Consequently, communications theory is not a natural science, but rather is concerned with the human being's unnatural aspects. It is one of the disciplines that were once called the "human sciences." It is concerned with the human being's unnatural aspects. The American term *humanities* appropriately describes the essence of these disciplines. It underscores that the human being is an unnatural animal.

Only in this sense is it possible to call man a social animal, a *zoon politikon*. If he has not learned to make use of the instrument of communication (i.e., language), he is an idiot (originally: a "private person"). Idiotism, incomplete being-human, shows a lack of art. Of course, there are other "natural" interpersonal relationships (such as between mother and infant, or in sexual intercourse). One can conclude that they are the most original, most fundamental forms of communication. But, they are not characteristic of human communication. Moreover, they have been considerably infected by artistic techniques ("influenced by culture").

People are not always fully conscious of the artificial character of human communication—the fact that man makes himself understood through artistic techniques. After learning a code, we have a tendency to forget its artificiality. If one has learned the code of gestures, then one no longer recognizes that head nodding signifies "yes" only to those who make use of this code. Codes (and the symbols that make them) become second nature, and the codified world in which we live—the world of significant phenomena, such as head nodding, traffic signs, and furniture—makes us forget the world of "first nature" (the signified world). In the last analysis, the purpose of the codified world is to make us forget that it is an artificial texture that imbues our essentially meaningless, insignificant nature with significance according to our needs. The purpose of human communication is to make us forget the meaningless context in which we are completely alone and incommunicado, that is, the world in which we are condemned to solitary confinement and death: the world of "nature."

Human communication is an artistic technique whose intention it is to make us forget the brutal meaninglessness of a life condemned to death. By "nature," man is a solitary animal, because he knows that he will die and that his community will not matter in the hour of his death: everyone must die alone. Moreover, every hour is potentially the hour of death. Certainly, no one can live with the knowledge of this fundamental solitude and meaninglessness. Human communication spins a veil around us in the form of the codified world. This veil is made from science and art, philosophy and religion, and it is spun increasingly denser, so that we forget our solitude and death, including the deaths of others whom we love. In short, man communicates with others. He is a "political animal," not because he is a social animal, but because he is a solitary animal who cannot live in solitude.

Communications theory is concerned with the artificial texture that enables us to forget our solitude, and it is thus a *humanity*. This is not the place to discuss the difference between "nature," on the one hand, and "art" (or "culture" or "mind"), on the other hand. But, the methodological consequence of the determination that communications theory is not a natural science must be addressed. At the end of the nineteenth century, it was generally agreed that the natural sciences explain phenomena, whereas the "human sciences" interpret them. (For instance, a cloud can be explained by pointing to its causes, and a book can be interpreted by pointing to its meaning.) According to this scheme, communications theory is considered to be an interpretive discipline: it is concerned with meanings.

Unfortunately, we lost the naïveté that allowed us to believe that the phenomena themselves require either explanation or interpretation. Clouds can be interpreted (prophets and some psychologists do it), and books can be explained (historical materialists and some psychologists do it). As soon as someone explains a thing, it becomes "nature," and as soon as someone interprets it, it becomes "spirit." According to this scheme, everything would be "art" to a Christian (that is, God's work), and everything would be "nature" (that is, theoretically explicable) to an enlightened philosopher of the eighteenth century. The difference between the natural sciences and the "human sciences" would have little to do with the subject matter. It would be a result of the researcher's attitude.

This, however, has nothing to do with the actual state of things. Certainly, one can "humanize" everything (for instance, read clouds) and "naturalize" everything (for instance, discover a book's original cause). But, one must remember that each of these approaches only uncovers different aspects of the phenomenon in question. Therefore, it makes little sense to speak of the "same phenomenon." An "interpreted" cloud is not the same as the meteorologist's cloud, and an "explicated" book has nothing to do with literature.

If one takes these statements and directs them at the phenomenon of human communication, then one recognizes the methodological problem mentioned earlier. If one tries to explain human communication (for instance, as a development of the communication of mammals, as a consequence of human anatomy, or a particular method of transferring information), as opposed to trying to interpret it (indicating what it means), then one has a different sort of phenomenon in mind. The present essay intends to preserve this distinction. As a result, "communications theory" is understood as an interpretive discipline (for instance, in contrast to "information theory" or "information sciences"), and human communication is seen to be a meaningful phenomenon that must be interpreted.

The artificiality of this phenomenon becomes apparent when viewed from the perspective of interpretation. The artificiality of its methods—the intentional production of codes—is only part of the problem. Human communication is unnatural. In fact, it is perverse, because it wants to store the information it acquires. It is "negatively entropic." One can assume that the transfer of acquired information from one generation to another is an essential aspect of human communication, a general characteristic of humankind: man is an animal that has discovered certain tricks for the purpose of storing acquired information.

These negentropic processes are also in "nature." For example, one way to understand biological development is to recognize the tendency toward ever more complex forms, toward an accumulation of information—as a process that leads to more improbable structures. It can be said that human communication represents, for the time being, a final stage in this process—at least from the perspective of an attempt to explain human communication. Of course, then one would be speaking about a different phenomenon than the one currently under consideration.

When viewed from the perspective of the natural sciences, the storage of information is a process that, so to speak, plays itself out as an epicycle on top of a much larger process toward information loss. Eventually, it is absorbed by the larger process. The oak is more complex than the acorn; but it will eventually become ashes, which is less complex than the acorn. The ant is more structurally complex than the amoeba; but our planet is inching closer to the sun and our entire biological epicycle will eventually be reduced to ashes; and these ashes will be less complex than the amoeba. The epicycles of information storage are improbable, but they are statistically possible. Statistically speaking, however, they must, according to the second law of thermodynamics, lead to what is probable.

If one interprets the negentropic tendency of human communication instead of trying to explain it, then it appears in a different light. In this case, the accumulation of information is not seen as a process that is statistically improbable but possible. Rather, it is seen as a human intention—not as the result of accident and necessity, but of freedom. The storage of acquired information is not an exception to the law of thermodynamics (such as in information sciences), but rather, it is the perverse intention of a human being condemned to death. And, in the following manner:

These two theses make the same assertion: the thesis that human communication is an artistic technique directed against the solitude unto death; and the thesis that human communication is a process directed against the general entropic tendency of nature. The impassive tendency of nature to move toward more probable conditions, toward masses, toward ashes (toward "heat death"), is nothing more than the objective corollary of the subjective experience of our own stupid solitude and condemnation to death. Viewed from an existential perspective (as an attempt to overcome death by enlisting the aid of others) or from a formal perspective (as an attempt to produce and store information), human communication seems to be an attempt to deny nature. This denial is concerned not only with "nature" out there, but also with human "nature."

If one interprets our engagement for communication in this manner, then statistical considerations (and quantifiable ones in general) become insignificant. Then, it is a false question to ask: How likely is it that bricks and mortar shape themselves into a city, and when will they disintegrate into a pile of rubble? The city is built owing to our human intention to give meaning to our meaningless existence unto death. Then again, it it is a meaningless question to ask: How many years does it take monkeys hammering on keyboards to "necessarily" type the *Divine Comedy*. Dante's work should not be explained in terms of its causes, but should be interpreted according to its intentions. Human engagement for the storage of information in opposition to death cannot be measured with the same scales used by the natural scientist. Carbon-dating tests measure the natural time according to the information loss of specific radioactive atoms. However, the artificial time of human freedom ("historical time") cannot be measured by simply turning carbon-dating formulas around, so that they now measure the accumulation of information. The accumulation of information is not the measure of history, but rather, it is the dead waste of a human intention that motivates history in opposition to death. In other words, of freedom.

It is important to remember that there is no contradiction between an interpretive and an explanatory approach to communication, between communication theory and information sciences. A phenomenon is not a "thing in itself," but rather, it is a thing that appears in an observation. It makes little sense to speak about the "same thing" when applying two different methods of observation. Communication viewed from the perspective of information sciences is a different phenomenon than communication viewed from the perspective of this essay. In information sciences, communication is a "natural" process that must be described objectively. In this essay, it is a "perverse" process that must be interpreted objectively. These two horizons will eventually meet: a third perspective will pick up where the two perspectives meet in agreement. Such an undertaking, however, lies beyond the original intention of this essay. Its point of view is "humanistic," for it is concerned with human communication as a phenomenon of freedom.

(1973–74)

On the Theory of Communication

The term *communication* can be defined in a wide and in a strict sense. The wide sense is: a process by which a system is changed by another system. The strict sense is: a process by which a system is changed by another system in such a way that the sum of information is greater at the end of the process than at its beginning. The wide sense thus covers two types of communication: the "natural" one, which is entropic, because it obeys the second law of thermodynamics, and the "cultural" one, which over-compensates entropy. It is true that there are some negentropic natural processes, such as crystallization and biological evolution, but these may be shown to be epiphenomena on the overall natural tendency toward entropy. This essay will consider "cultural" communications only.

The definitions proposed may create the impression that cultural communications succeed, as if by a miracle, in escaping from entropy. This may encourage various idealistic interpretations ("spiritual" communication free of natural determination, "the spirit blows where it wills," and so forth). Of course, this is not the case. Every communication, being a natural phenomenon, is subject to entropy. But cultural communications permit being analyzed from a point of view that shows a negatively entropic structure overimposed on the entropic structure. An example may illustrate this.

A lecture may be considered a natural communication in this way: A system (the public present) is changed by another system (the lecturer). The lecturer is a "sender" (he emits sound waves), the public is a "receiver" (it receives the waves), and the air in the room is a "medium" (it transmits the waves). Now, this is a thermodynamic process, and part of the energy invested in it is degraded into heat. The sum total of information in the room diminishes as the lecture goes on. But the lecture may be considered a cultural communication in this way: The lecturer is a "sender" (he emits words), the public is a "receiver" (it receives the words), and the language is a "medium" (it transmits the words). Seen thus, the lecture is not a thermodynamic process, but is of a different order. The sum total of information in the room increases as the lecture goes on, if seen thus. And this is in fact the reason why it increases information, why it is negentropic.

Two aspects in this are important: The first is that such a negentropy cannot be observed objectively. An observer ignorant of the fact that certain sound waves may be words—for instance, a Martian—can never observe it. To observe it, it is necessary to participate in some way in the cultural medium. Which means that the observation of such negentropy is "intersubjective" (made by participants of the process). This is important, because it suggests that the negentropic tendency of cultural communication (of the "human spirit") is not a phenomenon to be objectively verified.

The second aspect is that, although no objective observation of cultural negentropy is possible, it is still possible to observe it with a rigor that approaches the rigor of the natural sciences. The theory of information can calculate it under certain conditions. This means that intersubjective observation can accept criteria of verification similar to those of objective observation. This is so because the negentropic tendency of cultural communication is the result of codes that can be quantified. In the example, the language in which the lecture is read is such a code. Thus, the analysis of code may become a powerful weapon for the quantification of intersubjective phenomena, be they called mental, cultural, or whatever. In fact, it opens the field for "cultural sciences" in a methodologically acceptable sense of the term.

Codes are symbolic systems, which means that they are composed of elements that represent (substitute) something. Such elements are called "symbols," what they substitute is called their "meaning," and the sum of the symbols composing a code is called "the repertoire of the code." Codes are symbolic systems, which means that they systematize their repertoire of symbols. They order their symbols by rules, and the sum of these rules is called the "structure of the code." Both repertoire and structure are quantifiable. Which means that the total number of possible combinations of symbols within a code can be calculated. This total is called the "competence of the code" and the total meaning of the competence is called the "universe of the code." The universe is therefore anything that a code can mean, and this can be quantified. In other words, it is possible to say exactly what a specific code can mean (for what meaning it is competent), and what it cannot mean (for what meaning it is incompetent). This can be done with all sorts of codes, at least as a thesis. For instance, with languages, scientific codes, artistic codes, ideological codes, the code of dream symbology, and so forth. Thus, the theory of communication, with the methods of the theory of information, may become one of the "sciences of the spirit" in the rigorous, nonpsychological method that the nineteenth-century philosophers imagined.

The ultimate aim of the theory of communication would be to "explain" the negentropic character of cultural communication, to "explain" how man opposes nature. Thus, the theory of communication, like every theory, aims at stepping back from the opposition between man and nature, at "contemplating" human alienation and its consequent praxis, and at explaining that alienation and influencing that praxis. Any theory of communication, like every formal theory—for instance logic, mathematics, the theory of decision, and so on—aims at contemplating that opposition from the point of view of man, not that of nature. This is why it is not, like the natural sciences, objective. But, as in every theory, this ultimate aim tends to disappear over the horizon of attention, as specific problems appear that were unobserved before, or that now appear under a different viewpoint. These problems tend to absorb attention and obstruct the view of the ultimate aim. Probably, this is a good thing. When a new continent is discovered, its rivers and mountains become more interesting than the passage to India originally searched for. The purpose of this essay is to point to some of these rivers and mountains without losing sight of the passage to India altogether. It is therefore no introduction to the theory of communication, but a presentation of some of its problems, with a view of inserting the theory into the general context of present cultural investigations.

The first problem encountered may be called "genetic" and put this way: How do codes originate? This is so, because we know truly only those things of which we know "how they are made." There are codes that seem to furnish a clear answer to the question. For instance, the Morse code, or the various telegraphic codes, or those of formal logic. The answer is this: Certain phenomena (electrical impulses, groups of letters, or typographical signs) *are chosen* to make up the repertoire of the codes. And these phenomena are given deliberate meanings (letters of the alphabet, short sentences of a spoken language, logical concepts). Thus, these phenomena become symbols. Then, rules are established that indicate how to handle the symbols. Those who have learned the meaning of the symbols and the rules to handle them can now use the code as a medium for communication. In short, codes are results of conventions that establish symbols and rules.

But if we try and extend that answer to other codes, we are in trouble. It seems that the codes that serve our communications can be organized, from this point of view, into a sliding series, along which the conventional character seems to become ever more doubtful. The examples chosen are, of course, obvious. Less obvious are the codes of the sciences, such as physics and chemistry, although we still might say that they were established by a convention. But the Latin alphabet, which codifies letters to represent sounds, seems to be a product of historical and geographical accident as much as of convention. And the spoken languages, which codify sounds to represent ideas, do not allow us to imagine who made the convention where or when. And the gestures of dance, which codify gestures to represent sentiments, seem to spring from an inner necessity rather than from convention. And psychosomatic diseases, which can be shown to codify body symptoms to represent psychological phenomena, certainly were not conventionally established. And the symbology of dreams, which is the code by which the unconscious communicates with the conscious, cannot have been established by convention, if this implies a conscious activity. Now, this seems to suggest that the more conventional a code, the more it is artificial, and the less conventional, the more it is natural. But such a statement does not help to solve the problem. One can, of course, say that there are more or less conscious conventions, the Morse code being an example of an extremely conscious convention, and the dream symbology of an extremely unconscious convention. This would help to explain how we participate in a code. The Morse code would demand conscious training. A spoken language would demand more or less conscious learning, but also an "intuition," an unconscious grasp of the language. The code of dreams would demand no learning at all for us to use it. But, curiously enough, it would demand such learning for us to decode it. All this is very unsatisfactory, and the problem is still there.

The second difficulty in saying that codes result from convention is the following one: There are codes that do not seem to have chosen their rules by convention, but in an effort to copy the rules that order the meaning of their symbols. The chemical sentence "$Na + Cl \rightarrow NaCl$" does not seem to obey a conventional rule, but seems to mirror a relation that exists between the meaning of "Na" and the meaning of "Cl." The sentence "John loves Mary" seems to mirror, in its structure, the relationship between the meaning of "John" and the meaning of "Mary." Now, it is said by some that it is this mirroring of rules that makes these sentences "true." And this suggests that codes with conventional rules cannot communicate truth or falsity, but only other types of messages. But the matter is not that easy. We know that the rule of addition that orders the chemical sentence mentioned is not essential to its meaning. There are other chemical codes—for instance, the code of structural chemistry—that can communicate the same meaning without the rule of addition. And we know that the English sentence cited obeys rules, which are completely different from the rules of Chinese, and nonetheless there are Chinese sentences very similar in meaning to "John loves Mary." This aspect of the problem remains unsolved also, and becomes ever more virulent.

There are other difficulties opposed to the conventional explanations of codes, but the most formidable seems to be the following one: If codes are made by convention, how is that convention communicated to the future users of the code? Through the medium of the new code itself? This is not impossible, as the Berlitz method to learn languages without recourse to other languages seems to suggest. But it is difficult to understand. There seems to be a trick to these methods, for instance, the recourse to gesture codes, for the following reason: the convention that establishes a code must be prior to the code both historically and logically. Therefore, it must be stated in a previous code (a "metacode" of the new one). Sometimes, one can show this. The Morse convention was made in English, the chemical convention in the language of "common sense," and the English convention in vulgar Latin, Germanic, and so forth. Sometimes, it is not so easy to show this, but the possibility is open. The convention of the Islamic code must be looked for in Christian and Hellenistic codes, the convention of abstract painting in the code of cubism, and so forth. But sometimes this is very problematic—for instance, looking for the convention of dream symbols in the code of the archetypes. In fact, we are in a dilemma. Either we state that every code has a metacode, which is to state a *reductio ad infinitum,* or we state that some codes have no metacodes, which is to state a *creatio ex nihilo.* This seems to happen, by the way, whenever we look for the "origin" of something. So, the question of how codes are originated seems to allow for no answer. The best way out seems to be to look, in every code, for some sort of convention as a sort of provisional working hypothesis.

But we can abandon the "genetic" attitude in favor of a structural one, which seems to be more fruitful. At least the short history of the theory of communication suggests this. We shall then have to ask questions that ask for the relation between symbol and meaning, and for the relation between the symbols themselves within a code, and finally for the relation between codes.

The relation between symbol and meaning may oscillate between two extremes. On one extreme are codes in which each symbol of the repertoire has a single meaning in the universe, and each meaning in the universe is represented in the code by a single meaning. There is a bi-univocal relation between the code and its universe. Such codes are called "denoting." On the other extreme are codes in which each symbol of the repertoire may have various meanings in the universe, and each meaning in the universe may be represented in the repertoire by various symbols. Such codes are called "connotating." Such extreme cases are rare, an example of the first one being the code of formal logic, and an example of the second one being the code of dream symbology. Most codes are mixed, having in their repertoire both denoting and connotating symbols, and having in their universe both meanings represented by single and by various symbols. Examples of this are the spoken languages.

Now, this might suggest that the more denoting a code is, the more it was established conventionally, and the more connotating it is, the more it is unconscious. Such a view is supported by the scientific codes, which try to eliminate every connotation. Behind such an interpretation is the Cartesian ideal of a "clear and distinct message." But this is not supported by fact. There are highly conventionalized codes, such as the codes of some arts and the codes of commercial and political propaganda, that aim at maximum connotation. The key to the problem must be sought elsewhere.

Denoting codes transmit clear messages about their universes, but they lose many aspects of these universes in that clearness. Connotating codes transmit more "significant" messages (they capture more of their universes), but the messages are muddled. Denoting messages are "closed"; they allow their receivers only one interpretation. Connotating messages are "open"; they open a parameter of interpretation for their receivers. Now, this suggests that in establishing the relation between symbol and meaning, codes aim at certain behavior patterns in their receivers. They aim at denotation consciously, if they were established by conscious convention, or they may aim at connotation and denotation unconsciously, if we suppose that some codes were established by unconscious convention. Now, here is a very important point for the theory of communication: to discover the denoting or connotating character of a code—which might, and usually does, go undercover—is to de-ideologize it.

We can compare connotating and denoting messages, because it is possible, to some extent, to translate from one message to another, to "transcodify" the message. Were it not so, any comparison would be impossible and we would have to say that the denotation or connotation "reflects" the character of the universe meant by the message. The possibility of transcodification shows that one universe may have two or more codes to communicate messages about it, and that in some codes there may be an overlap of universes. They are partly translatable into certain codes, and partly not. And the limitations of translations show that no code refers to all the universes, and no universe is referred to by all codes. The series of universes is not bi-univocally related to the series of codes. Now, this is a disagreeable discovery both for the "realists," who claim that in the last analysis all codes refer to the same universe (to "reality"), and for the "idealists," who claim that every universe is a "projection" of a code. But the complex relationship between codes—some being partially translatable into others, some being totally untranslatable into others, and some being related closely to others, although of completely different structure—is a challenge to the theory of communication. Possibly, some sort of "families of codes" will be discovered in the future. This will not only influence the praxis of translation, but possibly contribute to overcoming ancient ontological quarrels.

The question of how symbols relate to each other within a given code concerns the structure of codes in two totally different ways. In one way, that structure will be regarded as the sum of rules that order the symbols physically within the code. In the other, it will be regarded as the sum of rules that order them logically within the code. Although these two views are interrelated, they must be considered separately.

What sort of physical phenomena are the symbols that make up the repertoires of our codes? The fact is that any sort of physical phenomenon may be established to represent any sort of phenomenon, physical or not. Symbols may be points, or lines, or surfaces, or bodies. Any aspect of a phenomenon—its shape, color, smell, its sound effect—may be thus established. And codes may be composed of a single type of phenomenon, or they may be mixed. In fact, at first sight, this situation seems to be so chaotic that any effort at cataloging it seems hopeless. And without a sketch of a catalog, no disciplined investigation is possible.

But, at second sight, the situation becomes far more simple. Possibly too simple. There might be a great number of existing codes, and an indefinable number of possible codes, but those codes that really do transmit the important messages in our situation are of very few types. In fact, we may distinguish three types: those that codify some visual aspects of phenomena (visual codes), those that codify some sound aspects (auditory codes), and mixed ones (audiovisual codes). The visual codes may be ordered in those that codify points and lines (for instance, alphabets), those that codify bodies and their movements (for instance, architecture and dance). The auditory codes may be ordered in those that codify sound produced by human mouths (for instance, spoken language), and those that codify any other type of sound (for instance, instrumental music and drum codes). And the audiovisual codes may be ordered in those that use traditional methods (for instance, the theater), and those that use advanced methods (for instance, TV).

Such radical, even excessive, simplification seems to show that the present situation is dominated by three codes only: a visual one (the Latin alphabet), an auditory one (spoken language, especially English), and an advanced audiovisual one (television). There are, of course, numerous other codes by which men communicate, advanced ones such as computer codes, traditional ones such as painting, and immemorial ones such as the codes of myth. But the three codes mentioned seem to characterize the present. This explains why so many of the theorists of communication have paid much of their attention to these codes and to allied ones, like posters and advertising. This is good in the sense that the results achieved may be applied to other codes as well. But it is bad in the sense that it tends to narrow the field of attention. The theory of communication should be applied to all codes.

The physical property of symbols influences decisively the structure of the codes. It is influenced more by this than by the criterion of meaning. The structure of a message reflects the physical character of its symbols more than the structure of the universe it communicates. This explains the famous sentence "The medium is the message." We can distinguish, *grosso modo*, three types of structures: those that order the symbols in linear sequences (the diachronical ones); those that order them in surfaces (the plain synchronical ones); and those that order them in space (the tridimensional synchronical ones). Examples of the first type are spoken languages and alphabets; of the second type, Chinese writing and painting; of the third type, theater and architecture. The three types can be combined variously, the structure of TV, for example, being a complex combination of diachronicity and plain synchronicity.

The effect of the structure on the message concerns the problem of translation. Can one translate a book into a film, or a newspaper article into a TV program? The problem is that diachronical messages use a different type of time from synchronical ones. It is no exaggeration to say that we know and experience the world, and that we act in it, within the structures that are imposed on us by the codes that inform us. The theory of communication must analyze this fact, and although the results are so far provisional and spotty, they even now open up unsuspected horizons. They show that our "being-in-the-world" can be changed, if the structure of our codes is changed, and this is important not only for the understanding of our situation, but also for any effort to change it.

A different view is offered if we consider the structure of codes logically. We have to ask now how symbols are ordered within codes formally. Whether there are hierarchies of symbols. A good method to approach the problem is to choose a code that has been thoroughly analyzed by other disciplines (the spoken languages that have been analyzed by formal logic and by linguistics), and to make of it a model for other codes, in order to see where they coincide with the model and where they differ from it.

In Western languages, we can distinguish three types of symbols (words): those that mean phenomena (for instance, substantives), those that mean relations (for instance, verbs), and those that mean rules (for instance, copulas). The languages order these three types of symbols in sequences called "sentences." There are many types of sentences, but they can be reduced to four: those that affirm, those that command, those that exclaim, and those that ask (indicatives, imperatives, exclamations, and questions). The difference between them stems from the difference in ordering the symbols. Questions can be reduced to indicatives, although this is somewhat problematic. Therefore, the structure of Western languages basically allows for the transmission of three types of messages: indication (knowledge, epistemological messages), command (behavior models, ideological messages), and feeling (experience models, aesthetic messages).

Before language is used as a model, some difficulties must be admitted. One has to do with the fact that many sentences order their symbols in disagreement with the structure of the language. Such wrong sentences are nonsense. They convey no message. But it is sometimes hard to find this out, because such sentences may be constructed purposely to convey no message. This may be called "demagoguery," and it possibly represents the greater part of all sentences communicated. Another difficulty concerns the fact that there are mixed sentences, and it is necessary to analyze their epistemological, ideological, and aesthetic aspects, which is often not easy. A third difficulty is that many ideological sentences mask their message epistemologically or aesthetically, and the analysis of this (the de-ideologization) is sometimes almost impossible. And there are other difficulties.

Now this admittedly difficult model must be applied to other codes for comparison, and the results, although provisional, are promising and surprising. In fact, a field is opened by the theory of communication that may give a totally new meaning to the word *criticism*—not only in the arts, although there it is most evident, but also in science. To give only one example: The film code, if it is compared to the language model, allows for criticism of its various messages (the films shown) that finally frees the critic from the barren attitude to give subjective value statements. He is now able, thanks to communicological methods, to analyze the film in the intersubjective exact method offered by the theory of communication. In this field, the theory is already working, although enormous tasks still await it.

It can be shown, thanks to the model, that there are codes eminently destined to transmit epistemological messages (e.g., the scientific ones), others eminently destined for ideological messages (e.g., the codes of the mass media), and others eminently destined for aesthetic messages (e.g., the artistic codes). But *eminently* does not mean *exclusively*, nor *evidently*. The theory of communication must show how much of ideology and aesthetics is masked as knowledge in the sciences, and how much of ideology is masked as aesthetics in the arts. But most of all, the theory of communication must show that the mass media, owing to their structure, transmit only ideology (namely, models of consumer behavior), but that they often mask this message as knowledge (for instance, through newspaper reporting), or aesthetically (for instance, in TV musicals). A systematic analysis of codes may thus become an effective method of de-ideologization.

A third attitude toward codes, after the genetic and the structural, is possible, and may be called, for want of a better term, "dynamic." It will ask the following question: Because communications is a process, and because, therefore, messages "flow" in the codes, what is the dynamic of that process? This transfers attention from the codes themselves to those who use them, to the senders and receivers. The danger of the two previously discussed attitudes is the "reification" of codes. They tend to forget their human function. The third attitude reinserts them into their cultural context, and shows that the theory of communication is a social science.

We may distinguish two types of codes: dialogical ones and discursive ones. To understand this classification, the two dynamics of communication must be considered. In one, messages flow from a sender toward a receiver, and this is called "discourse." In the other, messages oscillate between various participants in the process, and this is called "dialogue." Now, although this distinction cannot be maintained with rigor, because every dialogue can be considered a phase in a wider discourse, and every discourse a phase in a wider dialogue, it is important for the following reason: the function of information is different in each of the types of dynamics. In discourse, information is contained in the memory of the sender and transmitted to the memory of the receiver. Therefore, information precedes the discourse, and discourse serves the purpose of transmitting information from one participant to another participant of a culture. An example of this is a lecture. In dialogue, there is partial information in the memories of the participants that is being synthesized into global information by the process. Therefore, new information results from dialogue, and it serves the purpose of elaborating information for a culture. An example of this is parliamentary debate that elaborates a law. The dynamic of communication is the elaboration of information through dialogue and its transmission through discourse.

At first sight, it seems that there are two types of codes in this sense. Discursive codes (such as painting) and codes that permit both dialogue and discourse (such as the languages). But, at second sight, the situation is seen to be more complex. The painting given as an example of discourse may, for instance, be changed into a dialogical structure, as it is in Chinese scrolls, where comments may be inscribed successively upon the scrolls in a dialogical manner. Now, this is important for the following reason: The mass media seem to have an exclusively discursive structure. They are constructed so that very few senders emit messages toward enormously numerous receivers who are totally incapable of dialoguing with the senders. This is, in fact, what characterizes the present: a discursive culture without dialogical feedback. This means a culture that has a difficult time renewing its stock of information on many levels, because this is renewed by dialogue. A culture in which most participants have no access to the origin of information, therefore, tends to become totalitarian. A culture in which very few emit information, and therefore tend to manipulate society. A culture in which to participate means to receive discourse, and a highly unified discourse, therefore tends to become massified.

The situation may be shown, in this sense, to have the following structure: A small elite of specialists dialogically elaborates information, through codes that are becoming increasingly difficult to learn. This elite tends to divide into mutually incommunicable groups. The information thus elaborated is communicated discursively through almost equally difficult codes to a small number of elite receivers. These discourses have mostly scientific and artistic messages, and ideological messages tend to disappear. A new type of man is created this way—the nonideological functionary, the receiver of these messages. The functionary puts the information received discursively at the disposal of the holders of economic, social, and political power. These holders transmit the information through imperative discourses to functionaries specialized in mass communication. They manipulate the information to give it an ideological meaning and then transmit it discursively through the mass media toward the public. The public has, increasingly, only access to this type of information, which is basically only one: behavior models for the consumption of the material or ideal goods in which the holders of power are interested. It is in this situation that the theory of communication originated, partly as a means of defense of society.

Now, the theory of communication can show that, although mass media are being used almost exclusively for discourse, they could be changed in a way that would allow for dialogue as well. Even now, some dialogical islands seem to be there, for instance, "letters to the editor" in newspapers, and TV programs that ask receivers to call them back. But these islands are, of course, mere pretenses at dialogue, destined to create a false feeling of participation. A radical change in the mass-media structure is perfectly possible, and present techniques allow it. To give only one example: TV can be changed so that it becomes a true "network" (namely, a dialogical code), more or less like the telephone network. Closed circuits and manipulations of magnetoscopes point to this possibility, among other attempts. This would mean that people could dialogue over TV in a complex, both diachronical and plain synchronical, code. This would really change humanity into a global village, not only with idle talk in the cosmic marketplace, but with real participation of great numbers in the elaboration of information. This would be true democracy. And this is only a single example of how the theory of information can work at present.

But, of course, there are enormous difficulties. A practical one, for instance, is that the holders of power must resist such attempts, because they would make it far more difficult for them to manipulate society. A theoretical one is that a situation would come about that is the opposite of the present one. Now there is almost no public space left, namely, a space in which meaningful communication is possible for the participants of the culture. Then there would be almost no private space left, namely, a space into which communication cannot penetrate. An omnipresent dialogue is just as dangerous as an omnipresent discourse. But all this shows a wide field for the future activities of the theory of communication.

At the beginning of this essay, it was said that the ultimate aim of the theory of communication is to "explain" the negentropic character of human communication, an aspect of man in his opposition to the world. And it was said that this ultimate aim tends to be forgotten, as new and fascinating problems are being discovered and attacked. The situation seems to be as follows: Aside from the theory of communication, and in part within it, a purely quantifying discipline, the theory of information, is developing, and it is dedicated to the study of negentropy. The theory of information should be a method of the theory of communication, but it is often being confused with it. The proper theory of communication is leaving the problem of negentropy aside, and is dedicating its attention to other problems, some of which have been mentioned in this essay. But negentropy cannot be ignored, nor left for the theory of information to handle. It is a problem that touches the essence of man (his form-giving essence), and merely quantifying approaches do not grasp it. It is true that, with the help of the theory of information, the theory of communication may achieve a rigor comparable with the natural sciences. But it will never be a natural science, and should not be one. It is, owing to its problematic, and should also be through its methods, a "humanistic" discipline. Therefore, it cannot be, and should not be, a "pure" discipline. It requires a commitment alien to the commitment to natural science. It is more like medicine in this respect. And, as in medicine, there should be, in the theory of communication, no neat distinction between theory and praxis.

But because it is a new discipline, it is very difficult to say whether, when, and how it will solve its internal problems, and whether it will ever evolve a unified method.

(ca. 1986–87)

Line and Surface

Surfaces are becoming ever more important in our surroundings. For instance, TV screens, posters, the pages of illustrated magazines. In the past, these surfaces were rarer. Photographs, paintings, carpets, *vitreaux,* cave paintings surrounded men in the past, but these surfaces did not offer themselves either in the quantity or with the degree of importance of the surfaces that now surround us. Therefore, it was formerly not so urgent as it is today to try to understand the role surfaces play in human life. In the past, there existed another problem of far greater significance: to try to understand what lines meant. Ever since the "invention" of alphabetical writing (that is, ever since Western thought began to articulate itself), written lines surrounded men in a way that demanded explanation. It was clear: these lines meant the three-dimensional world in which we live, act, and suffer. But how did they mean it?

We know the answers that have been given to this question, the most decisive for modern civilization being the Cartesian one. This affirms that lines are discourses of points, and that each point is a symbol of something out there in the world (a "concept"). Therefore, the lines represent the world by projecting it as a series of successions, in the form of a process. Western thought is "historical" in the sense that it conceives the world in lines, therefore as process. It can be no accident that historical feeling was first articulated by the Jews—the people of the book, that is, of linear writing. But let us not exaggerate: only a very few knew how to read and write, and the illiterate masses distrusted (and *pour cause*) the linear historicity of the scribes and clerks who manipulated the civilization. The invention of the printing press vulgarized the alphabet, however, and it may be said that during the last hundred years or so the linear historical consciousness of Western man has formed the climate of our civilization.

This has now ceased to be the case. Written lines, although appearing even more frequently than before, are becoming less important than surfaces to the mass of people. (We need no prophets to tell us that the "one-dimensional man" is disappearing.) Now, what do these surfaces mean? That is the question. Of course, we may say that they mean the world, just as the lines do. But *how* do they mean it? Are they adequate to the world, and if so, how? And do they mean the "same" world that is conveyed by the written lines? The problem is to find out what adequation there is between the surfaces and the world on the one hand, and between the surface and the lines on the other. It is no longer just a question of the adequation of thought to thing, but of thought expressed in surfaces on the one hand, and thought expressed in lines on the other.

There are various difficulties to be encountered in merely stating the problem. One difficulty has to do with the fact that the problem can only be stated by writing it out in lines—in a way, therefore, that begs the question. Another difficulty has to do with the fact that although thought that is expressed in surfaces now predominates in the world, this kind of thought is not quite so much aware of its own structure as is thought expressed in lines. (We do not have a two-dimensional logic comparable in rigor and elaboration to linear Aristotelian logic.) And there are other difficulties that we cannot evade by saying, for instance, that thought expressed in surfaces is "synoptic" or "syncretic." Let us admit the difficulties, but let us try, nonetheless, to think about the problem.

Adequation of "Surface Thought" to "Line Thought"

To begin, we might pose the following question: What is the difference between reading written lines and reading a picture? The answer is apparently quite simple: we follow the text of a line from left to right; we jump from line to line from above to below; we turn the pages from left to right. We look at a picture, instead, by passing our eyes over its surface in pathways vaguely suggested by the structure of the picture. The difference seems to be that in reading lines we follow a structure imposed upon us, whereas in reading pictures we move rather freely within a structure that has been proposed to us.

This is not a very good answer to our question, however. It suggests that both readings are linear (because paths are lines), and that the difference between the two has something to do with freedom. If we think about this more closely, we realize that this is not so. We may in fact read pictures in the way described, but we need not necessarily do so. We may seize the totality of the picture at a glance, so to speak, and then proceed to analyze it by means of the above-mentioned pathways. (And that, as a rule, is what happens.) In fact, this double method—synthesis followed by analysis (a process that may be repeated several times in the course of a single reading)—is what characterizes the reading of pictures. This gives us the following difference between reading written lines and pictures: we must follow the written text if we want to get at its message, but in pictures we may get the message first, and then try to decompose it. And this points to the difference between the one-dimensional line and the two-dimensional surface: the one aims at getting somewhere; the other is there already, but may reveal how it got there. This difference is one of temporality, and involves the present, the past, and the future.

It is obvious that both types of reading involve time—but is it the "same" time? It is so apparently, because we can measure the time involved in both readings in terms of minutes. But this simple fact makes us pause. How can we explain that the reading of written texts usually takes many more minutes than does the reading of pictures? Is the reading of pictures more tiresome, so that we have to stop sooner? Or are the messages transmitted by pictures themselves usually "shorter"? On the other hand, would it not be more sensible to say that the times involved in the two processes are different, and that their measurement in minutes fails to reveal this difference? If we accept this last statement, we may say that the reading of pictures takes less time because the moment in which their messages are received is denser; it is more compacted. It also opens up more quickly.

If, then, we call the time involved in reading written lines "historical time," we ought to call the time involved in reading pictures by a different name, because "history" has the sense of going somewhere, whereas, while reading pictures, we need go nowhere. The proof of this is simple: it takes many more minutes to describe what one has seen in a picture than it does to see it.

This difference between the two types of temporality becomes even more virulent if, instead of comparing the reading of written lines to the reading of pictures, we compare it to viewing movies. We all know that a film is a linear sequence of pictures, but while reading or viewing a film, we forget this fact. Indeed, we *have* to forget it if we want to read the film. How, then, do we read it? This question has been asked by a number of sciences, and is eliciting detailed physiological, psychological, and sociological answers. (This is important, because knowing these answers enables film and TV producers to change films and filmmaking, and thereby to change the behavior of those who watch them, i.e., human-kind.) But the scientific answers, by being "objective," fail to show the existential aspect of reading films, which is the one that matters in considerations like these.

It may be said that films are read as if they were a series of pictures. But these pictures are not identical with the pictures of which the film is physically composed, with the photographs that compose its ribbon. They are more like moving pictures of scenes in a play, and this is the reason why the reading of films is often compared to the reading of staged drama, rather than to the reading of pictures. But this is an error, because the stage has three dimensions and we can walk into it, while the screen is a two-dimensional projection and we can never penetrate it. The theater represents the world of things through *things,* and the film represents the world of things through *projections of things*; the reading of films goes on in a plane, like the reading of pictures (although it is a reading of "talking pictures," a problem we will return to later).

How we read films can best be described by trying to enumerate the various levels of time in which the reading goes on. There is the linear time in which the pictures of scenes follow one another. There is the time in which each picture itself moves. There is the time it takes for us to read each picture (which is similar to, though shorter than, the time involved in reading paintings). There is the time that is meant by the story the film is telling. And, very probably, there are other, even more complex, time levels.

Now, it is easy to simplify all this, and say that the reading of films is similar to the reading of written lines, because it also follows a text (the first time level). Such a simplification is true in the sense that in films, as in written texts, we get the message only at the end of our reading. But it is false in the sense that in films (unlike written texts, but like paintings) we can first grasp each scene, and then analyze it. This discloses a central difference: the reading of films goes on in the same "historical time" in which the reading of written lines occurs, but the "historical time" itself occurs, within the reading of films, on a new and different level. We can easily visualize this difference. In reading written lines, we are following "historically" given points (concepts). In reading films, we are following "historically" given surfaces (images). The written line is a project toward the first dimension (an unfoldment from point to line). The film is a project that starts from the second dimension. Now, if by *history* we mean a project toward something, it becomes obvious that "history" as embodied in reading written texts means something quite different from what it means in reading films.

This radical change in the meaning of the word *history* has not yet become obvious, for a simple reason: we have not yet learned how to read films and TV programs. We still read them as if they were written lines, and fail to grasp their inherent surface quality. But this situation will change in the very near future. It is even now technically possible to project films and TV programs that allow the reader to control and manipulate the sequence of the pictures, and to superimpose other pictures upon them. Videoscopes and multimedia shows point clearly to this possibility. In consequence, the "history" of a film will be something that is partly devised or manipulated by the reader. It will even become partially reversible. Now, these developments imply a radically new meaning of the term *historical freedom*. For those who think in written lines, the term means the possibility of acting upon history from *within* history. For those who think in films, however, it will mean the possibility of acting upon history from *without*. This is so because those who think in written lines stand within history, and those who think in films look at it from without.

The preceding considerations have not taken into account the fact that films are "talking" pictures. But this is a problem. Visually, films are surfaces, but to the ear they are spatial. We are merged in the ocean of sound and it penetrates us; we are opposed to the world of images, and it merely surrounds us. The term *audiovisual* obscures this distinction. (It seems that Ortega, like many others, has ignored this difference when speaking of our *circunstancia*. Visionaries certainly live in a different world from those who hear voices.) We can physically feel how sound in stereophonic films adds a third dimension to the surface. (This has nothing whatever to do with possible future three-dimensional films, because they will not introduce the third dimension, they will "project" it, just as paintings do through the use of perspective.) This third dimension, which drives a wedge into the surface reading of films, is a challenge to those who think in surfaces; only the future can show what will come of this.

Let us recapitulate what we have tried to say in the preceding paragraphs. Until very recently, official Western thought has expressed itself much more in written lines than in surfaces. This fact is important. Written lines impose a specific structure on thought, in that they represent the world by means of a point sequence. This implies a "historical" being-in-the-world of those who write and read written lines. But, in addition, surfaces have always existed, and these also have represented the world. They impose a very different structure on thought in that they represent the world by means of static images. This implies an "unhistorical" being-in-the-world of those who make and read these surface images. Very recently, new channels for the articulation of thought have come about (e.g., films and TV), and official Western thought is taking increasing advantage of them. They impose a radically new structure on thought in that they represent the world by means of moving images. This implies a posthistorical being-in-the-world of those who make and read these moving images. In a sense, it may be said that these new channels incorporate the temporality of the written line into the picture, by lifting the linear historical time of written lines onto the level of the surface.

Now, if this is true, it means that "surface thought" is absorbing "linear thought," or is at least beginning to learn how to do so. And this implies a radical change in the climate, the behavior patterns, and the whole structure of our civilization. This change in the structure of our thinking is an important aspect of the present crisis.

Adequation of "Surface Thought" to "Things"

Let us now ask a quite different sort of question. We can take a stone as an example. How is that stone out there (which makes me stumble) related to a photograph of it, and how is it related to its mineralogical explanation? The answer *seems* to be easy. The photograph represents the stone in the form of an image; the explanation represents it in the form of a linear discourse. This means that I can *imagine* the stone if I read the photograph, and *conceive* it if I read the written lines of the explanation. Photograph and explanation are mediations between me and the stone; they put themselves between the stone and myself, and they introduce me to it. But I can also walk directly toward the stone and stumble over it.

So far so good, but we all know that the matter is not so easy. The best we can do is to try to forget all we were told at school about such matters, for the following reasons: Western epistemology is based on the Cartesian premise that to think means to follow the written line, and it does not give the photograph its due as a way of thinking. Let us therefore try to forget that, according to our school's tradition, to adequate thought to thing means to adequate concept to extension (point to body). The whole problem of truth and falsehood, of fiction and reality, must now be reformulated in the light of the mass media if we are to avoid the barrenness of academicism.

However, the stone we have offered as an example is not really typical of our present situation. We can walk right up to a stone, but we can do nothing of the sort with most of the things that determine us at present—either the things that occur in explanations or the things that occur in images. The genetic information or the Vietnam War, or alpha particles, or Miss Bardot's breasts are all examples. We may have no immediate experience of any of these kinds of things, but we are nonetheless determined by them. With such things, there is no point in asking how the explanation or the image is adequate to them. Where we can have no immediate experience, it is the media themselves that are the things for us. To "know" is to learn how to read the media in such cases. It does not matter at all whether the "stone" (namely, the alpha particle or Miss Bardot's breasts) is "really" somewhere out there, or whether it merely appears in the media; such "stones" are real in that they determine our lives. We can state this even more strongly: we know that some of the things that determine us are deliberately produced by the media, such as speeches of presidents, the Olympic Games, and important weddings. Is there any sense in asking whether the media are adequate to these things?

Nonetheless, we can go back to the stone as an extreme, though nontypical, example. Because, after all, we still have some immediate experience left, even though it is diminishing. (We live in an expanding universe: the media offer us more and more things of which we can have no immediate experience, and take away, one by one, the things with which we can communicate directly.) Now, if we still cling desperately to the stone, we may venture the following statement: we live, roughly speaking, in three realms—the realm of immediate experience (stone out there), the realm of images (photograph), and the realm of concepts (explanation). (There may be other realms we live in, but let us disregard them here.) For the purpose of convenience, we may call the first realm "the world of given facts," and the other two "the world of fiction." Now our initial question can be stated thus: How does fiction relate to fact in our present situation?

One thing is obvious: fiction pretends, very often, to represent facts by substituting for them or pointing at them. (This is the case of the stone, its photograph, and its explanation.) How can fiction do this? Through symbols. Symbols are things that have by convention been appointed as representatives of other things (be that convention implicit and unconscious, or explicit and conscious). The things that symbols represent are their meaning. We must therefore ask how the various symbols of the world of fiction relate to their meanings. This shifts our problem to the structure of the media. If we take advantage of what was said in the first paragraph, we may answer the question as follows: Written lines relate their symbols to their meanings point by point (they "conceive" the facts they mean), while surfaces relate their symbols to their meanings by two-dimensional contexts (they "imagine" the facts they mean—if they truly mean facts and are not empty symbols). Thus, our situation provides us with two sorts of fiction: the conceptual and the imaginal; their relation to fact depends on the structure of the medium.

If we try to read a film, we must assume a point of view that the screen imposes upon us; if we do not do this, we can read nothing. The point of view is from a chair in the cinema. If we sit on the chair, we can read what the film means. If we refuse to take the chair, and approach the screen, we see only meaningless light spots. On the other hand, if we try to read a newspaper, we need not assume a point of view imposed on us. If we know what the symbol "a" means, it does not matter how we look at it—it always means itself. But we cannot read the newspaper unless we have learned the meaning of its symbols. This reveals the difference between the structure of conceptual and imaginal codes and their respective means of decodification. Imaginal codes (like films) depend on predetermined viewpoints; they are subjective. And they are based on conventions that need not be consciously learned; they are unconscious. Conceptual codes (like alphabets) depend on predetermined viewpoints; they are objective. And they are based on conventions that must be consciously learned and accepted; they are conscious. Therefore, imaginal fiction relates to fact in a subjective and unconscious way, while conceptual fiction relates to fact in an objective and conscious way.

This may lead us to the following interpretations: Conceptual fiction ("line thought") is superior and posterior to imaginal fiction ("surface thought") in that it makes facts and events objective and conscious. Indeed, this kind of interpretation has dominated our civilization until recently, and it still explains our spiteful attitude toward the mass media. But it is wrong, for the following reason: when we translate image into concept, we decompose the image—we analyze it. We throw, so to speak, a conceptual point-net over the image, and capture only such meaning as did not escape through the meshes of the net. Therefore, the meaning of conceptual fiction is much narrower than the meaning of imaginal fiction, although it is far more clear and distinct. Facts are represented more *fully* by imaginal thought, more *clearly* by conceptual thought. The messages of imaginal media are richer, and the messages of conceptual media are sharper.

Now we can better understand our present situation, so far as fact and fiction are concerned. Our civilization puts two types of media at our disposal: those of linear fiction (e.g., books, scientific publications, and computer printouts) and those of surface fiction (e.g., films, TV pictures, and illustrations). The first type may mediate between ourselves and facts in a clear, objective, conscious, or conceptual way, but it is relatively restricted in its message. The second type may mediate between ourselves and facts in an ambivalent, subjective, unconscious, or imaginative way, but it is relatively rich in its message. We can all participate in both types of media, but participation in the second type requires that we first learn how to use its techniques. This explains the division of our civilization into a mass culture (those who participate almost exclusively in surface fiction) and an elite culture (those who participate almost exclusively in linear fiction).

For both of these groups, getting at the facts is a problem, but it differs for each. For the elite, the problem is that the more objective and clearer the linear fiction becomes, the more it is impoverished, because it tends to lose contact with the facts it wants to represent (all meaning). Therefore, the messages of linear fiction can no longer be made satisfactorily adequate to the immediate experience we still have of the world. For the mass culture, the problem is that the more technically perfect the images become, the richer they become and the more completely they substitute themselves for the facts they may have originally represented. Therefore, the facts are no longer needed; the images can stand for themselves, and thus lose all their original meaning. They no longer need to be made adequate to the immediate experience of the world; that experience is thus abandoned. In other words, the world of linear fiction, the world of the elite, is more and more disclosing its merely conceptual, fictitious character—and the world of surface fiction, the world of the masses, is masking its fictitious character ever more successfully. We can no longer pass from conceptual thought to fact for lack of adequation, and we can no longer pass from imaginal thought to fact for lack of a criterion that enables us to distinguish between fact and image. In both instances, we have lost our sense of "reality," and thus we have become alienated. (For instance, we can no longer say whether the alpha particle is a fact, or whether Miss Bardot's breasts are real, but we can now say that both questions have very little meaning.)

But it may well be that this alienation of ours is nothing but a symptom of a passing crisis. It may be that what is happening at present is the attempt to incorporate linear thought into surface thought, concept into image, elite media into mass media. (This is what the first paragraph tried to argue.) If that should turn out to be the case, imaginal thought could become objective, conscious, and clear, while remaining rich, and could therefore mediate between ourselves and the facts in a far more effective way than has so far been possible. How might this take place?

This development involves a problem of translation. So far, the situation has been approximately thus: Imaginal thought was a translation of fact into image, and conceptual thought was a translation of image into concept. (First there was the stone, then the image of the stone, then the explanation of that image.) In the future, the situation may become thus: Imaginal thought will be a translation from concept into image, and conceptual thought a translation from image to concept. In such a feedback situation, an adequate model can finally be elaborated. First there will be an image of something, then there will be an explanation of that image, and then there will be an image of that explanation. This will result in a model of something (this something having been, originally, a concept). And this model may fit a stone (or some other fact, or nothing). Thus a fact, or the absence of a fact, will have been disclosed. There would once more exist a criterion of distinction between fact and fiction (fit and unfit models), and a sense of reality would have been recovered.

What has just been said is not an epistemological or ontological speculation. (As such, it is very problematical.) It is, rather, an observation of tendencies at work in the present situation. The sciences, and other articulations of linear thought such as poetry, literature, and music, are having increasing recourse to imaginal surface thinking; they are able to do so because of the technical advance of surface media. And, in a similar way, these surface media, including painting, graphics, and posters, are having increasing recourse to linear thought, and they can do so because their own technical advance permits it. Although what has been said may be theoretically problematic, therefore, it has already begun to be realized in practice.

Fundamentally, this means that *imaginal thought is becoming capable of thinking about concepts.* It can transform a concept into its "object," and can therefore become a metathought of conceptual thinking. So far, concepts have been thinkable only in terms of other concepts, by reflection. Reflective thought was the metathought of conceptual thinking, and was itself conceptual. Now, imaginal thought can begin thinking about concepts in the form of surface models.

No doubt this is all far too schematic. The actual situation of our civilization is far more complex. For instance, there are tendencies toward thinking in the round, in the third dimension. Of course, such three-dimensional media have always existed, as proved by Paleolithic sculpture. But what is happening now is very different. An audiovisual TV program that can be smelled and that provokes bodily sensations is no sculpture. It is one of the advances of thought toward representing facts bodily, the results of which cannot yet even be suspected. It will no doubt enable us to think about facts that are presently unthinkable. Certainly, there are also other tendencies within our civilization that have not been taken into account in the foregoing schema. But we hope it will serve its present purpose: to show an aspect of our crisis, and one of the possibilities that might enable us to overcome it.

To return to our argument, at present we dispose of two media between ourselves and the facts—the linear and the surface. The linear are becoming more and more abstract, and are losing all meaning. The considerations before us indicate that they may be conjoined in a creative relationship. A new kind of medium may thus emerge, permitting us to rediscover a sense of "reality"; in this way, we may be able to open up fields for a new type of thinking, with its own logic and its own kind of codified symbols. In short, the synthesis of linear and surface media may result in a new civilization.

Toward a Posthistorical Future

Let us now ask ourselves what appearance this new kind of civilization might have. If we examine the present civilization from a historical point of view, it initially appears as a development of thought from imagination toward concept. (First there were the wall paintings and the Venuses of Willendorf, and then there were the alphabets and other linear modes, ultimately like Fortran.) But such a simple historical view at some point begins to fail us. Our present imaginal media (films, etc.) are obviously developments from conceptual thought; for one thing, they result from science and technology, which are conceptual. And, in addition, they are developments from conceptual thought in that they advance along linear discursive lines, which are conceptual. (A Venus of Willendorf may tell a story, but a film tells its story differently; it tells it historically, along a line.) Thus we must rectify our explanation: the present civilization does not look like the result of a linear development from image to concept, but rather like the result of a sort of spiral movement from image through concept to image.

We may state this as follows: When man assumed himself subject of the world, when he stepped back from the world to think about it—when he became man—he did so mainly thanks to his curious capacity to imagine the world. Thus, he created a world of images to mediate between himself and the world of facts with which, because of this distance-taking process, he was beginning to lose contact. Later, he learned how to handle his imaginal world, thanks to another human capacity—the capacity to conceive. Through thinking in concepts, he became not only subject to an objectified world of facts, but also subject to an objectified world of images. Now, however, by again having recourse to his imaginal capacity, he is beginning to learn how to handle his conceptual world. Through imagination, he is now beginning to objectify his concepts and thus to free himself from them. In the first position, he stands in the midst of static images (in myth); in the second position, he stands in the midst of linear progressive concepts (in history); in the third position he stands in the midst of images that order concepts (in "structures"). But this third position implies a being-in-the-world so radically new that its manifold impacts are difficult to grasp.

Let us therefore use a metaphor—the theater. The mythical position would correspond to that assumed by a dancer enacting a sacred scene. The historical position is represented by the role assumed by an actor in a play. The structuralist position then might correspond to that assumed by the author of the play. The dancer knows that he is acting the ritual; he knows that the symbolic mode is demanded by the reality he is to represent. If he were to act differently, it would be a betrayal of reality, a sin; his only freedom therein is to sin. The actor also knows that he is acting; he knows that the symbolic quality of his performance is a theatrical convention. He may therefore interpret this convention in various ways, and thereby change or modify the convention; herein lies his freedom, which is, strictly speaking, historical. The author of the play knows that he is proposing a convention within limits imposed upon him by the theatrical medium, and he tries to give meaning to his convention; his freedom is structural. Seen from the point of view of the dancer, the actor is a sinner and the author is a devil. Seen from the point of view of the actor, the dancer is an unconscious actor, and the author is an authority. Seen from the point of view of the author, the dancer is a puppet, and the actor is a conscious tool from which he (the author) continuously learns.

The example of the theater is, however, not a very good one. It does not adequately display the third position, because this does not truly exist in the theater as yet; it is too recent. Let us therefore try another example, which may reveal the third position more clearly: the future role of a TV spectator. Such a spectator will have at his disposal a video theater, including a magnetic tape library of various programs. He will be able to mix them in many ways, and thus compose his own programs. But he will be able to do more: film his own program, include himself and others, register this on a tape, and then project it on his TV screen. He will thus see himself in his program. This means that the spectator will control the beginning, middle, and end of the program (within the limitations of his video theater), and that he will be able to play any role in the program he desires.

This sketch reveals more clearly the difference between the historical and the structural being-in-the-world. The spectator is still determined by history (by the video theater) and he still acts within history (by appearing on the screen himself). But he is beyond history in the sense that he composes a historical process, and in the sense that he may assume any role he desires in the historical process. This may be stated even more forcefully: although he acts in history and is determined by history, he is no longer interested in history as such, but in the possibility of combining various histories. This means that history for him is not a drama (as it is for the historical position); it is a game.

This difference is, basically, a difference in the temporality of the two positions. The historical position stands in historical time, *in* the process. The structural position stands in that sort of time wherein *processes are seen as forms*. For the historical position, processes are the method by which things become; for the structural position, processes are the way things appear. Another perspective on things from the structural position is to view processes as parameters or dimensions that determine things. The historical method decomposes things into phases; it is diachronical. The structural method joins phases into forms; it is synchronical. For this method, whether processes are facts or not depends on one's perspective.

Furthermore, those things that stand in opposition for the historical position (matter-energy, entropy-negentropy, positive-negative, and so on) are complementary for the structural position. This means that historical conflict, including wars and revolutions, does not look like conflict at all from the structural position, but like sets of complementary moves in a game. This is why the structural position is often called inhuman by those who see things from a historical point of view. It *is* inhuman, indeed, in the sense that it is characteristic of a new type of man who is not as yet recognized as such by members of the older type.

Herein lies a problem. All that has been said concerning the third position has been composed into written lines, and is therefore a product of conceptual thinking. But if the argument is even partly correct, the third position cannot be conceptualized; it must be imagined with the kind of imagination that is now being formed. Therefore, this essay can only be suggestive. On the other hand, unless we try to incorporate concept into image, we shall fall victim to a new form of barbarism: confused imagination. This fact may offer a kind of justification, *quand même,* for this essay. For it is a present truth that the third position is now being assumed, whether we can conceive it or not, and it will certainly overcome the historical position as time goes on.

Let us, then, recapitulate our argument, in order to try to suggest what form the new civilization might take. We have two alternatives before us. First, there is the possibility that imaginal thinking will not succeed in incorporating conceptual thinking. This could lead to a generalized depoliticization, deactivation, and alienation of humankind, to the victory of the consumer society, and to the totalitarianism of the mass media. Such a development would look very much like the present mass culture, but in more exaggerated or gross form. The culture of the elite would disappear for good, thus bringing history to an end in any meaningful sense of that term. The second possibility is that imaginal thinking will succeed in incorporating conceptual thinking. This would lead to new types of communication in which man consciously assumes the structural position. Science would then be no longer merely discursive and conceptual, but would have recourse to imaginal models. Art would no longer work at things ("oeuvres"), but would propose models. Politics would no longer fight for the realizations of values, but would elaborate manipulable hierarchies of models of behavior. All this would mean, in short, that a new sense of reality would articulate itself, within the existential climate of a new religiosity.

All this is utopian. But it is not fantastic. Whoever looks at the scene can find everything already there, in the form of lines and surfaces already working. It depends very much on each one of us which sort of posthistorical future there will be.

(1973)

The Codified World

The revolution in the world of communications whose witness and victim we are influences our lives more than we usually tend to recognize. We know, for example, the consequences that television, advertising, and film can have. What is meant here is much more radical. The present reflections will propose that the meaning of the world in general and of life in the world transforms itself under the pressure of this revolution in communications.

If we compare our situation with the one that existed before the Second World War, we are impressed by the relative colorlessness of the time before the war. Architecture and machinery, books and tools, clothes and food, all of these things were comparably colorless. Our environment is filled with color, which, day and night, in public and in private, sometimes loud and sometimes quiet, demands our attention. Our socks and pajamas, cans and bottles, displays and posters, books and maps, beverages and ice creams, films and television, everything is in Technicolor. With these things we are dealing not simply with an aesthetic phenomenon, but with a new "artistic style." The red traffic light means "Stop!" and the obnoxious green of peas means "Buy me!" This explosion of colors means something. We are exposed to a constant stream of colors. We are programmed by colors. They are an aspect of the codified world in which we have to live.

Colors are the manner in which surfaces appear to us. Thus, if a significant number of the messages programmed for us appear in color, it means that surfaces have become important as carriers of messages. Walls, screens, paper surfaces, plastic, aluminum, glass, textiles, and so on have become important "media." The situation before the war was relatively gray, because at that time surfaces played a smaller role in communications. Lines dominated: letters and numbers, which were ordered in rows. The meaning of these symbols is, for the most part, independent of color: a red "A" and a black "A" signify the same sound, and, had it been printed in yellow, the present essay would not have another meaning. For this reason, the current explosion of colors points to an increase in the importance of two-dimensional codes. Or vice versa: one-dimensional codes like the alphabet now begin losing importance.

Premodern and Postmodern Images

The fact that humankind is being programmed by surfaces (images) should not be considered a revolutionary piece of news. On the contrary, it apparently signifies a return to a primitive origin. Before the invention of writing, images were a decisive means of communication. Because most codes are ephemeral, such as the spoken word, gestures, and song, we are dependent on images to decipher the meaning that man has given both his deeds and his suffering from the time of Lascaux to the time of Mesopotamian tiles. Moreover, surface codes, such as frescoes and mosaics, tapestries and church windows, played an important role even after the invention of writing. Only after the invention of printing did the alphabet truly begin to dominate. For this reason, the Middle Ages—including the Renaissance—appear so colorful to us in comparison to modernity. In this sense, our situation can be interpreted as a return to the Middle Ages, which is to say, a *retour avant la lettre.*

It would be unfortunate if we wanted to think of our situation as a return to illiteracy. The images that program us are not really the kind that dominated before the invention of printing. Television programs are different from Gothic church windows, and the surfaces of soup cans are different from surfaces of Renaissance paintings. In short, the difference is this: premodern images are the products of skilled handworkers ("works of art"), and postmodern images are the products of technology. One can recognize a scientific theory at work behind the programmed images, but the same is not necessarily true for the premodern images. Premodern man lived in a world of images, which meant the "world." We live in a world of images, which theories regarding the "world" hope to symbolize. This is a revolutionary new situation.

Excursus on the Concept of Codes

In order to grasp this, the present reflection will attempt an excursus on the concept of codes. A code is a system of symbols. Its purpose is to make communication between people possible. Because symbols are phenomena that replace ("stand for") other symbols, communication is a substitute: it replaces the experience of "that which it intends." People must make themselves understandable through codes, because they have lost direct contact with the meaning of symbols. Man is an "alienated" animal, who must create symbols and order them in codes if he wants to bridge the gap between himself and the "world." He must attempt to "mediate." He must attempt to give the "world" meaning.

Wherever one discovers codes, one can infer human presence. The circles that are constructed from stone and the bones of bears and that surround the skeletons of African anthropoids who died two million years ago allow us to recognize these anthropoids as men. For these circles are codes, the bones and stones are symbols, and the anthropoid was a man. For he was "alienated" (insane) enough to have given the world a meaning. Although we have lost the key to these codes—we do not know what these circles mean—we know that we are dealing with codes: we recognize the meaning-giving intention, the "artistic" in them.

Later codes, such as cave drawings, can be deciphered with less effort—because we use similar codes. For example, we know that the drawings in Lascaux and Altamira signify hunting scenes. Symbols that consist of two-dimensional codes, as is the case in Lascaux, signify the "world" in that they reduce the four-dimensional situations of time and space to scenes. In that they "imagine" them. Taken literally, "imagination" means: the ability to reduce the world of situations to scenes. And vice versa: to decipher the scenes as substitutes for situations, to make "maps" and to read them—including the "maps" that designate desired situations, for example, a future hunt (Lascaux) or gadgets to be built (blueprints).

The scenic character of codes gives rise to a specific way of life of societies that they program. One can call it the "magical form of being." An image is a surface whose meaning is suspended in a moment: It "synchronizes" the situations that it represents as a scene. But, after this moment of suspension, the eye has to wander around the image, to receive its meaning as it is. It has to "diachronize synchronicity." For example: It is clear from the first moment that this scene signifies a situation of the type "walking." But, only after the diachronization of synchronicity does one realize that what is meant are the sun, and two people and a dog going for a walk.

From Image to Line

For people programmed by images, time flows through the world the way the eye wanders across the image: it diachronizes, it orders things into positions. It is the time of the return from day to night to day, of sowing to reaping to sowing, of birth to death to rebirth, and magic is the technique that is called for in this experience of time. It orders all things in the manner in which they relate to each other within the cycle of time. The world, the world of images, the "imaginary world" thus codified, possesses the same form of being as that of our ancestors who were programmed and cultivated for untold centuries: for them, the "world" consisted of a bunch of "scenes" that demanded magical attunement.

And then we came to an eruption, a revolution with such violent consequences that we are still breathless when we consider the event that took place six thousand years ago. One can illustrate this event according to the manner it appears on "wedge-shaped" Mesopotamian tiles.

The invention of writing consisted not so very much in the invention of new symbols, but rather in the unrolling of the image into rows ("lines"). We say that with this event prehistory ends and history in the true sense begins. But we are not conscious of the fact that with this event we mean the step that was taken outside of the image and into the yawning void, making it possible to roll the image out into a line.

The line that stands on the right side of the image in the illustration rips the things from the scene, to arrange them anew, that is, to count them, to calculate them. It rolls the scene out and transforms it into a story. It "explains" the scene in that it enumerates each individual symbol clearly and distinctly *(clara et distincta perceptio)*. For this reason, the line (the "text") does not directly mean the situation, but rather the scene of the image, which for its part means the "concrete situation." Texts are a development from images, and their symbols do not directly signify something concrete, but rather images. They are "concepts" that signify "ideas." For example, ☼ in the illustration does not directly signify the concrete experience of the "sun," but rather ☼ in the image, which for its part signifies "sun." Texts are one step further away from concrete experience than images, and "conceptualizing" is an additional symptom of being one step further away than "imagining."

If one wants to decipher ("read") a text, one must let the eye glide along the line. Not until the end of the line does one receive the message, and then one must attempt to bring it together, to synthesize it. Linear codes demand a synchronization of their diachronicity. They demand progressive reception. And the result is a new experience of time, that is, linear time, a stream of unstoppable progress, of dramatic unrepeatability, of framing: in short, history. With the invention of writing, history begins, not because writing keeps a firm hold on processes, but because it transforms scenes into processes: it generates historical consciousness.

This consciousness was not immediately victorious over the magical. It overcame it slowly and with great effort. The dialectic between surface and line, between image and concept began as a battle, and it was not until later that texts sucked up images. Greek philosophy and Jewish prophecy are battle cries against images on behalf of texts: Plato, for example, despised image making and the prophets inveighed against idolatry. Not until many centuries later did texts (Homer and the Bible) begin to program society, and, throughout antiquity and the Middle Ages, historical consciousness remained the distinguishing mark of a small literary elite. The masses continued to be programmed by images, although these images were gradually infected by texts. They petrified, so to speak, in a magical consciousness, remained "pagan."

The invention of printing cheapened manuscripts and allowed a rising middle class to push through to the historical consciousness of the elite. And the industrial revolution, which tore the "pagan" villagers from their magical existence, in order to crowd the masses around machines, programmed this mass with linear codes thanks to elementary schools and the press. In the so-called developed countries, historical consciousness became widespread during the nineteenth century. On the other hand, it is just becoming so for the rest of humankind, because it is only now that the alphabet is actually beginning to function as a universal code. If one considers scientific thinking as the highest expression of historical consciousness—because it raises the logical and procedural thinking of the linear text up to the level of method—then one can say: the victory of texts over images—of science over magic—is an event of our most recent history and far from being counted as conclusive.

From Text to Techno-Code

In case the first section of these demonstrations is correct, it is important, on the contrary, to be clear about the disappearance of historical consciousness. To the extent that surface codes dominate, that images replace alphabetical texts, this is the end of an experience of time made conceivable by categories of history, that is, as irreversible, progressive, and dramatic. The codified world in which we live no longer signifies processes, or becoming. It does not tell any stories, and living in this world does not mean acting. The fact that it does not mean this any longer is called a "crisis of values"; for we are still generally programmed by texts, and thus for history, for science, for a political program, for "art." We "read" the world, for example, as logical and mathematical. But the new generation, which is programmed by techno-images, does not share our "values." And we still do not know for what meaning the techno-images that surround us are being programmed.

Our ignorance about the new codes is not surprising. After the invention of printing, centuries passed before writers learned that writing means storytelling. At first they only documented and described scenes. It will take just as long before we comprehend the virtualities of techno-codes, before we learn what photography, filming, videomaking, or analog programming signifies. Meanwhile, we are still telling TV stories. But these stories already partake of the posthistorical climate. It will take a long time before we achieve a posthistorical consciousness; but we recognize that we are close to taking the next decisive step, either stepping back from texts or all the way past them. This is a step that reminds us of the risky adventure of the Mesopotamian tiles.

Writing is a step away from images, because it allows images to dissolve into concepts. With this step, the "belief in images," that is, magic, became lost, and a new level of consciousness was reached that led much later to science and technology. The techno-codes are a further step away from texts, because they allow us to make images out of concepts. A photograph is not the image of the facts at hand, as was the case with the traditional image, but rather the image of a series of concepts, which the photographer has come up with in the scene that signifies the facts at hand. Not only can the camera not exist without texts (for example, chemical formulas), but also the photographer must first imagine, then understand, to be able to "techno-imagine." With this step backwards out of the text and into the techno-image, a new degree of alienation has been reached: the "belief in texts"—in explanations, in theories, in ideologies—is lost, because texts are now recognized as "mediations," just as images were once upon a time.

That is what we mean by "crisis of values": that we step out of the linear world of explanations and into the techno-imaginary world of "models." The revolutionary originality of techno-images is not that they move themselves, that they are "audiovisual," that they shine in light of the cathode ray, and so on, but that they are "models," the image of a concept of a scene. That is a "crisis," because the reaching beyond texts disempowers old programs, such as politics, philosophy, and science, but does not replace them with new programs.

There are no parallels in the past that allow us to learn how to use techno-codes, for example, when they manifest themselves as an explosion of colors. But we have to learn it; otherwise we are condemned to endure a meaningless existence in a techno-imaginary codified world that has become meaningless. The decline and fall of the alphabet points to the end of history in the narrow sense of the word. The present reflection hopes to raise the question concerning the commencement of the new.

(1978)

Criteria—Crisis—Criticism

The Greek verb *krinein* corresponds to English "to divide," "to separate," or "to break." We recognize this verb in nouns such as *criterion, crisis, criticism,* or *criminality.* If we translate it with the words "to judge," "to decide," or "to perpetrate," rather than with the words "to divide," "to separate," or "to break," we come closer to its true meaning. It signifies an action that splits oneness, breaks it down, breaks in half: it casts doubt on oneness. This is not a comfortable doubt, but rather the sort of doubt that makes judgments, decisions, and perpetrates crimes. At this meeting, we bring these doubts to bear on photography.[1] This is not a meeting that takes place on Mount Olympus, but rather, it takes place in a concrete situation, and this particular situation is stuck in a crisis. We are presently coming to a fork in the road: we must come to a decision, and we are bathed in a criminal attitude. I am calling these things to mind before I take up the task of talking about a critique of photography. We should not forget the criminal undertone, the *basso continuo* of criminality, that accompanies all our thoughts, deeds, and sufferings.

Critical Thinking

Our ability to break oneness in two in a disciplined way is the result of a very specific praxis, just as all our other talents result from specific actions. Critical thinking results from the praxis of linear writing. It can be proven that linear writing was invented in the second millennium B.C. with the intention of counting. Counting is the act of tearing things out of their context, to arrange them in rows. Counting is the core of critical thinking. We have developed our critical capacity to the extent that we have mastered writing. We have achieved a high degree of critiquing in the form of logical and mathematical analysis, especially in the domain of calculation. We have developed the capacity to divide, to separate, and to break down into dot elements all the phenomena of the external and internal world, all objects, processes, thoughts, feelings, and actions.

At this meeting, it is important to remember that linear writing is both the origin of critical thinking and its tool. Its original purpose was not to critique objects in the world out there or the phenomena of the interior world, but rather to critique images. The first critics were critics of images. The prophets were critics of the images of gods (idols), and the pre-Socratics were critics of mythical imagination. The reason for the invention of writing as a tool for the criticism of images is found in the internal dialectic of the images themselves. Images conceal the world they are supposed to represent. If images are the preeminent intermediary between human beings and their world, as they were at the origin of writing, then it is a necessity of life to critique them and reveal the access to the world concealed by them. For example, if I only had pictorial representations of the drinking pitchers in my storeroom, I would have to detach the represented drinking pitchers from the surface of the image one by one, to organize them in numbered rows. I must critique images.

Originally, critical thinking meant the criticism of images. It was directed against the image, it was directed against pictorial thought: it was iconoclastic thinking. Its intention is to emancipate people from the mythical power of images and, thus, to replace the magical praxis following from it with another, "rational" one. Critical thinking divides images—separates them into elements—judges them—makes decisions about them—breaks them apart—perpetrates crimes against images—because it casts doubt on myth and magic. The result of critical thinking is Western history, with all its triumphs and its barbarities. Essentially, this means Western science and technology.

In this essay, I want to defend the following thesis: If we consider how the criticism of images has been elaborated during the course of our history, then critical thinking cannot be applied to photography or other technical images, because these images are based on science and technology—produced by apparatuses—and are therefore themselves based on critical thinking. Photo criticism, including the criticism of other technical images, is therefore essentially a critique of critical thinking. Technical images force critical thinking to turn against itself. If people believe they can critique photography the way they critique traditional images (paintings, mosaics, or stained-glass windows), then they are mistaken. In terms of photography and other technical images, critical thinking is in crisis. It is being pressured to elaborate new criteria, to critique the myths projected into the world by photographs and the particular magic that results from photography. For these myths and this magic have themselves been produced by critical thinking. They are based on scientific techniques. In short, my thesis is: critical thinking is presently experiencing its own crisis, because it does not possess the appropriate criteria allowing it to critique its own products.

Criteria

One has to possess criteria—the units of measurements and rules—to be able to critique: the yardstick that one applies to the thing one critiques, to judge and decide over it. The tradition knows three kinds of measurement standards: the epistemological ("true-false"), the ethical ("good-bad"), and the aesthetic ("beautiful-ugly"). The critic is a "measurer" *(Messer)*—not to call him a "carper" *(Beckmesser)*.

He carries these three measurement standards around in his pocket the way a tailor might, applying them to his material and cutting the material according to these standards. This tradition is, indeed, sanctified (for example, the "true," the "good," and the "beautiful"), but it can no longer be sustained. It has always been dubious, but it falls apart when confronted with photography and other technical images. Whoever judges and decides that a photographic image is true, good, or beautiful, that it is either a document or a code of conduct or even a work of art, is simply speaking nonsense. But this is exactly what the media that distribute photographic images are doing. The media are presently the real critics. As I just mentioned, they apply criteria that fall apart in the face of technical images.

The three traditional measurement standards have always been suspicious. A Stone Age knife only cuts well when it is true—mechanically correct—and it is beautiful because it is made well and cuts well. Critics believe they can distinguish between the search for the true, the good, and the beautiful. However, an examination of the blade reveals the manufacturer's intention to cut something. The criteria "true," "good," and "beautiful" are simply aspects of the intention to cut. Finally, these criteria can only be distinguished from a critical distance.

So long as the critic maintains this distance, there is nothing wrong with his criteria. They are of no consequence to the Stone Age knife itself. If, however, the critic engages the manufacturer in conversation, then this sort of criteria can have disastrous consequences. To name only the most

impressive example: The Platonizing criticism of the Renaissance believed that man was searching for perfect beauty. Those who were influenced by this idea became pure artists. Consequently, museums, exhibitions, and academies amassed beautiful objects that were neither true
nor good for anything. On the other hand, the daily life of industrial society was flooded with a great number of scientifically true insights and
good machines and products that were inhuman, because they were
robbed of their beauty. The critics have expelled beauty from daily life.
Thus, they have not only inundated industrial society with ugliness, they
have also dehumanized everything good, true, and beautiful.

Certainly, the three traditional measurement standards have always
been suspicious. The traditional division of man's involvement in the
transformation of the world into science, politics, and art has always
been a mutilation of the unity of existence, a crime against humanity.
But, this division of "true, good, and beautiful" has lost all meaning in
the face of photographs and other technical images. Based on science,
photography is a technical gesture toward the production of aesthetic
phenomena. It is true to the extent that science is true, good to the extent
that the camera works well, and beautiful to the extent that the media,
which distribute the photographs, allow photographs to model the experience of the observer. The photograph has one thing in common with
the Stone Age knife: in photography, the epistemological, ethical, and
aesthetic parameters fuse together after having experienced their fateful
division in modernity. However, there is one difference between the
Stone Age knife and photography: in photography, the criteria precede the
photograph. In comparison to the Stone Age knife, photography results
from critical thinking.

In the first stage, represented here by the Stone Age knife, something
is produced. The critic does not arrive until after the fact to make his
judgment. In the second stage, called the "modern," there is a conversation between the manufacturer and the critic during production. This is
true even if the critic is the manufacturer. In the contemporary stage,
criticism precedes production. Criticism accompanies the production
and distribution of manufactured objects, so that we receive the manufactured object as something that has already been thoroughly critiqued.
This means that we, as the addressees of photographs, have to critique
the criteria according to which photographs have been produced: that is,
those criteria according to which the apparatus that produced them has
itself been produced and programmed, and through which they have
been distributed, until they finally reach us.

When I think about the scene of photo criticism, I do not have the impression that we have worked out the criteria necessary for a criticism of criteria, these "metacriteria." Instead, I have the impression that we are holding on to the traditional criteria, despite the fact that they are no longer operative. If we apply criteria such as "true," "good," and "beautiful" to the photograph—documentary photography, politically engaged photography, artistic photography—we have not criticized it, but rather, we have been taken in by the criteria that have been foisted onto the photograph. Armed with these criteria, which are no longer operative, we confront the photograph uncritically—with all the unforeseeable consequences that an uncritical reception of technical images brings.

Our critical blindness can be explained by the fact that human beings are involved in the production of photographs, whenever the means of production is not fully automated. We call them photographers—not just scientists, technicians, and camera operators, not just the apparatuses of science, technology, and the media, but also individual beings with their own individual intentions. We confuse these individual beings, these photographers, with the makers of Stone Age knives or the producers of modern images. Thus, we often critique photographs as if they were Stone Age knives or oil paintings. Unlike the producer of Stone Age knives or oil paintings, the photographer does not struggle with the object (with stone or oil), but rather, he struggles with the criteria of scientific, technical, and media apparatuses. As long as we do not recognize that we need to critique photography's struggle against criteria—against programs—we remain incapable of working out newer and more appropriate criteria. Our critical capacity will find itself in a crisis vis-à-vis the photographic images that program us.

Crisis

Normally, this concept describes the point on a curve where it changes identity. To suit my own purposes, I use this concept to describe the critical point where critical thinking begins to turn on itself. At this point, one begins critiquing criteria. It is just that "point" is not the right expression. As a "point," the crisis lasts too long, because we have been caught up in it at least since Kant's *Critique of Pure Reason*. This entire project requires a tiresome revaluation of all values, because "criterion" is nothing more than the attempt to say something less controversial than "value," and "criticism" is nothing more than evaluating. The criteria "true," "beautiful," and "good" are the so-called highest values. And, if they fail in photographic images, then even the highest values will find themselves in crisis. In the face of photography, the highest values show how they fail. They become meaningless.

Let us assume that I ask whether a given photograph is true. Truth is a relationship between a statement and its meaning. For example, a scientific statement is true if and only if it agrees in some way with its meaning. It turns out that it is incredibly difficult, if not impossible, to formulate this "in some way agreement." The term *truth* is experiencing a moment of crisis in the scientific realm (see Popper). But, in a photograph, the relationship between a statement and its meaning is even more opaque than in scientific propositions. An entire complex of apparatuses and their criteria as well as photographers and their intentions, about which I have already spoken, is interpolated in the space between a photograph and its meaning. This complex is practically opaque. Therefore, it makes little sense to ask if a photograph is true or false, for example, "posed." Theoretically, there are methods to answer this question. But these methods are meaningless, because photography turns the relationship between statement and meaning completely around. The photograph does not discover meanings, but rather, it gives them. It does not matter if they are true or false—even if this could be established. The critical question is, Which meaning does it intend to give according to which criteria? The criterion "true"—the value "truth"—is no longer operative in photography and must be abandoned.

It goes without saying that the criteria "good" and "beautiful" must also be abandoned. It makes little sense to ask if a photograph is good the same way we think of bread and butter—or, for example, noble actions—as good. Instead, the critical question is, Why does it desire the good, and according to which criteria? In addition, it makes little sense to ask if a photograph is beautiful the same way we think of a girl—or, for example, Beethoven—as beautiful. Once again, the critical question is, Which experiences does it desire to program into the addressee, and according to which criteria?

Photographs did not originate in their search for truth, goodness, and beauty, and these values are not unattainable ideals that stand above them. Photographs originate in apparatuses and are distributed through apparatuses whose intention it is to preserve themselves and multiply. The true, the good, and the beautiful are pretexts in the service of this intention. They are not unattainable ideals but criteria for programming. In photography, values have been demoted to criteria for programming.

The beauty of an advertising sign serves as an example here. If a critic establishes its beauty, then he has not critiqued the sign, but rather, he has uncritically accepted a criterion of the sign. This is called a "crisis": the so-called highest values are in the service of programs, and we do not have the criteria that allow us to say in the service of which higher values the programs are. Unless we say that they are absurd—which is precisely what we do.

Photographers try to defend themselves against the absurd and the value-free inertia endemic to apparatuses. They try to defy the crisis of criteria. This attempt is recognizable in a number of photographs. In defiance of absurdity, photographers try to produce true or good or beautiful photographs. It is a charming undertaking that is sure to fail. For nothing can compete with the programmed truth, goodness, and beauty of photographs created automatically (for instance, by NASA). If one wants to overcome this crisis, new criteria must be developed. This is not the task of the photographer but of photo criticism. It is the task of critical thinking directed against itself and its own criteria.

Photo Criticism

Considering what has been said, we need to differentiate between two diametrically opposed definitions of this term. On the one hand, "photo criticism" signifies a critical, judgmental, decision-making activity that programs photographic apparatuses and directs the photographs pouring from them into channels through which we receive them. On the other hand, "photo criticism" signifies the attempt to critique photo criticism in the first sense. This is not yet completely successful. Owing to our situation, the distinction we have here arrived at is unfortunately difficult to put into practice.

The one who decides which photographs will appear and which will not appear in the media—in newspapers, magazines, on signs, on canned goods, in exhibitions—is a functionary of the media apparatus. He not only censors photographs, but he also decides through which of the available channels they should appear—whether as documents, whether suitable for politics or advertising, or as art. The judgment calls and decisions of the media functionary are directed back into the photographic industry through feedback channels, such as specialized publications and market research institutes. There, functionaries use them for the reprogramming of photographic apparatuses to be developed in the coming year. This cybernetic feedback loop between media and industry functionaries produces ever truer, better, and more beautiful photographic images, that is, photographs that always fit more exactly the programming criteria of the apparatuses. This is photo criticism in the first sense of the word. Photographers are caught in its gears and are crushed by it.

Media functionaries are often those people who practice photo criticism in the second, opposite sense of the word. They write articles and books that are supposed to reveal criteria hidden from the view of the photograph's addressees. The articles and books that critique photographic criteria are a form of self-criticism or a form of public confession for media functionaries. However, the conclusiveness of their findings is doubtful, not just because every confession is necessarily dishonest, but because it is extremely difficult to achieve critical distance from oneself. To achieve the distance necessary to observe the apparatus criteria, photo critics in the second sense of the word would have to be people who neither are employed by the apparatus nor work for newspapers, museums, or advertising agencies. Yet, it is not clear how such photo critics in the second sense of the word should make a living. This explains our inability to critique photographs.

As apparatus functionaries, photo critics can theoretically be programmed and automated just like any other apparatus function. One can imagine boxes that sort photographs automatically, throwing out some, marking others with labels, such as "true," "good," and "beautiful," and directing them into their respective channels. For example, these automated photo critics could be programmed with equations drawn from information sciences and function according to the principle of Maxwell's demon. If we look at the work of most photo critics, we truly get the impression that the automation of photo criticism is close at hand. However, the same cannot be said for photo criticism in the second sense of the word. Because the criteria here are lacking for the time being, it is difficult to foresee how they could be automated. Moreover, the function of this sort of photo criticism consists in critiquing apparatus functions. Therefore, it is first necessary to invent an anti-apparatus, to program this sort of antifunction. The thought process that we are pursuing here indicates just how much we need a photo criticism in the sense of a critique of photographic apparatuses and photographic distribution apparatuses. It has to uncover the apparatuses behind the apparatuses that program apparatuses. Through photographs, it has to critique the entire apparatus culture and all its totalitarian tendencies, including the apparatuses that program us. In doing so, it will discover a type of photographer who fights directly against the photo camera and the media—and, through them, totalitarianism. Thus, the task of this sort of photo criticism is to emancipate the photographer and, through him, to contribute to the emancipation of society as a whole.

(1984)

Note by the Editor

1. Bielefeld Symposium on Photography in November 1984.

Habit: The True Aesthetic Criterion

Everything that is new is terrible, not because of what it is, but because it is new. The degree of terror may be taken as a measure of novelty: the more terrible, the newer.

In fact, this statement is nothing but a translation of the second law of thermodynamics into English. It states that novelty is an improbable inversion of the general tendency toward ever greater probability, and that it is "terrifying" precisely because it is an inversion. But implicitly it also states that whatever is new must of necessity grow old (return to the general tendency toward becoming ever more probable). However, if the statement just quoted were nothing but a translation from mathematics into English (one among numerous possible translations of the second law), it would be of limited interest. The statement is radical because it proposes quantifiable aesthetic criteria: it states that mathematical categories may be applied to art criticism. It translates the second law from an algorithm into an English sentence in order to use that algorithm as a criterion to judge art by. This is indeed interesting and requires some consideration.

All those who experience the tremor of beauty (in other words, every one of us) know by intuition what is implied in the terror of newness. Rilke, for instance, says that we admire beauty so much because it scorns, with nonchalance, to destroy us: each of the angels is terrible. But understanding something by intuition and understanding something exactly (theoretically) are two different things. Speaking about terrible angels is quite different from speaking about measurable amounts of noise. In this age of computation, we are beginning to learn that exact theoretical understanding is not necessarily less "human" than is intuition, and that measurable amounts of noises are not necessarily less "beautiful" than are terrible angels. On the contrary, because noises are newer than angels, they are, according to Rilke himself, more beautiful than angels. This needed saying.

The word *new* here means objectively any situation that emerges from the tendency toward ever-increasing probability, and such an improbability may be exactly quantified by probability calculus. Thus an atom of helium is four times newer than an atom of hydrogen—or, inversely, hydrogen is four times older than helium. (This is what the carbon test is about.) And the word *new* means subjectively any situation that makes us tremble because it is unexpected. Thus a cow with a horse's head (Russell's example) is newer than is an ordinary cow because it makes us tremble more. The problem here is to have the objective and the subjective meaning of *new* coincide: to calculate exactly how much more we tremble at the sight of a cow with a horse's head. If this should succeed, exact art criticism would become feasible: any work of art could then be subject to a carbon test. This is not yet feasible, but we may even now guess at what the structure of such a future art criticism might look like. Probably as follows:

"Art" is any human activity that aims at producing improbable situations, and it is the more artful (artistic) the less probable the situation is that it produces. Such a "new" situation is terrifying if seen from the context it emerges from, because it is unexpected and therefore experienced as something hateful, ugly. Thus "art" is that human activity which aims at producing hateful, ugly situations, situations that cause terror. Such a definition of "art" may recall romanticism, but it is nonetheless quite unromantic. Because any future art criticism will start from the assumption that anything improbable will of necessity reemerge within the tendency toward ever-increasing probability, and therefore any deliberately produced improbable situation will of necessity grow more probable with time. In an aesthetic context like this one, it is more adequate to say "habit" instead of "probability," so that any future art criticism will start from the assumption that even the most improbable situations created by art will in the long run become habitual—will no longer be experienced as being hateful and ugly. Thus future art criticism will be structured by the measuring of the various phases of ugliness as it grows habitual: it will measure exactly how one gets accustomed to ugliness, how the new grows old.

Obviously, "habit" here means the aesthetic equivalent of "entropy" in physics. And, as entropy is a basic category in physics (and in ontology in general), so habit must become a basic category in aesthetics. "Art" is that which opposes habit but must of necessity return to habit. However, in aesthetics there prevails a different nonontological climate than in physics. "Aesthetic" means "capable of being experienced" and "habit" implies anaesthetics: that which has become habitual is no longer experienced at all. Thus habit as a fundamental category in aesthetics is a measuring rod for experiences, for perception. For instance: the less habitual, the more it may be experienced (perceived), and the older, the less existentially interesting. In other words, habit (ordinariness) as a future carbon test for aesthetic evaluation. Or, to say the same thing in more acoustic and informatic terms: everything aesthetic begins as a terrifying enormous noise ("big bang"), and as it grows more habitual ("redundant") it ends in a quiet whisper (whimper). Thus one succeeds not only in making objectivity coincide with subjectivity, the sciences of nature with the sciences of culture, but even Eliot with Rilke.

The problem for such a future art criticism will be how to scale the measuring rod of habit. To solve this problem, informatics (that mirror of the algorithm for entropy) will become useful, but it will not be sufficient. The two extremes of such a rod are immediately obvious: the one is total noise, total improbability, meaning a situation that approaches the impossible; the other extreme will be total redundancy, almost total probability, meaning a situation that approaches tautology, the absence of information. Both extremes are unattainable, and they constitute the two horizons of the universe of aesthetics. Close to the first extreme, one will have to identify those works of art that were previously absolutely unexpected and that thus transform our lives. Close to the second extreme, one will have to identify the great mass of habitual ordinary products that surround us day and night and that we hardly perceive. This is the easy part of the problem of scaling.

But the problem is not the two extremes of the scale of values, but rather the fact that the scale will have to be dynamic. The aesthetic phenomena will have to glide from one extreme to the other. It will become necessary to show that the value of works of art is not "eternal," but that all works tend to slide in the direction of habit. To put this differently: it must be shown that habit rises like a flood of slime along the scale of values and that it swallows all values. Such a relativistic vision of the universe of the arts poses a problem, because it is inhabitual: we do not usually consider the "great works" to be provisional, and it is difficult for us to accept that they all tend to become redundant (which is the case, for instance, with some compositions by Mozart). It is difficult to admit that the flood of habit is about to devour even Mozart's chamber music. Such a view is inhabitual, which means that future art criticism is at the present moment felt to be detestable, ugly.

This dynamic of the scale of values demands that it be marked not with clear and distinct segments like a yardstick, but rather with zones that overlap, to permit the measurement of the sliding of aesthetic phenomena. Thus uppermost there should be a zone for the entirely inhabitual, for pure terror. Possibly, within that almost invisible zone, phenomena we call "sacred" should be located. Such a zone for the consuming irradiation that the ancients called "hierophania" (the appearance of the sacred) may also be named "wonder," because it points beyond the aesthetic universe. From where we stand, down here where art criticism is located, it cannot be made out whether there are works of art that merit inclusion in that zone, although we sometimes do speak of "wonderful" works of art.

Much more interesting (more graspable), however, is the imprecise passage between that extreme zone and the one that we can just stand without cracking. It is that gray zone where we say of a Schubert melody that we can hardly stand it because it is too beautiful for us. Therein a few passages from Shakespeare and Dante, a few Chinese drawings, possibly some Hindu ragas should be located. It is that gray zone where terror turns into enthusiasm, ugliness into beauty. Or, to put it differently, where that thundering noise begins to turn into information, because a minimum of redundancy has infiltrated. And there is yet another way to put it: this is that gray zone into which those artists have climbed who have attempted, at the risk of their lives, to utter that which is unutterable, to render audible that which is ineffable, to render visible that which is hidden.

If one slides along the scale of values somewhat more down to earth, one needs no longer to stammer, one can speak reasonably. This is because the gray zone of beauty grows ever more gray, and thus beauty changes imperceptibly into prettiness. Theoretically this process may be measured exactly, and informatics offers the tools to do so. The more convenient the reception of the information contained within a work of art is, the prettier that work is. If one applies the basic law of communication, which states that information and communication are inversely proportional, one may measure how much a specific work communicates: the better it communicates (the more redundancies it contains), the less it informs. In other terms: the easier it is to decipher a work of art, the prettier it is, and therefore the more successful. Thus one may measure (although indirectly) the sliding of a work from beauty toward prettiness by the success of that work. The less it disturbs habit, the prettier it becomes.

This sliding from beauty toward prettiness, from the unexpected toward habit, from the difficult toward the easy, finally comes up against a critical point at which it turns against itself. This critical point (this "catastrophe," in the precise sense of that term) can be exactly quantified. It is that point at which the amount of redundancies exceeds the amount of noise, so as to render impossible the transmission of any information at all. Products that transmit no information communicate perfectly and without any effort on the part of their receiver (he may insert them without effort into his habits), but he can no longer perceive them. Because their reception is effortless, they cannot be experienced (they are covered up by habit). Such products "anesthetize" their receiver. They are called "kitsch," and with them the sliding along the scale of values is over. Those products plunge again into the ocean of habit, or redundancies, of entropy, and they head, thanks to inertia, toward "thermic death." By far the largest segment of the scale of values (as used by future art criticism) will have to be reserved for that black and noiseless zone of kitsch.

However: the considerations advanced so far have not yet really touched the problem of habit, if habit is taken as the basic criterion for art criticism, because it now looks as if the problem were to build a linear scale of values marked by zones to be called "ugly," "beautiful," "pretty," and "kitsch," and to have the phenomena glide along the scale in order to evaluate them. It is true: such a scale permits the notion that values are provisional ("historic"), because phenomena tend of necessity to glide toward habit, and thus no "eternal" values can be stipulated. Still: such a linear criticism is no longer feasible where habit is the criterion of judgment. The novelty of such a criticism, its terror, its ugliness, is not so much the fact that it denies absolute values, but rather that it can no longer be linear, and thus confounds the upper with the lower, the sublime with the infernal.

There is a passage in Sartre in which the circularity of the aesthetic universe is clearly articulated. He describes a honey pot in which we are immersed, and where we spend our time licking that sweet stuff—up to the point that we are overcome with nausea in regard to the honey and to ourselves, and we begin to vomit. That nausea, which propels us out of sweet habit into terror and which shows us our own emptiness as opposed to the excessive fullness of kitsch, is precisely what we might call our "humanity." We are hollow, the world is full, and the moment we become aware of this we begin to vomit that fullness from out of our hollowness. And this vomit is not only a sign of our becoming human, it is also what we mean when we use the word *art*. *Art* and *human* are synonymous, and they both mean that we deny the fullness of the world (its being such). They both mean that we are not animals governed by habit, but human beings, meaning artists.

This is the central point of any future art criticism—that point at which habit turns into terror, kitsch into what is ugly. It is too easy to say that we must imagine our scale of values to be a loop wherein kitsch turns into ugliness again, and then glides on from beauty to prettiness to return to kitsch. This is too easy because such a loop is the aesthetic equivalent of the negatively entropic epicycles in physics and in cosmology that lie on the straight line that points at entropy. And this will not do in the realm of aesthetics. Because if all art is motivated by that nausea called habit, by ordinariness, by vulgarity, how can we account for that quite different terror that shakes us when we face the totally unexpected? Is there a dialectics that includes both extremes (the extreme probability and the extreme improbability) and that has those two extremes coincide

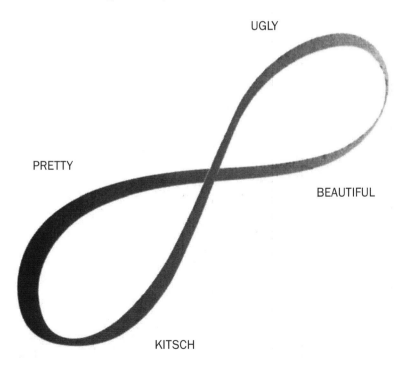

and then fall apart? This is the type of question that cannot be faced without the danger of falling into religiosity, or even into mysticism. It is, to be sure, an unavoidable kind of question, but not a "good" one.

Therefore, this is where these reflections must stop. In spite of this, they may have resulted in something useful. Namely, in the discovery that a quantifying art criticism will become possible in the future, because it will become necessary to abandon the notion of eternal unchangeable values. Such a quantifying criticism, which will use both physical and informatic theories, will measure all artworks with a loop that will contain zones marked "ugly-beautiful-pretty-kitsch-ugly," and the measurement will show the slide of works of art toward habit. Thus it will answer questions of the type: "How long will this specific work remain within the zone of beauty before, licked by habit, it slides into prettiness?" Those may not be very grandiose questions and answers, if compared to those formulated by present-day criticism, but they spring from the experience of terror in the face of the totally unexpected and of the totally habitual. In other terms: it may be that the future art and art criticism will again, as they were in the Middle Ages, be dedicated "ad maiorem Dei gloriam," although obviously under quite different presumptions.

(1990)

Betrayal

This is a strong word. So are most of its synonyms, such as *treachery* or *deception*. But there is a near synonym that is less strong, namely, *divulgence*. *To divulge* means, of course, to betray a secret. But the word is used to mean something like publication. The purpose of this essay is to consider the connotation of treachery hidden within the concept of publication. In this age of media culture it might not be wise to repress this hidden meaning.

An apparently harmless example might illustrate this purpose. A scientist publishes an article in a magazine destined for the general educated public. That man is a traitor. He is betraying the scientific discourse by transcoding it into the code of common speech, and thus changing its message. Through such a reformulation, the message loses its original clear and distinct structure, and it becomes open to nonscientific interpretations. It is divulged, made vulgar. In fact, that man betrays himself: he becomes unfaithful and untrue to his responsibility for the rules of disciplined reason. This harmless example shows what is meant by "trahison des clercs," betrayal by the intellectuals. Media culture as a whole may be seen as the result of this kind of treason.

It may be seen as a network that divulges secrets. There are knots within that net (for instance, TV stations) that suck in secrets. They suck in the secrets either by sending out spies (reporters) or by seducing people who hold secrets to divulge them (people who permit themselves to be interviewed or quoted). Those knots then transcode the secrets into a sort of slang: they "process the information." That slang, which is even more vulgar than is common speech and which is even easier to learn, permits everybody who connects to the net to participate in the secrets. Which of course are no longer secrets. The question to ask is this: How did this situation come about? And only then may one ask whether to divulge secrets, to betray, is a good or a bad thing.

This is a chicken-and-egg question. Is the present cultural situation as vulgar as it is because the media feed it, or do we feed on media because we have become so vulgar? The progressive feedback between vulgarity and the media, "The more there are media, the more we become vulgar, and the more vulgar we become, the more we become media addicts," sets in only later. Here is the chicken answer: we have become as vulgar as we are because the declining bourgeoisie has merged with the emerging proletariat to form a plebeian gray zone in which the media flourish. And here is the egg answer: scientific and technical progress has resulted in communication gadgets that permit the media to work, and the result of the media is a plebeian "silent majority," a vulgar culture. Is there a common root to the chicken and the egg, one that would permit us to spot the original betrayal?

There is such a common root: the invention of the printing press. That invention divulged the secret of alphabetic writing. Prior to it there was an elite of "literati" (mostly monks and priests) who manipulated the secret alphabetic code in order to rule the illiterate masses, to impose rules on them that they were unable to decipher, and that they had to follow blindly. Printing has cheapened all the texts, they became ever more profane, and ever wider groups of the population gained access to them. The masses became capable of deciphering the rules, and somewhat later of writing them themselves (or at least of believing that they did so). The secret of the elite (the alphabet) having been disclosed, there was no longer any place where the elite could hide, and it withered. This progressive disclosure of the secret is called "enlightenment," and the withering of the elite is called "social progress." Media culture is the triumph of enlightenment and social progress.

"Elite" means an elected group, but not elected through democratic elections. It means a group chosen to participate in a secret. The obvious example are the Jews, who were chosen by God's unfathomable council, and the church is the heir to this election. The opposite of the elite are the laypeople. The progressive laification of society is a measure of enlightenment and of social progress. This process of disclosure of secrets, of profanation and vulgarization, achieves a culminating point in Nazi Germany and Stalinist Russia. This is the high point of the radio and of film. The present situation may be seen as a less murderous stabilization of general profanation and vulgarization. It is less murderous because there are almost no secrets left to be betrayed, and those that are left are not really worth being disclosed: they have themselves become vulgar ("open secrets"). The age of television is thus less murderous than was the age of the radio, but it shows even better what is at stake in media culture: not only moral and intellectual, but even more so aesthetic vulgarization. By watching TV, we can concretely see not only that stupid murder is kitsch, but even more impressively that kitsch must in the end lead to stupid murder. Which leads to the second question: Is it a good thing to divulge secrets, and are the spying reporters and interviewed people committed to a good cause? Is betrayal a commendable method?

It is, if you are all for enlightenment and for social progress, without asking yourself where this has led to in the past, and where it must lead to in the future: to kitschy, stupid murder. But you cannot avoid asking yourself that question. Our generation is blessed with a lesson: the motives of the betrayers of secrets in Russia were noble ones. They were all for enlightenment and social progress. This was a lesson that is (was) hard to swallow, and we should not forget it. But if you do not avoid the question of where enlightenment and social progress lead to, you are cornered in an uncomfortable position. You are being forced into defending an elitist culture, one that could rule the plebeian masses by hermetically encoded rules that those masses would have to follow blindly, because they are not capable of deciphering them.

Let us assume, for argument's sake, that an elitist position is called for. Let us assume that the press that "did its duty" during Watergate and Irangate, and that is about to do the same thing in Russia ("glasnost"), is committed to the propagation of vulgarity, and thus will lead to kitschy, stupid murder. And that those who try to establish secret codes to which the masses do not have easy access (and of which the computer codes are the best examples) are doing the right thing. In that case, we will have to face two problems: (1) Can such an elitist culture establish itself in opposition to the prevailing mass culture—as the elitist monastic culture established itself in opposition to the mass culture of the circus during what we used to call the "Dark Ages"? (2) If those Dark Ages were to be reestablished, what would be the secret the elite would have to keep from being disclosed to the masses? The first problem is a technical one, and it is therefore relatively easy. Technical problems are formulated in a way that always admits a solution. The second problem is of a quite different order.

1. We may observe, even now, how monastic communities come into being. An early example are the kibbutzim; other examples are the "alternative" communities all over Europe, the groups that form around computers in the Western world, and the communities that gather in the artificial oases in the North American deserts. It is not difficult to imagine that a worldwide network of elitist groups linked by material and immaterial cables might crystallize in the not far distant future, and that such a network might elaborate rules that would govern society at large without being discovered by the masses. Such a thing has become technically feasible even now, and no doubt those techniques (and the codes that they would serve) will become ever more powerful.

2. However, if we compare such a future situation to the one that prevailed during the Dark Ages, one difference strikes us. Then, the monasteries were surrounded by barbarians (pagans), and they were committed to the preservation of civilized culture. This commitment had a meaning, because the monks had faith in individual and collective salvation. The future monasteries would be surrounded by plebeians (consumers), and their commitment would be a negative one: against kitsch and progressive stultification. It would not be a religious, but an aesthetic commitment. The secret the new monasteries would have to keep might well be the knowledge that there is no meaning, that life is absurd, and that the sole purpose of culture is to hide that knowledge. Now, this implies (if it were true) that the monks were an elite quite different from the one that is emerging at present. Their commitment was to lead society on to salvation, and paradoxically the result was modern civilization. The elite that is emerging at present could lead society nowhere, and it is precisely this lack of purpose (this "ludic commitment") that would constitute its secret. In this curious sense, the new Dark Ages we might be approaching would be even darker than were the early Middle Ages.

I believe that such is the true reason why it is so uncomfortable to defend an elitist culture at present. Not because it is "undemocratic," but because it is disillusioned, and therefore hopeless. The disgust many of us feel when exposed to mass culture may justify our wish to escape from it, but if we consider the technically feasible alternative, we despair of its justification. And instead of committing ourselves to a future elitist culture, we tend to opt for retreat into isolation.

Consider the inner contradiction that pervades this essay. If you read it, you will find that it is an argument against any publication. But of course it is meant to be published. It is a conscious betrayal of a secret.

Let me try to justify that treason. Erasmus wrote an essay in praise of folly. This is an essay in praise of media culture, which is a pernicious form of folly. Hopefully, this paper is treacherous in the same sense as are Erasmus's writings.

(ca. mid-1980s)

The Future of Writing

This essay will not consider the problems concerning the future of teaching the art of writing in the face of the growing importance of nonliterate messages in our surroundings, although those problems will become ever more important both in the so-called developed countries and in societies where illiteracy is still widespread. Instead, it proposes to consider a tendency that underlies those problems: namely, the tendency away from linear codes such as writing and toward two-dimensional codes such as photographs, films, and TV, a tendency that may be observed if one glances even superficially at the codified world that surrounds us. The future of writing, of that gesture which aligns symbols to produce texts, must be seen against the background of that tendency.

Writing is an important gesture, because it both articulates and produces that state of mind which is called "historical consciousness." History began with the invention of writing, not for the banal reason often advanced that written texts permit us to reconstruct the past, but for the more pertinent reason that the world is not perceived as a process, "historically," unless one signifies it by successive symbols, by writing. The difference between prehistory and history is not that we have written documents that permit us to read the latter, but that during history there are literate men who experience, understand, and evaluate the world as a "becoming," whereas in prehistory no such existential attitude is possible. If the art of writing were to fall into oblivion, or if it were to become subservient to picture making (as in the "scriptwriting" in films), history in the strict sense of that term would be over.

If one examines certain Mesopotamian tiles, one can see that the original purpose of writing was to facilitate the deciphering of images. Those tiles contain images impressed upon them with cylindrical seals and "cuneiform" symbols scratched into them with a stylus. The "cuneiform" symbols form lines, and they obviously mean the image they accompany. They "explain," "recount," "tell" it. They do so by unrolling the surface of the image into lines, by unwinding the tissue of the image into the threads of a text, by rendering "explicit" what was "implicit" within the image. It may be shown through text analysis that the original purpose of writing, namely, the transcoding of two-dimensional codes into a single dimension, is still there: every text, even a very abstract one, means, in the last analysis, an image.

The translation from surface into line implies a radical change of meaning. The eye that deciphers an image scans the surface, and it thus establishes reversible relations between the elements of the image. It may go back and forth while deciphering the image. This reversibility of relations that prevails within the image characterizes the world for those who use images for the understanding of the world, who "imagine" it. For them, all the things in the world are related to each other in such a reversible way, and their world is structured by "eternal return." It is just as true to say that night follows day as that day follows night, that sowing follows reaping as that reaping follows sowing, that life follows death as that death follows life. The crowing of the cock calls the sun to rise just as much as the rising sun calls the cock to crow. In such a world, circular time orders all things, "assigns them their just place," and if a thing is displaced it will be readjusted by time itself. Because to live is to displace things, life in such a world is a series of "unjust" acts that will be revenged in time. This demands that man propitiate the order of the world, the "gods" of which it is full. In sum: the "imagined" world is the world of myth, of magic, the prehistorical world.

The eye that deciphers a text follows its lines, and thus establishes the univocal relation of a chain between the elements of which the text is composed. Those who use texts to understand the world, those who "conceive" it, mean a world with a linear structure. Everything in such a world follows from something, time flows irreversibly from the past toward the future, each instant lost is lost forever, and there is no repetition. Each day is different from every other day, each sowing has its own characteristics, if there is life after death it must be a new sort of life, and the links of the causal chain cannot be exchanged one for the other. In such a world, every human act is unique, and man is responsible for it. The elements of such a world are, at least theoretically, distinct from each other like the beads on a string, and they can be counted. On the other hand, the string that orders the beads, the "univocal flow of time," is what holds such a world together. In sum: the "conceived" world is the world of the religions, of salvation, of political commitment, of science, and of technology—the historical world.

One may well ask why, six thousand years ago, the effort was made to substitute the world of conception for the world of imagination, why writing was invented. One may ask this at present precisely because a "new civilization of images" seems to be dawning. The answer is, of course: because, six thousand years ago, some people thought that some images needed explaining. Images are mediations between man and his world, a world that has become inaccessible to him immediately. They are tools to overcome human alienation: they are meant to permit action in a world in which man no longer lives immediately but that he faces. Cave paintings are meant to permit hunting of ponies, cathedral windows to permit praying to God, road maps to permit motoring, and statistical projections to permit decision making. One must learn how to decipher those images, one must learn the conventions that give them their meaning, and one may commit mistakes. For instance: it would be a mistake to decipher road maps as if they were cave paintings (magic for hunting tourists), or as if they were projections (proposals to build roads). The "imagination" that produces road maps is not the same as the "imagination" that produces cave paintings and projections. Explaining images with the help of texts may therefore be useful.

But there is yet another, and more profound, reason for the invention of writing and of historical consciousness. There is in images, as in all mediations, a curious inherent dialectic. The purpose of images is to mean the world, but they may become opaque to the world and cover it, even substitute for it. They may come to constitute an imaginary world that no longer mediates between man and the world, but, on the contrary, imprisons man. Imagination no longer overcomes alienation, but becomes hallucination, or double alienation. No longer are such images tools, but man himself becomes a tool of his own tools; he "adores" the images he himself has produced. It is against this idolatry of images, as a therapy against this double alienation, that writing was invented. The early writers in our tradition—the prophets, for instance—knew this by committing themselves against idols and idol making. And so did Plato when he announced his hatred of what we now call the "plastic arts." Writing, historical consciousness, linear, rational thought were invented to save humankind from "ideologies," from hallucinatory imagination.

Now, if we consider history to be the period of writing, which implies that history is a development of prehistory, a rendering explicit of what was implicit in prehistorical myths, we find that it is a slow and painful, not to say tragic, process. For most of its course, historical consciousness was the privilege of a small elite, while the vast majority continued to lead a prehistoric, magico-mythical existence. This was so because texts were rare and expensive, and literacy the privilege of a class of scribes and literati. The invention of printing cracked this clerical class open, and it made historical consciousness accessible for the rising bourgeoisie, but it was only during the industrial revolution and through the public primary school system that literacy and historical consciousness can be said to have become common in the industrialized countries. But almost immediately a new kind of image, the photograph, was invented, which began to threaten the supremacy of writing, and it now looks as if the days of historical, rational, conceptual thinking were numbered, and as if we were approaching a new type of magico-mythical age, a posthistorical image culture.

The reason why rational, conceptual thinking (and acting) is an exceptional form of existence, why history seems to be a brief interlude within the ageless "eternal return" of myth and magic, is that writing, just like images, is torn by an internal dialectic, and that this dialectic takes a more pernicious aspect in writing than it does even in image making. The purpose of writing is to mean, to explain images, but texts may become opaque, unimaginable, and they then constitute barriers between man and the world. The vectors of meaning of such texts turn around and point at their authors, instead of pointing at the world. This inversion of writing may be observed very early in the course of history, but during the nineteenth century it becomes obvious: scientific texts (which are the most characteristic form of writing, and therefore the "aim of history") tend to become explicitly unimaginable (one reads them erroneously if one tries to imagine their meaning), and scientific research "discovers" the rules that order its own texts (mainly logic and mathematics) "behind" the phenomena it is explaining. Such unimaginable explanations that mirror the structure of literate thought are existentially devoid of meaning, and in such a situation texts begin to constitute a kind of paranoid library wall that triply alienates man from his world. It is against the threatening lunacy of formal rationalism, of a meaningless existence amid speculative, opaque explanations, that the rise of the new image culture must be seen.

However, it would be an error to suppose that life amid posters, traffic signs, TV programs, illustrated magazines, and movie pictures will be like life before the invention of writing, that illiteracy will be restored. The new type of images are unlike their prehistoric predecessors in that they are themselves products of texts, and in that they feed on texts. They are products of history. The essential difference between a TV program and a tapestry is not (as one might believe) that the one moves and talks while the other stands still and is mute, but that the TV program is the result of scientific theories (texts) and that it needs texts (for instance, telegrams) for it to function. The new types of images are best called "techno-images," and the convention they are based on is best called "techno-imagination," if one is to distinguish the world of the future from prehistoric existence. No doubt techno-images are a sort of image, and they therefore mean, like every image, a world of myth and of magic. But life in the threatening future will be mythical, magic, in a sense quite different from prehistoric myth and magic. This difference may be stated as follows: prehistoric images mean the world, posthistoric ones mean texts; prehistoric imagination tries to seize the world and posthistoric imagination tries to be text illustration. Therefore, prehistoric myths mean "real" situations and posthistoric myths will mean textual prescriptions, and prehistoric magic is meant to propitiate the world, whereas posthistoric magic will be meant to manipulate people.

The easiest way to imagine the future of writing, if the present trend toward a culture of techno-images goes on, is to imagine culture as a gigantic transcoder from text into image. It will be a sort of black box that has texts for input and images for output. All texts will flow into that box (news about events, theoretical comments about them, scientific papers, poetry, philosophical speculations), and they will come out again as images (films, TV programs, photographic pictures): which is to say that history will flow into the box, and that it will come out of it under the form of myth and magic. From the point of view of the texts that will flow into the box, this will be a utopian situation: the box is the "fullness of time," because it devours linear time and freezes it into images. From the point of view of the images that come out of the box, this will be a situation in which history becomes a pretext for programs. In sum, the future of writing is to write pretexts for programs while believing that one is writing for utopia.

It is not important for the understanding of such a future of writing to try to whiten the black box, to try to understand how it works. The attempt to "demythify" the transcoding apparatus of the future is, of course, one of the most important challenges of "forecasting and planning for the future." But it is not indispensable where writing is the problem. One may disregard the wheels and screws that constitute the apparatus (the countless "media," "programmers," and other human and quasi-human operators who compose it), and concentrate upon the images as they come out of the box left black, if one wants to see what it will mean to be a "writer" in such a future. In other words, it is not necessary to analyze the whole hopelessly complex system that stands behind a TV program if one wants to understand the present crisis of rational thinking and acting. It is sufficient to analyze that program.

If one does so, one discovers the root of the present crisis: it is an inversion of the historical roles of reason and imagination. History may be said to be the attempt to submit imagination to the criticism of reason. Texts are meant to be critiques of images, and writing, as a code, is an analysis of surfaces into lines. Therefore, during history, imagination was the source of reason: the stronger the imagination, the greater the challenge of critical reason, and rich images permit more powerful linear explanations. There is something iconoclastic about historical reason: the better the icons against which it advances, the stronger is reason. But now writing is becoming subservient to image making, reason to imagination: one can observe this while analyzing any TV program. The better the reasoning, the richer becomes imagination. Planning has become a highly rational process in the service of highly irrational aims. The crisis is therefore not one of oblivion of the art of writing, of reason's decadence. It is one of reason's prostitution, of a "betrayal of the intellectuals." One may sum this up as follows: when it became obvious that reason might be a kind of paranoia, the intellectuals stopped being iconoclastic and became idolatrous, and present TV programs are among the results of that conversion.

TV programs are not, of course, the most impressive examples of what happens when reason betrays itself and serves imagination. Nazism is a better illustration. Still, it may be held that Nazism is one of the cruder advances in the direction of a future culture of images, or that the future techno-image culture will be Nazism perfected. This is why the battle cry "L'imagination au pouvoir!" that shook so many intellectuals out of their dogmatic slumber in May '68 has such a dubious ring to it. No doubt, rebellion against paranoid reason, against meaningless explanations, is necessary and healthy. But intellectuals are writers. They are committed to clear and distinct concepts, to reason. They are the historical consciousness of their society. If they adhere to the claim that imagination should take over, the dignity of man as a free actor, which means "history," will be over.

It may be asked, however, what else writers can do in the immediate future but serve imagination. If all the texts are going to be devoured by the gigantic transcoder to become images, how can this trend be resisted? Is it not so that if a text deliberately resists the trend, it becomes even better fodder for the transcoding apparatus? Actions committed to history and against the apparatus, like monks burning themselves to death or students being killed in riots, are even better pretexts for TV programs than are deliberate scripts made by TV programmers. It may look as if the trend, in which writing is becoming subservient to image making, planning to irrationality, and reason to magic, is increasingly automatic and autonomous of individual decisions.

This would be a perniciously wrong interpretation of the present crisis of writing. The purpose of writing is to explain images, and the task of reason is to criticize imagination. This is doubly true in the present crisis. At present, the purpose of writing is to explain techno-images, and the task of reason to criticize techno-imagination. Of course, this implies a sort of qualitative jump onto a new level of meaning on the part of reason. In the past, writing explained images of the world. It will have to explain illustrations of texts in the future. To write meant, in the past, to render opaque images transparent for the world. It will mean, in the future, to render opaque techno-images transparent for the texts they are hiding. In other words, reason, in the past, meant analysis of myths, and in the future it will mean de-ideologization. Reason will still be iconoclastic, but on a new level.

Nothing guarantees that reason will be able to perform such a jump, although there are some symptoms (for instance, cybernetics and structural analysis) that point in such a direction. It is perfectly possible that the general trend toward techno-images will become irresistible, and that reason will degenerate into the planning of programs—that to write will mean not to make "grams" but "programs," and that all texts will become pretexts. Thus, in fact, we may discern, at present, two possible futures of writing: it will either become a critique of techno-imagination (which means an unmasking of the ideologies hiding behind a technical progress that has become autonomous of human decisions) or it will become the production of pretexts for techno-imagination (a planning for that technical progress). In the first alternative, the future will be unimaginable by definition. In the second, history in the strict sense of that term will come to an end, and we may easily imagine what will follow: the eternal return of life in an apparatus that progresses by its own inertia.

(1983–84)

Images in the New Media

Among other things, an image is a message. It has a sender and it searches for an addressee. This search is a question of its portability. Images are surfaces. How does one transport surfaces? It all depends on the physical bodies on whose surfaces the images are affixed. If these bodies are the walls in a cave (as in Lascaux), they are not portable. In cases such as these, the addressees must be transported to the pictures. There are more convenient and more portable physical bodies to which images can be affixed, such as wooden boards and framed canvases. In such cases, one uses an improvised method of transportation. One transports the images to a specified meeting place, such as a church or an exhibition, and then one transports the addresses to the designated place. Of course, these cases make another method possible. An individual can acquire (buy, cheat, steal) one of these portable images for himself and thus become the exclusive addressee of the message. Recently, something new has been discovered. Disembodied images, "pure" surfaces, and all the images that have so far been in existence can be translated (transcoded) into images of a new kind. In this situation, the addressees no longer need to be transported. These pictures are conveniently reproduced and transmitted to individual addressees wherever they might be. However, the question of portability is a little more complicated than it has been described here. Photographs and films are transitional phenomena somewhere between framed canvases and disembodied images. There is, however, one unambiguous tendency: images will become progressively more portable and addressees will become even more immobile.

This tendency is characteristic of the current revolution in culture. All messages (information) can be reproduced and transmitted to immobile addressees. This is truly a revolution in culture, not simply a new cultural technique. To demonstrate this, it is necessary to compare three different situations of images to each other: the image of a bison in a cave painting, an image in an oil painting placed in front of a painter's studio, and an image on a television screen in someone's bedroom.

Hunting bison is a necessity of life. One should not approach this task without thinking (the way a jackal does it). One should reflect on this task from the outside (beyond subjectivity) and orient oneself to what one sees. By doing this, one will hunt better. But what one sees is fleeting. It needs to be suspended on the walls of a cave and in such a way that others will also be able to orient themselves to what has been seen. The bison's image on the cave wall is a suspended perception, a suspended experience, a suspended value, and it is a model for all future intersubjective perception, experience, and conduct, for all future hunting parties. It is an "image" in the true sense of the word. The portability of the image is out of the question. The addressees, such as the tribe, have to gather themselves around the image, to practice hunting in the presence of the image, for instance, through dancing.

The painter has learned to code his experiences, perceptions, and values in color surfaces. Like the codes of the alphabet and those of musical tones, this code has been transmitted from generation to generation. The painter swims in history. In his private chamber, he is preoccupied with putting whatever is specific to him (his own experiences, etc.) into these universal, intersubjective codes. These "noises" enrich the code. This is his contribution to history. If the manufactured image is nearly complete—it cannot be perfect, because both code and material work object to the idea of perfection—then the image must be transported from the private sphere to the public sphere, to make its way into history. The master painter places his painting in the marketplace in front of his house, so that those who walk by will critique it. They will establish the value of the image in a twofold manner: first, according to its usability with respect to a future history (exchange value); second, according to its degree of perfection (intrinsic value). The painter paints images because he is engaged with history by making the private public. This is what he lives for, and how he makes his living.

In order to legislate a complex society like that of the postindustrial age, one must be able to foresee how it will conduct itself. The proper method is to prescribe models of behavior. The situation of the cave demonstrates that images are good models of behavior. Images have an additional advantage in that they function as good models of experience and perception. Thus, legislators appoint specialists who manufacture such images. In addition to these specialists, other specialists are required who transport images into society or who measure their efficacy. These specialists are not the original senders, but rather the functionaries who oversee the transmission.

The Paleolithic hunter crawls into the dark, hidden, and secretive cave, to leave the open tundra behind and "to come to himself." He looks for and finds images that keep him from losing himself in the tundra. Together with other hunters, he uses the images there to help orient himself. In this manner, the world becomes meaningful to him. Shimmering in the torchlight, the images on the cave walls are responsible for making him into a hunter. They are a revelation of himself and his world. They are sacred.

The citizen leaves his private home and walks to a public place such as the marketplace or the church, to participate in history. He looks for images and other publications. Every publication calls out for his critique, which is to say, it calls out for integration into a reservoir of historical information. The more difficult the integration is, the more "original" and interesting the publication. And the less "original" it is, the easier integration can be accomplished. This is the criterion of all information criticism, including the criticism of images. If the citizen wants to enrich himself, then he purchases an original image and brings it home, to process it there. His reservoir of information—which is to say, he himself—is transformed by this process. If he wants to forgo the sacrifice of purchasing the object, he can be satisfied with the processing of information and images done in passing. This is the risk the painter takes, for his livelihood depends on sacrifices.

The postindustrial functionary (man or woman) and the children of these functionaries allow themselves to be exposed to images on a screen. Because so-called free time—time without any apparent function—is increasing, this exposure takes on greater dimensions and eventually gives evidence of its functionality. The functionary who appears not to be functioning—for example, the objectified office worker relaxing in a comfortable chair—is programmed by images. He is to function in a particular manner, because he is to be both producer and consumer of things and points of view. The images are programmed so that they reduce the addressee's criticism to a minimum. There are different methods for accomplishing this, for example, by means of an inflation of images that makes freedom of choice impossible, or a speeding up of the sequence of images. The addressee cannot interrupt his exposure to images simply by disconnecting the apparatus, to end objectification and become a subject; for he would thus give up his function and take himself out of society.

After close analysis of the three cases compared here, one regrets that the word *image* is being used for all three situations; for the word has a different meaning in each situation. In the first one, it signifies a revelation resulting from stepping back from the life-world. In the second one, it signifies a private offering to a public history, calling out to others for its integration. In the third one, it signifies a method for programming the behavior of functionaries in a postindustrial society. However, it is unavoidable to speak of the "image" in each of these three cases. And this is not only because the prehistorical and historical meaning of *image* resonates in the contemporary—"posthistorical"—significance of the word. The images flickering on the television screen contain remnants of prehistoric sacrality as well as of historical engagement, and, indeed, in both the political and the aesthetic sense of the word. This is exactly what makes an objective assessment of the contemporary situation so difficult.

There is a tendency to confuse the reception of screen images with that of cave images: as if the new images propelled us backwards to a prehistoric, uncritical siuation, and as if they were therefore depoliticizing. In addition, there is a tendency to confuse the reception of screen images with that of exhibited images: as if the new images were still transmissions sent by aesthetically and politically engaged individuals, the only difference being that the original images were no longer available for purchase, but rather had been made available as universally accessible reproductions. Each of these two tendencies leads to a different assessment of the contemporary situation: the first tendency to a pessimistic assessment, the second to an optimistic one. Both are in error. We must attempt to judge the contemporary situation according to its own characteristics, but we should also not lose sight of the previous interpretations of the "image." Thus, we will perhaps make the following judgment:

Owing to the manner in which images are currently transported, they must serve the same function as the codes of conduct just described. They must transform their addressees into objects. This is the intention of portability. However, the current methods of transport do not necessarily correspond to new media technologies, but rather only correspond to the intention behind them. The media can just as well—or perhaps even more effectively—be connected differently: not bundled, so that a sender is connected to countless addressees, but rather networked, so that individual addressees are connected with one another by reversible cables—thus, less like the television, more like the telephone network. Images do not have to be broadcast out of any sort of technical necessity. They can just as well be sent back and forth. The contemporary image-situation should therefore simply be considered an example of one technical possibility among others.

The intention behind the current mode of transmission is indeed powerful, but it is not impossible to overcome. We are in the beginning stages of a major change in the transmission of images, especially in the sphere of computer images. There, we can see how images are sent out from a sender to an addressee, to be then processed and returned. The beginning stages of this major changeover demonstrate how it is technically possible to outplay the intention behind the current mode of transmission. They demonstrate that technical means make it possible to take the political, economic, and social "powers" out of commission.

Should this change be successful, the notion of "image" would acquire a new, fourth meaning. The image would be a "disembodied surface." Many different participants would cooperate to project different meanings on this surface. In this manner, the previous meanings of *image* would be "negated," thus taking on a new, higher level of significance. The image would remain universally accessible, the way it currently is. It would still be a multiple of itself that is easily transported. It would regain the political, epistemological, and aesthetic potential that it possessed during the time when painters were responsible for its production. And, perhaps, it would regain some of its original sacred character. All of this is technically possible today.

My conclusions are relevant not just for what I have said about images, but for future existence in general. In our contemporary society, the new media are currently geared toward making images into models of behavior and people into objects. However, they can be connected differently. The new media can turn images into carriers of meaning and transform people into designers of meaning in a participatory process.

(1989)

On the Crisis of Our Models

(Theoretical Considerations and a Practical Proposal)

The motive of this essay is the suspicion that some new media of communication might offer possibilities for the elaboration of new types of models. This suspicion was provoked by some experiments with videotapes and films now in progress. This essay is therefore addressed to both theoretical thinkers and those who experiment with the new media. It will be structured as follows: A. It will consider some aspects of the present crisis of models; B. It will submit a rudimentary proposal for the elaboration of a model of the human body through the TV medium; C. It will criticize the proposal and suggest that such an attempt is worthwhile in spite of technical difficulties and possible objection.

A. Models are tools for the understanding of phenomena, they are made by those who seek understanding, they may be improved upon and replaced by better models. This statement is characteristic of the modern age, and it distinguishes it from other ages. For the Greeks and the medieval Christians, for instance, models were eternal ideas or forms, and "wisdom" for them was the contemplation of unchangeable models hidden behind the phenomena. For moderns, "knowledge" is in part the result of manipulations of models. This is an aspect of "progress." The question arises why models are being changed. The answer is that they tend to become unsatisfactory for two main reasons: (a) they become unsatisfactory if one no longer trusts their "fidelity"; (b) they may become unsatisfactory if they are hard to read.

(a) One may lose trust in the fidelity of models for various reasons, but at present there is a growing general mistrust with regard to a whole type of models. Models are projected from points of view on the phenomena that one wants to understand and handle. In the course of the modern age, one such point of view proved itself to be especially fertile: the "objective" one. It is the point of view of a subject standing above the phenomenon, which is then seen as an object. Objective models show phenomena to be understandable and manipulable objects. There were always theoretical difficulties with this point of view, because it was never quite clear how the subject can climb above the phenomenon to see it. But these difficulties did not diminish the trust in objective models, because they worked so well in the praxis of manipulating objects. This is now changing. It is becoming ever more obvious that one cannot really separate subject from object in praxis. The mere observation of an object by a subject may change the object. The Heisenberg uncertainty principle and the praxis of ethnology are merely two among many examples. And once a model is projected, the phenomenon tends to adjust itself to the model. This disagreeable feedback is experienced in the economy, sociology, politics, and many other fields of action. Thus the difficulties about objective models are no longer only theoretical ones, but are also practical, because the fact that the subject interferes in the object in the process of knowledge can no longer be practically discounted. Consequent loss of trust in objective models may be called "the crisis of objectivity."

Now, objective models are among the most important ones we possess. The greater part of all models supplied by the sciences and humanities belongs to this type. If we lose confidence in them, it becomes difficult for us to find our way in the world. This is why new points of view are being experimented from which to project new types of models. Phenomenological vision provides one such point of view. It does not stand above, but within, the phenomenon to be understood and manipulated. Models projected from it do not show the phenomenon to be an object, but a living experience. This type of model might be called the "intersubjective" one. A good example is the human body. In objective models, it is shown to be an object among many others, and to be of the type "organisms." In phenomenological models, it is shown to be the way through which people are in the world and change it. Such models provide a knowledge of the human body that may be trusted better, because it takes the interference of subject within object as its point of departure. It cannot, for sure, substitute for existing objective models (anatomical, physiological, biomolecular ones, and so forth), but it can work with them. This is the reason why this essay will propose such a model of the human body.

Such models are being proposed all over at present. For instance, there is an ever-growing literature that might be called "phenomenology of the human body." Still, one cannot escape the feeling that such models are not yet capable of competing with objective ones, let alone of replacing them. The crisis of models as an objectivity crisis has not yet been overcome by these models. The reason why this is so may have to do with the medium in which those models are being articulated. The medium in which phenomenological researchers articulate their models is mostly books. Books do not seem to be adequate media for such a type of model. More adequate media for such a purpose are at our disposal. At least this is the suspicion this essay harbors. The next paragraph will argue the point.

(b) The second main reason why models may become unsatisfactory is technical. The way one uses models is this: first, one projects it from a point of view with regard to a phenomenon; second, one feeds it with information supplied by the phenomenon; third, one understands the phenomenon as represented by the model. A geographical map might illustrate this. First, one projects a map from a point of view with regard to a landscape (for instance, the Mercator point of view); second, one fills in information supplied by the landscape (for instance, mountains and rivers); third, one understands the landscape (for instance, one can use the map for driving). But the model can store only a limited amount of information. If that amount is exceeded, the model can no longer be read easily and becomes unsatisfactory. New types of models must then be elaborated that can store the information. For instance, if information on a map becomes crowded, one can elaborate three-dimensional maps in which mountains appear in relief.

Such difficulty in reading models for excess of stored information is an important aspect of the present situation. We feel that we are being bombarded by new information that we cannot digest, because we cannot store it in the models at our disposal. Therefore, we look for new types of models, not only to store available information in a legible way, but also to leave room for new information. Only then may we become "curious" again, namely, interested in new information.

But to change technically the types of models is to change one's vision of the world. History supplies examples of this. For instance, at one point in the history of Mesopotamia, traditional models such as painted scenes were probably felt to be unsatisfactory for the storage of available information. The distance in time does not allow us to reconstruct the situation, but we can see it in outline. New types of models were elaborated that were able to store more information (the deeds of kings and so forth)—namely, linear writing. This was made possible by the technique of tile manufacture. The result was a new vision of the world: "historical vision." At one point in the history of Europe, traditional geographical maps became unsatisfactory for the storage of information brought in by travels. A new type of map, namely, globes, was elaborated. The result was a change in the vision of the world too well known to be discussed. At one point in the eighteenth century, traditional mechanical models (as, for instance, supplied by the French *Encyclopedia*) became unsatisfactory for the storage of information brought in by the various sciences. A new type of models, namely, dynamic ones, was elaborated. We still are under the impact of the change in world vision that resulted from it. To change technical models is literally to change the understanding of the world and man's place within it.

Practically all the models now at our disposal are space models. They are either linear (such as sentences, or equations, or curves); or they are on a plane (such as maps, or sketches, or two-dimensional statistics); or they are three-dimensional (such as atomic models, prototypes of machines, or models of architecture). Even our mental models are of this type, because a mental model is an effort to imagine a material model. Which means that most of our available models can show time only indirectly. Now, this is as it should be for objective vision, because from that point of view phenomena are objects within time. But it is not satisfactory for phenomenological vision, because from that point of view phenomena are events. The more objective models fail us because of the practical difficulty mentioned earlier, the less are they able to store incoming information concerning time. Only models of the type "space-time continua" can now satisfy us. One reason present models as elaborated by phenomenologists fail us may be the fact that phenomenologists still write books, instead of using space-time media.

Films, videotapes, and so forth are such media. They allow the elaboration of models better suited for phenomenological vision. And they allow the storage of a larger amount of information than do traditional media, because they have one more dimension. Such media may therefore contribute to the superation of both the "objectivity crisis" and the "information inflation crisis." If they were used for the elaboration of models in this sense, our vision of the world would probably change in a way we cannot begin to imagine.

All over, and mostly in the United States, experiments are under way to use the new media in this sense. Especially experiments with videotapes and holograms seem to be very promising. But those who undertake such experiments tend to consider themselves to be "artists." They therefore tend to supply us with subjective models, not phenomenological ones. If scientists do recur to the new media (chemists, biologists, and so forth), they tend to elaborate variations of objective models. The use of the new media for the elaboration of phenomenological models—for instance, by philosophers—does not seem to happen. Which is surprising, given our situation. *One of the purposes of the present essay is to propose a collaboration between philosophers and those who experiment with the new media.*

B. The human body is a good example of the crisis of our models. We have at our disposal a great number of objective models of our body. They increasingly show us the objective aspect of our body as a living organism. They do not show the phenomenological aspect of our body, namely, the fact that our body is how we experience the world and act in it. Literature does show this aspect, but does not provide us with good models. On the other hand, we dispose of an enormous amount of information concerning our body, but can no longer store it in our models. For instance, we cannot coordinate the information coming from ecology with the information coming from molecular biology. Possibly a space-time continuum model could help? To illustrate such a possibility, a primitive model of our body in the TV medium will now be proposed.

A hollow, translucid sphere appears on the screen swimming within a context. The context is composed of elements of various shapes that are dense around the sphere and spare toward the horizon of the screen. Some of the elements penetrate the sphere more or less deeply. The sphere sometimes secretes liquids that condense to form elements of the context. The sphere changes constantly its shape and color, and so do the elements of the context. At times the sphere breaks open and closes again. At times other similar spheres appear on the screen and make contact with the original one either directly or through elements of the context. The vacuum within the sphere and the horizon of the screen remain always black. This action is accompanied by sound. It should cause a dramatic impression.

Labels are to be introduced. The vacuum within the sphere is to be labeled "myself," the wall of the sphere "my body," the context "my world," and the horizon "my death." The stream of elements toward my body is to be labeled "my future," the secretions from my body "my past," incoming elements "my problems," outgoing ones "my works," the places on my body where elements come in "my passive presence," and where they go out "my active presence." Now, one can try to insert information into the model as it is being supplied by body experience.

Coming from my future, a problem reaches my passive presence. Let us label it "liver pain." One should resist the temptation to label the spot where it comes in "my liver," and thus start a mapping of my body. Experience shows that my liver cannot be experienced unless it is part of an incoming problem. It is therefore not, phenomenologically speaking, part of my body. The model can show this. The moment the problem "liver pain" presents itself, the sphere emanates a red aura and a specific sound appears in the sound track. It is within this aura that my liver is to be located, in an intermediate region between my body and my world. This region is to be labeled "theoretical aspect of my body." Other problems that present themselves may also be located within that region. For instance, the problem "my genetic information." In that case, the region will have a different color and the sound will be different. The various phases of that region may be synchronized on the screen. The region will then appear to largely coincide with the traditional objective models of the body. Those models should be used for the mapping of that region.

Coming from my future, a different problem of different shape, color, and sound reaches my passive presence. Let us label it "a newspaper." The wall of the sphere opens up, forms a channel, and the newspaper drifts through it toward the inner vacuum. The channel is to be labeled "my eyes." At that moment my body becomes, as a whole, an organ for the sucking in of the newspaper. It changes its color and becomes green. At the next moment a different problem presents itself, to be labeled "my pipe." My body opens a different channel of a different shape to be labeled "my finger." It turns partly pink. Thus various channels have to be shown diachronically and synchronically, to be labeled "my mouth," "my sex," and so forth, and the color of the sphere has to change to show the interplay between the various channels. The sound track will have to show the intensity of the channels. The model will also have to show how the incoming problems are being molded by the various channels. They will have to change shape and color as they pass through the channels.

The model will also have to show how the various channels relate to the vacuum. For instance, it will have to show the difference of the experience of my eyes from the experience of my fingers. My body has various fingers, and one may finger the other. But although my body has two eyes, one cannot see the other. Therefore, my finger is a channel more obviously than is my eye; it is more obviously part of my body. In other words, my eye is more like myself, and my finger is more like my world. Therefore, the model must show my eye to be like myself (blackish), and my finger to be like my world (variously colored). And the whole body must be shown at moments to be myself-like, and at others to be my-world-like.

A secretion begins to condense on the inner wall of the sphere, it penetrates the wall in complex curves, erupts on the outside at the spot of my active presence, and flows toward my past to form an element of my world. Let us label the secretion "my gesture of writing," and the new element of my world "a letter written by me." During the process, the shape of my body changes and becomes a pointed cone. The point of the cone is to be labeled "my hand." At this point the secretion leaves my body. But an even more dramatic event happens. One of the elements of my world leaves its context, turns around to face the context, and attaches itself to my hand to form the true point of my body. Let us label this element "my fountain pen." At the same time, all other problems of my world recede, and my body points at the single problem "my letter." This event is to be shown through various shapes, sounds, and colors. The model must also distinguish between turnable problems and others. Turnable problems are to be labeled "tools," and their totality "culture."

It serves no purpose to continue inserting information into the model. The amount of available information is enormous, especially if one considers that more than one sphere may be shown within the same context. What is interesting about this experiment is the fact that the information inserted is not new. On the contrary, the information is of a type so common that it tends to be forgotten. This is the purpose of a phenomenological model: to reveal forgotten available information. This does not exclude, of course, that the model here proposed may not reveal new information, but that is not its purpose.

Its purpose is to supply a new structure for available information. This seems to be important. Now, available objective models of our body permit us to know and manipulate our bodies even better as objects. This leads to an increasing alienation of a special type from the body (specialized medicine, sports, robotization, and so forth). We also have excellent subjective models of our body, as supplied by artists and so forth. This leads to an increasing alienation of a different type from our body (abandon to body sensation, drugs, the whole complex of the "anticulture"). The two forms of alienation go together, and result from the lack of intersubjective models. Models like the one proposed here may therefore contribute toward a de-alienation from our body. And what is true of the body is very probably also true of many other phenomena in the midst of which we live.

The model proposed here is obviously primitive, and it suffers from the lack of practical experience of the possibilities offered by the new media. Only those who have this practical experience may judge whether such a model is feasible, and, if so, whether it can provide a new type of experience and a new type of knowledge. It must do both if it is to be a truly phenomenological model. *One of the purposes of the present essay is to suggest to those who experiment with the media to try to elaborate such a type of model.*

C. The model proposed here is very vulnerable to theoretical objection. Such objections must be raised, and it would be intellectually dishonest were this fact not mentioned in the present essay, although it may be hoped that they can be met better during the process of experimentation than at the outset. But two of the objections at least must be stated right away, because they seem to question the very basis of this proposal: *(a)* the epistemological, and *(b)* the religious objection.

(a) Models are epistemological tools; their purpose is to know the phenomena they model. Therefore, they are reifications of a specific theory of knowledge held by the one who projects them. Consequently, new types of models cannot really change our vision of the world. Only a new theory of knowledge can do this, a theory of which new models are only manifestations. This can be seen from the examples taken from history offered here. The theory had to change in all the examples offered before new models could be elaborated. And this can also be seen from the model proposed here. One can see the theory of which it is a reification. In its middle stands the knowing subject, around it is the knowable object, and around it an empty horizon. This is the structure of the theory of knowledge of existentialist philosophy. Therefore, not the medium of a model is decisive, but the theory that underlies its structure.

The objection is correct, but does not attain the essence of the proposal. It aims at a change in world vision through the practical application of an already existing theory of knowledge. Thus, the model proposed here will certainly not contribute to a theoretical resolution of the "subject-object" problem. It leaves it untouched, but tries to remove it from praxis. In praxis, the knowledge of our body is hampered by the barren antinomy between body and soul, or spirit. Phenomenological vision shows that "body" is an objectivation of "body experience," and "spirit" is an objectivation of the way "body experience" happens, and that the concrete reality is only the body experience itself. This phenomenological vision structures the proposed model and therefore should permit a knowledge of the phenomenon "body experience" from which the antinomy has been removed. But, of course, this does not abolish the epistemological problem. It now appears one step removed, in the question: "What is the relationship between the model and its users on one side, and the phenomenon on the other?" In this sense, the objection is valid: the model does not provide answers to questions of theory of knowledge. But that the epistemological question is in fact removed one step, which is to say that it is put into brackets in practice, is the true purpose of the model. In sum: it must be admitted that basically revolutions in world vision are the results of changes in theories of knowledge. In our case, such a change might have happened in Husserl. But this revolution can only manifest itself in the form of new types of models. And the model proposed is meant to suggest that the new media of communication are very useful for the practical manifestation of the revolution in world vision. In this sense, the present proposal can live with the epistemological objection.

(b) Models are tools for the orientation in the world. They are meant to facilitate answers to questions of the type: "Where am I and what can I do to go someplace else?" Now, this type of question is basically the religious type of question. Because it asks: "What is my 'Befindlichkeit,' that is, how do I find myself in the world?" It may be shown that we find ourselves in the world in a way that is imposed on us by the religions of our tradition, whether we accept these religions or not, and whether we are conscious of it or not. Which is a way of saying that we find ourselves in the world within the structure of Western civilization. All the models we elaborate are manifestations of the way we find ourselves in the world. Indeed, the fact that we do elaborate models is a manifestation of our specific finding ourselves in the world. Therefore, models can only answer this type of religious question, because the answer is already contained in the model. This can be seen clearly from the proposed model. The vacuum called "myself" in its center corresponds to the place occupied by "soul" in Western religious structure, and the vacuum called "my death" on its horizon corresponds to the place occupied by the "transcendent God" in Western religious structure. That those two places are vacuums in the proposed model corresponds to a stage that Western traditional religions have reached for many at present. Therefore, new types of models, whatever the medium they are made of, can never change the way we find ourselves in the world. Such changes are results of religious revolutions (however we want to define the word *religion*).

The objection is correct, but curiously enough, it does not attack but sustains the proposal, if carefully considered. It is true that all models hide a specific "*Befindlichkeit,*" a specific religious structure. But the problem is exactly the fact that they hide it. For instance, the models of our natural sciences do not seem to be the results of Judeo-Christian transcendence, and therefore the knowledge they provide seems to be independent of our religious tradition. Only a phenomenological analysis of those models will reveal this. Now, it is an advantage of phenomenological models that they show their dependence on religious structures. For instance, it is an advantage of the proposed model that it shows our body experience to be modeled by the tradition of "incarnation"; that it shows that our body experience follows the structure of "incarnation" whether we know of it or not, and whether we accept "incarnation" or not. In fact, it is one of the purposes of phenomenological models to reveal such aspects. In this sense, of course, neither the proposed model nor any other can provide new answers to the religious question. It cannot be used as a tool to answer the question of the salvation of the soul, nor as a tool for the removal of the soul myth. But this is not what it was meant to do. It was meant to reveal, among other things, our religious determination while experiencing our body. And to suggest that this can be done better with the new media of communication. In this sense, the objection is no objection, but sustains the proposal.

The short consideration of these two objections has pointed to some limitations of the effectivity of all models, including the new type proposed here. No doubt, the consideration of other objections would reveal further limitations. But the consideration also suggests that, within those limits, the new type of models proposed here might have revolutionary results for our vision of the world. *One of the purposes of the present essay is to contribute to a discussion of the limits and possibilities of such an undertaking between philosophers and those who experiment in the new media.*

We find ourselves, with respect to numerous problems, in an ambivalent position. On the one hand, we have a feeling of decadence and disappointment; on the other hand, a feeling of challenge, of adventure. As if we were living simultaneously in the evening and in the morning. This applies also to the problem posed by models. The fundamental purpose of this essay is to infect others with the feeling of adventure.

(ca. 1980s)

Change of Paradigms

Translated by Elizabeth Wilson and Andreas Ströhl

The division of the history of the West into antiquity, the Middle Ages, and modernity is questionable, but nevertheless not arbitrary. In these cases, the issue was a change of paradigms, involving changes in living, feeling, and thinking, changes obvious not only to us, at our historical distance, but also to those affected by them.

Equally dubious, but still not arbitrary, is the present talk about "postmodernism" and/or "posthistory." This lecture has the intention of confirming that we too can and must note a profound change in our modes of living and thinking up to now and in our feelings and wishes.

In order to realize this intention, it would be necessary first to sum up the actual paradigms, in order to illustrate the present change. This, however, is not advisable. Instead, the attempt will be undertaken to get a grip on some aspects of the transition from the Middle Ages to modernity and then to use this as a starting point for describing the current shift.

1. *Material and form.* Artisans are people who stuff material into forms. For instance, wood into the form of a table. This gesture is called "work." The medieval interpretation of this gesture goes like this: the forms are hidden behind the appearances, the theoretical glance can see them; and they reveal themselves to faith. One of these forms is the form of a table. The artisan sees it and he tries as well as he can to stuff it with wood. He does not completely succeed in this because the material defends itself from being informed. The theoretically trained and faith-enlightened glance of the bishop penetrates the work (the wooden table) and establishes the degree to which the artisan has managed to stuff the

material into the form. He establishes the value of the work. The authority of the bishop rules the market: *praecium iustum.*

The bourgeois revolution of the Renaissance can be seen as dismissing
the authority of the bishop and introducing the free market. This implies
an alteration in the question of forms. The revolutionary artisan denies
having theoretically recognized the form of a table or having experienced
its revelation in faith. He claims that previous artisans invented it and
that he, in the process of his own work, can improve it. This modern notion that forms are not fixed ideas but plastic models, that they can be
modeled, that they can be progressively improved, and that therefore the
works express fashions or modes is expressed in the word *modern.*

Thus, the word *theory* also changes its meaning. It no longer denotes
the contemplating of fixed, unchanging ideas but active modeling. It dia-
lectically opposes observation, on the one hand, and experiment, on the
other; for I have to observe the appearances before I work out a model for
them and I must try out my model in order to see how good it is. So
modern scientific technique enters the stage.

Thus the attitude toward value also changes. Work, then, is that gesture
thanks to which models are worked out and progressively improved. This
is why work is the source of all values. There are no eternal values that
can be recognized theoretically or reveal themselves to faith. There is no
idea of a perfect table, of a perfect society, of a perfect human being. All
values have to be worked out. The modern work ethic—recently crystallized as liberalism, on the one hand, and Marxism, on the other—follows
from this.

We are no longer modern. We can no longer ask the question of the
relation of material and form like this because we no longer share the
modern analysis of work and therefore the modern work ethic. We have
been led to a postmodern view of this problematic by the industrial revolution. To us, the work process looks like this: machines work. These de-
vices are an opening (input) through which raw material flows in order
to flow out of another opening (output) as products. In the middle of the
machine is a tool. It bears the form of the product that is to be created
and it mechanically stamps this form onto the raw material that flows by
it. An example is a machine through whose input plastic flows, whose
tool bears the form of an ink pen, and out of whose output plastic ink
pens stream. A critique of these mass-produced ink pens shows that their
value results neither from the raw material nor from the machine nor
from the human beings who work at this machine, but from the form in

the tool. It is thanks to this form that ink pens can write. This is why the source of all work is to be found not in the worker but in the software.

From this point of view, work consists of two phases: a soft phase in which human and artificial intelligence design forms, often from numeric calculations, and a hard one in which these forms are mechanically, often automatically, stamped upon raw material. The second phase, that is, the one that in modernity was regarded as true labor, is inhuman because it can be mechanized. A constantly decreasing part of society participates in this phase. A constantly increasing part is occupied with producing forms, information taken in the widest sense, in the so-called tertiary sector. This quantitative shift alone explains the downfall of Marxism. For the question of who has power and makes decisions has thus shifted. It is not the owner of machines but the information specialist (not the capitalist but the systems analyst and programmer) who holds the power.

But this shift has not only quantitative consequences. The word *theory* has recently undergone a change in meaning. The numerically generated forms of all values that are to be materialized, that appear on computer screens (projects for ink pens, airplanes, or also for formerly unimaginable objects), are without space and time, though able to be modeled. Because they have been numerically generated, they are just as free of space and time as algorithms. That is, whoever contemplates these forms on computer screens has an understanding of theory that is related to that of the classical period and the Middle Ages. The postmodern science that is based on a purely formal theory such as this will necessarily have to lead to a no longer modern technology. The issue will no longer be to work out models for materials, but rather materials for models: no longer a form of a table for wood, but not yet existent materials for worked-out forms. From this technique emerging from formal theory, we can expect alternative worlds. *Cyberspaces,* for instance, give a foretaste of this. We postmoderns are no longer subjects of a given objective world but projects for alternative objectified projections.

2. *Heaven and earth.* In order to make the preceding easier to comprehend, let me refer to a second aspect of the transition from the Middle Ages to modernity. The medieval image of the world looked approximately like this: The world is a ball. In the middle, the earth, above it water, above that air, on the outside fire. Between air and fire, the orbit of the moon draws an ontological limit. The eternal, perfect harmony of spheres, the heavenly order, rules above the moon. Thanks to astronomy and faith, we gain some insight into this. The sublunary world is a mess.

Stones (pieces of earth) are being thrown into the air, water penetrates the earth, air gets into the water, but divine justice brings everything into order again: tossed stones fall back to the earth, water rises from the earth as a spring and falls from the air as rain, and every fire rises as flames to the sky. Down here under the moon, every movement is unjust and must be righted, and everything we do on our own is sin. Judgment Day will come and the heavenly order will also be erected in the sublunary world. Heaven on earth will be established.

This image of the world is recorded in written form in Aristotle and in the Bible; its correctness can be empirically perceived everywhere. All scientific, philosophical, and theological theories offer proofs of it. The medieval political and social order reflects this Weltanschauung. And the sharp division of the world into heaven and earth is also the basis for the division into spiritual and worldly power: pope and emperor. The image of the world is therefore incontestable; it is always everywhere and by everybody taken as valid. It is in this sense catholic.

This image of the world collapses, nevertheless, in a catastrophe that is no longer comprehensible. Disorders in the heavens (for instance, mountains on the moon) become visible and transgress the separation of heaven and earth. Newton finally succeeds in trying to blend the heavenly and the earthly mechanics (Copernicus and Galileo) into one. In this modern image of the world, the Copernican revolution (sun [that is, fire] instead of earth in the center) is less revolutionary than that of Galileo. The things of the world (on earth as well as in the heavens) now move without a motive because of inertia. They no longer commit sins and they are also no longer judged. Any mover of the world becomes a superfluous hypothesis. The law of inertia alone is sufficient as an explanation for movement. The world, heaven as well as earth, is an inert, inanimate, absurd structure, and we can rule it.

In order to do that, we first have to perceive it. Omniscience (science) is necessary for omnipotence (technology). And here appears an epistemological problematic that is characteristic of modernity. The inert world is a thing with extension. We, who stand opposite it, are thinking things. To perceive means to assimilate thinking to extension. The world is geometrical and we ourselves think clearly, that is, arithmetically. Therefore, to know the world is to tag all the places of the world with numbers. But this Cartesian method of analytic geometry is not sufficient. We have to fill up the intervals between the numbers or else the world slips through our fingers. Thanks to differential calculus, we actually succeeded in this. But even after Leibniz, the Kantian epistemological question is still open: how is science possible? This doubt characterizes the whole of modernity. The radiant building of the Newtonian image of the world comes into being on the rubble of the old, catastrophically destroyed medieval image of the world. However, it cannot pass on the lost faith.

We no longer share this doubt in the same way: we now doubt differently. We are no longer modern. The unification of the heavens and the earth into a single universal world in which the same mathematically formulatable laws are valid everywhere has proven to be temporary. The Newtonian building has fallen apart—not into two parts, as in the Middle Ages, but now into three. And these three parts are not distinctly separated, as were heaven and earth in the Middle Ages; rather, they deeply interlock everywhere. And that looks approximately like this:

We are forced to split up the things and processes of the world into three orders of magnitude. In the medium order of magnitude, which is measurable in our measures, that is, in centimeters and seconds, Newton is still valid. In the big order of magnitude, that is, the one measurable in light-years, the Einsteinian rules are valid. In the small one, which is measurable in micromicrons and nanoseconds, the rules of quantum mechanics are valid. In each of these three worlds, we have to think differently, try to imagine differently, and act differently.

And yet we cannot separate the three worlds, in order, for instance, to make a sandwich image of the world. For everywhere, the small world interferes with the medium one (for instance, Chernobyl), the medium one with the big one (for instance, astronautics and aeronautics). The formal incompatibility of the three worlds and their interpenetration makes the following doubt appear on stage: Is it not so that our mathematical way of thinking is projected from us outwards to strike back at us in the shape of three worlds? Is it not as if we had designed out of ourselves the structure of algorithms and theorems, which is the framework of the world, and as if we then had forgotten about it and now laboriously fetched it back? Is it not as if we only discover what we ourselves have invented? This is the postmodern, posthistorical doubt.

And at this point, the reflections concerning heaven and earth meet the other ones concerning material and form. The doubt just mentioned means that the pluriverse with its three worlds is perhaps our own projection. And this means implicitly that we can also put next to the universe of science other worlds that can just as well be known, experienced, and treated. It means that it makes little sense to differentiate between what is given and what is made, between data and facts, between true and false, between real and fictitious, between science and art. It means that all these modern categories have to be thought differently in favor of different ones, if we are no longer subjects but projects. It means, for example that, instead of "true and false," we have to put "probable and improbable." Instead of "real and fictitious," "concrete and abstract." And instead of "science and art," "to formulate and to project."

This attempt to catch hold of the present change of paradigms at two ends and then knot them together is necessarily fragmentary. And it can lead to errors: for instance, if it were proclaimed here that postmodernism were solipsistic. On the contrary, if we assume that the world is our projection, then we assume as well that we ourselves are nothing but this projection. And this reversible ontology (no subject without an object, as well as no object without a subject) is a basic posthistorical feature. As I said before, all this has only been indicated in a fragmentary manner in this lecture. And the forms of consciousness and action that come into being out of the paradigms that I have sketched have not even been indicated. This has necessarily been so and has only partially to do with the time limits that were imposed on this lecture. The real reason for this is that we, I think, are situated within a change of paradigms that we cannot yet foresee. I have nevertheless dared speak about it because this is the first opportunity to utter, in the town of my birth, some of the thoughts that keep me busy.

(1991)

Taking Up Residence in Homelessness

It goes against my own nature, but, having been seduced by my own topic, "Home and Homelessness," I now intend to make the secret of my homelessness a little clearer. I was born a citizen of Prague, and it seems that my ancestors lived more than a thousand years in the Golden City. I am a Jew, and the saying "Next year in Jerusalem" has been with me since my youth. For decades, I was involved in an experiment to synthesize Brazilian culture from a larger mix of Western European, Eastern European, African, East Asian, and Indian cultural phenomena. I live in a village in Provence, and I have become woven into the life fabric of this timeless neighborhood. I was raised in the German culture, and I have been involved in German cultural life for several years. In short, I am homeless, because there are so many homelands that make their home in me. This fact of life is expressed daily in my work. I feel at home in at least four languages. I sense a necessity and a certain amount of pressure to translate and retranslate everything that still needs to be written.

It is burdensome, but it is also exciting for me that I am interested in the phenomena of interpersonal communication, that is, in the gaps between different positions and in the bridges that cross these gaps. Perhaps this interest of mine can be related back to my own tendency to hover over different positions. It causes me to experience the transcendence of homelands and to work through it concretely, but it also forces me to understand it theoretically. The following lecture will document this concrete experience. It will recount the daily work and theoretical considerations of the topic "Home and Homelessness."

First, I want to differentiate as much as possible between "home"

(Heimat) and "a home" *(Wohnung)*. Indeed, I am painfully aware that this causes me to play with the German language. In the languages with which I am familiar, the German word *Heimat* has an equivalent only in the Czech word *domov*. This is most likely owing to the fact that German had a strong influence on Czech for hundreds of years. Perhaps the term *Heimat* is only native to German—the term, but not the experience? After all, I also have my doubts about the experience itself. Does the Provençal farmer living in Robion experience his own historical, multi-stratified homeland (whose archaeological structure has been put in place by late-Paleolithic, Neolithic, Ligurian, Greek, Roman, Visigothic, Burgundian, Arabian, Frankish, Provençal, Italian, and French ancestors) in the same manner that the traveling Brazilian farmworker experiences his *terra* or the Israeli kibbuznik his *Eretz Israel*?

During the lengthiest epoch of human existence, man has dwelled in "a home," a house, but he has not possessed a "home." If all the signs are to be believed, then we are now ready to leave the ten-thousand-year-long Neolithic period behind us. This experience teaches us just how short, relatively speaking, the prevailing epoch of human settlement has been. We are about to discard our so-called values along with our settled forms of existence, such as property, the second-class citizenship of women, the division of labor, and the notion of homeland. In this manner, we demonstrate that these are not eternal values, but rather a function of agriculture and cattle breeding. The painful departure from agriculture and its industrial legacy for the uncharted lands of postindustrial society and posthistory ("hic sunt leones") will become easier once we take up these considerations. We, the uncounted millions of emigrants (whether we are guest workers, expellees, or intellectuals traveling from one seminar to another),[1] do not recognize ourselves as outsiders, but rather as pioneers of the future. For this reason, the Vietnamese in California, the Turks in Germany, the Palestinians in the Persian Gulf, and the Russian scientists at Harvard should not be considered pitiful victims in need of aid. One should not give aid so that they can go back to their homelands. Instead, they should be considered role models whose examples we follow in case we are sufficiently daring. Certainly, only the expelled and emigrants can allow themselves such thoughts, not the expellers or those who stayed behind; for emigration is a creative activity, but it also entails suffering. Just as we know that doing comes from suffering ("Whoever has not eaten his bread with tears . . .").

Home is not an eternal value, but rather the function of a certain technique; yet, whoever loses his home, suffers. He is bound to his home by many threads, most of which are secret threads beyond his consciousness. If the threads tear or are torn, then this tear is experienced as a painful surgical incision into his most private self. When I was expelled from Prague (or mustered up the courage to flee), I experienced this moment as if it were the collapse of the universe. For I made the mistake of confusing what is intimate with what is public. In pain, I realized that the threads now amputated had tied me down. I was overcome with a sense of vertigo resulting from my liberation and newfound freedom. Allegedly, this vertigo is the mark of a wayward spirit. I experienced freedom during the first year of World War II in London, a place that seems like China to someone from the Continent. I experienced freedom while anticipating the coming horror of humanity in the concentration camps. The changing of the question "freedom from what?" into the question "freedom for what?"—this turning of one thing into another, which is characteristic of hard-won freedom—followed me like a *basso continuo* through all my future migrations. We are all like this, we nomads who have surfaced after having experienced the breakdown of a settled form of existence.

Secret threads tie the person with a home to people and the things of home. They reach beyond the consciousness of our adult life into regions that are at once childish, infantile, and perhaps even fetal and transindividual, into the poorly or barely articulated and unarticulated memory. A prosaic example: The Czech dish *svíčková* (pork loin) awakens feelings in me that are difficult to analyze but that the German word *Heimweh* ("homesickness") expresses well. The loss of home sheds light on this secret. It brings fresh air where there was once a comfortable fog. It discloses what it really is: the seat of most (perhaps all) of our prejudices—the judgments made before any conscious judgments.

The famous desire for home much celebrated in prose and poetry, this secret rootedness in infantile, fetal, and transindividual regions of the psyche, cannot stand up to the kind of cool analysis that the man without a home is bound to and is capable of. Certainly, in the initial stages of this analysis, the desire for home being analyzed tears at the guts of the man analyzing himself, as if it wanted to turn them inside out. The German word *Heimweh* or the French *nostalgie* does not capture this feeling as well as the Portuguese *saudade*. However, once the fact of expulsion has led to the state of freedom—once the question "freedom from what?" has changed into the question "freedom for what?"—the secret rootedness in home becomes an obscure involvement that calls out to be split in half like the Gordian knot. Thus, the man who analyzes himself recognizes the degree to which his secret rootedness in home has obscured his clear view of the scene. He recognizes not only that every home blinds those involved in its own way, but also that in this sense all homes are equal. Most of all, noncoercive judgments, decisions, and actions become possible only after overcoming this involvement in home. In my case, after splitting one Gordian knot after another—one in Prague, one in London, and one in São Paulo—I recognized the equality (or the equal worthlessness) of all prejudices residing there, anticipating those that reside in Robion. But, above all, I recognized that my freedom to make judgments, to decide for myself, to act, increases with every splitting of a knot. This knowledge allows me to split one knot after another with ever-growing virtuosity. The emigration from Prague was a terrible experience, whereas leaving Robion would probably only require the free decision of stepping into a car and driving away. This is the reason why Zionism, despite all my sympathy for it, does not appeal to me existentially.

The mysterious desire for home chains people to other people and things. Both people and things are drenched by its mystery. I do not think it is necessary to speak about the perniciousness of a mysterious attachment to things. Sanctified things not only set limits (that is, they reduce freedom), but also become personalized (that is, one loves them). This confusion of things for persons, this ontological error of taking an It for a Thou, is exactly what the prophets called paganistic. It is the magical thinking that the philosophers wanted to overcome. The mysterious attachment to people deserves some reflection, however. For it poses the true question of freedom.

In this respect, I have two experiences that contradict one another. All of the people to whom I was mysteriously bound in Prague were murdered. All of them. The Jews in gas chambers, the Czechs in the Resistance, the Germans on the Russian front. All of the people to whom I was mysteriously bound in São Paulo are living, and I am still in contact with them. Paradoxically, the splitting of the Gordian knot in Prague was easier for me than the one in São Paulo, even though the secret that bound me to Prague was murkier than the one in São Paulo. An incredibly macabre experience.

The mysterious ties that bind a man to the people at home (meaning love and friendship as well as hate and enmity) also tear at the emigrant, because they call into question the freedom he suffered for. These are the dialogic threads of responsibility and of answering for another. Is the freedom of the migrant, this "spirit" who belongs nowhere, a solipsistic freedom devoid of responsibility? Has he attained his freedom at the cost of being with others? Or is solitude devoid of responsibility not, rather, the migrant's fate (just as the Romantic poets described it)? As I mentioned earlier, the transition from expulsion into freedom negates this question. It was my birth that threw me into my first homeland, without anyone asking me if this was something I wanted. The chains that bound me there to my neighbors were, for the most part, placed on me. In my now hard-won freedom, it is I who ties the binds that connect me to my neighbors, in cooperation with them. The responsibility that I have toward my neighbors is not something that has been imposed upon me, but rather that I have accepted for myself. Unlike the one who is left behind and who remains mysteriously chained to his neighbors, I am instead bound to them by my own free will. These ties are not less emotionally and sentimentally charged than his chains, but rather just as strong and more independent.

This, I believe, demonstrates what freedom means: not cutting off all relationships with others, but weaving these connections in cooperation with them. The migrant does not become free by denying his lost home, but by overcoming it. I am a citizen of Prague and of São Paulo and of Robion. I am Jewish, and I belong to the so-called German culture. I do not deny this. Indeed, I emphasize it, to be able to negate it.

The sociologists would have us believe that the secret codes of home can be learned by strangers (for instance, by sociologists or by those without a home), because natives had to learn them. The initiation rites of so-called primitive peoples prove this. Thus, a person without a home could travel from home to home and find his way into each of these, if he were able to bring with him a master key that unlocked all these homes. The reality is different. The secret codes of homes are not made of conscious rules, but rather spun from unconscious habits. What characterizes the habit is the fact that one is not conscious of it. The person without a home must first consciously learn the secret codes and then forget them, to be able to immigrate into a home. However, if the code becomes conscious, then its rules turn out not to be sacred but banal. The immigrant becomes even more unsettling to the native, uncannier than the traveler out there, because he reveals the banality of the sacred to the native. He is hateful; he is ugly, because he exposes the beauty of home as nothing more than pretty kitsch. His immigration causes a polemical dialogue between the ugly stranger and the beautiful native. The dialogue either escalates into pogroms or into modifications of the home or into the native's liberation from the ties that bind. In this respect, my involvement in Brazil provides a good example.

First, I want to liberate the term *Brazil* from the Eurocentric prejudices that conceal it (such as Third World, underdevelopment, or exploitation). (After all, these prejudices and judgments that are made preconsciously are native to all homelands.) Until well into the nineteenth century, the Brazilian population consisted of three different groups that overlapped one another. There were Portuguese, some of whom had fled their homeland and some of whom administered Brazil on behalf of Portugal. There were Africans, who were brought to Brazil as slaves. And, there were indigenous peoples, who were driven even further and further into the outback. (These indigenous peoples could be separated into a ruling class, the Tupis, and a dominated lower class, called Tupinambas in a derogatory way.) When slavery was abolished in the second half of the nineteenth century, unemployed Africans began crowding the cities, so that European immigrants, especially northern Italians, were called in to cultivate the land (coffee, cotton, sugar cane). Others followed the first wave of immigration; for instance, there were Poles, Syrio-Lebanese, Japanese, and, of course, Portuguese. At the time of my arrival in Brazil, the last of these waves was the Jews. Yet, others have come in the meantime, until the flow of immigrants finally dried up in the 1960s. It is important to remember that this flow of immigrants impacted the south but barely affected the north, so that the country eventually split into two regions. Currently, there is a massive influx from the northeast into the south. The images that European television has given us are mostly related to this massive influx.

Before the emancipation of the slaves, there was a lot of Romantic talk about a Brazilian homeland in poems and prose, but reality (the notorious *realidade brasileira*) exposed this Romantic talk as a lie. There was the thin Portuguese upper class that crowded around the harbors, to receive the latest news from their lost homelands, Lisbon and Paris. One felt oneself exiled. Africans made up a majority of the people, but there was no conscious connection to Africa. These people were naked when they were thrown from the slave ships onto the Brazilian shores. Only, in their inner selves deformed by hard work they carried with them and then brought out their cultural traditions in the form of music, dance, and religious rites, to build the foundations of a future Brazilian homeland. The indigenous peoples who were driven further into the background were never an actual part of Brazilian life, but rather part of a myth of the outback that was worshiped and brutally destroyed at the same time. The difference between Brazil (as well as Argentina and Uruguay) and other Latin American countries is that the indigenous peoples of these countries exist only as an ideologically charged background.

The European, Near Eastern, and Far Eastern immigrants began asking questions about the status of Brazil as a possible home. Using these heterogeneous elements, would it be possible to create a fabric of mysterious relationships like the one familiar from the old homes? There was one common thread: the Portuguese language. On the one hand, Luso-Brazilian is archaic in comparison to the language spoken in Portugal (Renaissance elements can be identified); on the other hand, it is wild (African elements had made their way in). Still, this is what enabled Portuguese to become a lingua franca for speakers of Arabic and Japanese. Another question: Is it possible to construct a Brazilian language that can both support and transmit a Brazilian culture and thus make the country of Brazil into a home for a future society? In my opinion, this controversial question is the breeding ground for everything that Brazil has produced in the last century, beginning with Brasília and ending with bossa nova.

When I arrived in Brazil and as soon as I managed to free myself from the gas chambers to a certain extent, I was carried away by this fever. I indulged myself into building a new, humane home free of prejudice. It was not until the *golpe,* the army's coup d'état, that I became more humble. But, not because I understood the Brazilian coup to be a reactionary intervention—the way most European observers interpreted it— but because I recognized it as the first manifestation of a Brazilian homeland. I would like to discuss my disappointment with the Brazilian homeland (indeed, with all homelands) in somewhat more detail.

Existentially speaking, Brazil was a "no-man's-land" when the first waves of immigration began during the nineteenth century. It was nobody's home. Thus, the patriotic battle cry that demanded the creation of a home: "Esta país tem dono" (This country has an owner). It was not an African, an Asian, or an Andean colony, where colonists ruled over natives, but rather, it was like the United States, an empty land from which the natives were expelled. Thus, the immigrants were not greeted as ugly strangers, but rather, without prejudices, as partners in destiny without a home. (For reasons of time, I cannot go into the differences between Brazil and the United States at this moment.) This unprejudiced attitude was very different from the European attitude about homelands from which the immigrants had been expelled, and it would almost have been selfish not to get involved. After all, in a "no-man's-land" such as this, one was a pioneer in everything one wanted to do. In my case, a Brazilian philosophy was yet to be created with the help of a few partners in destiny. One began spinning out threads of dialogue with one's neighbors. Unlike at home, where these threads were imposed by birth, the new ones were established freely. Thus, I recognized what makes patriotism (whether local or national) so devastating: it anoints the human ties that bind and thus neglects the ties that we accept freely; it privileges family ties to elective affinities, the real or imagined biological relations to those of friendship and love. I fell into a fever of freedom: I was free to choose my neighbor.

This weaving together of future secret codes, of a future Brazilian home, of a transformation of adventure into habit, and of a sacralization of habit was exciting as long as new waves of immigration continued to find acceptance. Preoccupied with making new connections, the network remained open. For example, there was the philosophical institute, where Italian students of Croce, German Heideggerians, Portuguese Ortegans, East Jewish Positivists, Belgian Catholics, and Anglo-Saxon Pragmatists participated in debate. It had to open itself to the ideas of Japanese devotees of Zen, to a Libyan mystic, and to a Chinese writing scholar, and it had to give room to a West Jewish Talmudist. Despite this open attitude, the institute was professionalized. The acceptance of new people became more difficult. The reigning prejudices crystallized. Which is to say, the attempt to build a new home was beginning to be a success.

Added to this, there were two experiences in the 1950s that had to be taken into account. The first one is described by the term *defasagem* (something like "de-phasing"); the second one by the term *populismo*. To the extent that an autonomous Brazilian social core was developing, the previously dynamic contact with major centers of the world (above all in America) was lost. I recognized what I had given up once I had become involved in Brazil—namely, the freedom from geographical ties. Confronted with the present information revolution, I began to have doubts. I was not sure whether geographical ties were not reactionary, or whether one should surrender the advantages of not having a home.

The second experience, that of *populismo,* is more radical. The socioeconomic class structure of the 1950s went along these lines: The majority of the people lived a half-nomadic existence; they followed the harvests of the monocultures into suffering, hunger, and disease; and the challenge was to create a homeland from these masses devoid of culture. Above this stratum, there was the proletariat living in the cities and made up mostly of immigrants. And, beyond this, there was the bourgeoisie made up partly of immigrants and partly of the offspring of Portuguese conquistadores. The weaving together of a homeland was the bourgeoisie's task. And the question was: To whom should we turn? To workers in the city, to awaken them? Or to the passive crowd, to make it part of the social fabric? Both objectives could not be achieved at the same time. For, to mobilize the cities, one had to politicize them. And, to confront the masses, one had to depoliticize them and create economic options. In short, one had to fight either for freedom or against hunger and disease. It is very difficult to make a clear decision when one is confronted with choices so grim. I tried, and I failed.

The "populist" tendency that came to power with Vargas, and that had as its aftermath the president who died before taking office, believed it could avoid this impossible dilemma.[2] And, in the following manner: First, one had to mobilize the workers politically and then be able to absorb the masses at a later date. This led to fascistic demagoguery and to a vulgarization of all cultural undertakings. Second, a "technocratic" tendency took the bull by the horns. One had to remove need, and to be able to do this, one had to use central planning. This sort of planning requires a dictatorship and a "provisional" stopping of all social, political, and cultural disruptions of central planning. The army—a group that consisted of the bourgeoisie—embodied this "technocratic" tendency. After 1964, it became clear to me that the only possible way to build a Brazilian homeland was through the eventual victory of technocracy over populism. Moreover, it became clear to me what this homeland would look like: a gigantic, progressive apparatus that would be equal in every way to the closed-mindedness, fanaticism, and patriotic prejudices of every European homeland. And yet, my involvement in Brazil lasted until 1972, when I made the painful decision to give it up and to live in Provence, which is for me an anti-Brazil.

The disappointment with Brazil was the discovery that every home is nothing more than the sacralization of the banal, whether one is born into it or one is involved in its synthesis. Whatever its shape, home is nothing more than a place to live surrounded by mysteries. If one wants to preserve the hard-won freedom of homelessness, then one must withstand participating in this mystification of habits. In the case of my Brazilian experience, I have to preserve the connections that I established there, because I am responsible to my Brazilian neighbors, just as they are responsible to me. However, I have to establish other connections outside Brazil, and I have to integrate my Brazilian experience into my new connections. Brazil is not my home. Instead, "home" is the people to whom I am responsible.

The freedom gained by homelessness is not to be confused with philanthropy, cosmopolitanism, or humanism. I am not responsible for all mankind—for example, one billion Chinese. Instead, freedom is the choice to take responsibility for one's "neighbor." It is the kind of freedom taught by the Judeo-Christian tradition, where freedom is love of one's neighbor. Also, it says that man is an outcast in the world who must seek his home elsewhere.

"Home" is considered to be a relatively permanent location, but "a home," a house, is a transient, dispensable location. The contrary is true: one can exchange homes or dispense with them altogether, but one has to live in a house, no matter where. The Parisian clochards live under bridges, Gypsies in caravans, and Brazilian farmworkers in huts. Moreover, people lived in Auschwitz, even though this may sound terrible. For, if one is without a home, then one literally dies. There are different ways to describe this sort of death, but the following is the least sentimental: when one is without a home and unprotected from the usual and what one is used to, everything that comes to us is noise and nothing is information. In a world without information, a world of chaos, one can neither feel, nor think, nor act.

I built myself a house in Robion, so that I could live there. My usual writing desk stands in the middle of the house with the usual disorder of books and papers. I have gotten used to the village surrounding my house. There is the usual post office and the usual weather. Things become more and more unusual the further I get away: Provence, France, Europe, the earth, the ever-expanding universe. Also, the past year, the lost homelands, the adventurous abysses of history and prehistory, the coming adventurous future, and the unforeseeable future behind it. I make my bed in the things I am used to, so that I can let in the unusual, and do unusual things. I make my bed in redundancy, to receive noise as information and to produce information. My home, this network of habits, serves as a net that captures adventure and serves as a springboard to adventure.

According to Hegelian analysis, the dialectic between a home and the unusual, between redundancy and noise, is the dynamic of unhappy consciousness, which is consciousness in general. Consciousness is the back-and-forth between a home and the unusual, between private and public. According to Hegel, if I find the world, then I lose myself; if I find myself, then I lose the world. Without a home, I would be unconscious; that is, without a home, I would not actually exist. A home is how I find myself in the world—if at all. It is primary.

There is an external dialectic between a home and the world, between the familiar and the strange. But, there is also an internal dialectic of habit, a dialectic of the home. If habit is open to the strange, if it recognizes the strange as information, then it cannot be recognized itself. If I am sitting at my writing desk, then I do not recognize the books and papers lying around, because I am used to them. I only recognize the books and papers that have recently arrived. Like a cotton blanket, habit covers up all phenomena. It rounds off the edges of the phenomena that it covers, so that I no longer run into them but make use of them unconsciously. With respect to this, there is the well-known Heideggerian study of the slippers lying under the bed. I do not recognize my home, but I dully experience it, and, aesthetically speaking, this dull experience is prettiness. Everyone's home is thought pretty by its resident, precisely because he is used to it. This demonstrates the well-known cycle of aesthetics: "ugly-beautiful-pretty-ugly." The noises coming into the home are ugly, because they disturb familiarity. If one uses them to create information, they become beautiful, because they are built into the home. Habit transforms this beauty into prettiness, because it is dully experienced. Ultimately, the home throws superfluous things into the trash, and they become ugly.

This excursus into aesthetics was necessary, so that we could get a handle on the phenomenon of love for homeland (and for fatherland). Natives confuse home with a home. They think their homes pretty, just as we all think our homes pretty. Consequently, they confuse prettiness with beauty. This confusion stems from the fact that natives are involved in their homes. They are not open to the ugliness that confronts them and that could be transformed into beauty. More than anything, patriotism is a symptom of an aesthetic disease.

In every homeland, prettiness wrongly passes for beauty. In most homelands, this confusion of the unusual and the familiar, of the extraordinary and the ordinary, is not only an aesthetic catastrophe, but also an ethical one. If I consider the French Provence or the German Allgäu beautiful—because I am used to them, and not because I discovered them myself—then I am the victim of an aesthetic fallacy. However, I am not necessarily the victim of an ethical fallacy. But, if I consider São Paolo beautiful, then I have committed a sin. For habit is like a cotton blanket: It covers up and rounds off the edges of phenomena. It prevents me from recognizing the misery and injustice prevailing there, and I can only vaguely feel them. They become part of the prettiness of home that I confuse with beauty. This is what is so catastrophic about habit.

A home is the foundation of everyone's consciousness, for it enables us to recognize the world. But it also dulls the senses, for it cannot be recognized, and we barely acknowledge its existence. If one confuses a home

(Wohnung)—a house—with home *(Heimat),* the primary with the secondary, then the internal contradictions become clearer. Because the native is involved in his homeland, only a conscious effort enables him to recognize the world outside.

The migrant is a man of a coming future world without homes. In his subconsciousness, he carries the mysteries of all the homes he has once passed through. But he does not embody any of these mysteries. In this respect, he is not mysterious. He is transparent to his others. He does not live in mystery but in evidence. He is both a window and a mirror: natives can see the world through him and, at the same time, they see themselves, if only in a distorted view. Nevertheless, the migrant's lack of mystery gives the native an uncanny feeling. Evidence of the migrant's existence cannot be denied. The ugliness of the unfamiliar comes from everywhere and penetrates every home. It calls the prettiness and beauty of home into question. Moreover, because the native confuses home with a home, it calls his consciousness and his existence in the world into question. The uncanniness of a homeless man is that he gives evidence to the native that there are not only numerous homes, but also numerous mysteries. Moreover, he is evidence that there will not be any more mysteries of this sort in the near future.

Living in evidence does not present the migrant with an uncanny feeling, but rather with a problem. The loss of the original, barely acknowledged mystery of home opens him up to a different sort of mystery: to the secret of being with the Other. His problem is this: How can I overcome the prejudices that lie inside the mysteries that I have carried with me? How can I break through the prejudices of my neighbors who embody mystery? How will I join together with them to create beauty out of ugliness? In this respect, every person without a home is—at least, potentially—the clear consciousness of all natives as well as a messenger of the future. Thus, I believe that we migrants must accept this function as our profession and our calling.

(1987)

Notes by the Editor

1. This text is based on a lecture at the second "Kornhaus-Seminar" on the topic "Home and Homelessness" in Weiler im Allgäu (Germany).

2. Getúlio Dornelles Vargas (1883–1954), twice president of Brazil

(1930–45, 1951–54), was a very popular dictator who was forced by the army to resign from office. After twenty-three years of military presidents, the civilian Tancredo Neves was selected by Congress and in January 1985 was elected president. However, he contracted a fatal disease and died in April 1985, thus making way for his deputy, José Sarney (born 1930), who was unable to improve the desperate economic situation in Brazil.

Exile and Creativity

This essay will explore neither the existential nor the religious connotations of the concept of the term *exile*. However, we should keep in the back of our mind the Christian story of man's expulsion from Paradise and his entrance into the world, the Jewish mystic's story of the exile of divine spirit in the world, and the existentialist story of man as a stranger in the world. All of these stories should be kept in the back of our mind without being verbalized. For the intention here is to interpret the exile situation as a challenge to creative activity.

This is the proposed hypothesis: The expelled has been torn out of his customary surroundings (or else he has done it himself). Habit is a blanket that covers up the facts of the case. In familiar surroundings, change is recognized, but not permanence. Whoever lives in a home finds change informative but considers permanence redundant. In exile, everything is unusual. Exile is an ocean of chaotic information. In it, the lack of redundancy does not allow the flood of information to be received as meaningful messages. Because it is unusual, exile is unlivable. One must transform the information whizzing around into meaningful messages, to make it livable. One must "process" the data. It is a question of survival: if one fails to transform the data, one is engulfed by the waves of exile. Data transformation is a synonym for creation. The expelled must be creative if he does not want to go to the dogs.

Before I begin defending this hypothesis, I want to point out that it proposes a positive assessment of expulsion. In a situation where one is accustomed to pitying the expelled, this positive assessment is itself unusual, and, according to the hypothesis, it should itself be informative.

For it seems—according to this hypothesis—that those people who want to "help" the expelled to become ordinary again are, in fact, engaged in reeling him back into their ordinariness. This is an informative assumption, because it forces us to think about what is usual. The assumption does not justify the expellers, but rather, it exposes the vulgarity of the expellers: the expelled were bothersome factors who were expelled to make the surroundings even more ordinary than before. Indeed, this assumption leaves the following question to our discretion: Even without intending to do so, have the expellers not done the expelled a service?

I use the word *expelled* rather than *refugees* or *emigrants,* to bring the totality of the problem before our eyes. For I do not only refer to phenomena like the "boat people," Palestinians, or Jewish emigration from Hitler's Europe, but also, the expulsion of an older generation from the world of their children and grandchildren—or even the expulsion of humanists from the world of apparatuses. We find ourselves in a period of expulsion. If one values this situation positively, the future will appear a little less dark.

This essay has been written by one who has been expelled not only many times, but also in a number of different ways. Thus, it comes from one who knows the suffering that characterizes every form of exile. Also, the shadow that this sort of suffering casts and for which the German language has coined the term *Heimweh* ("homesickness"). Nevertheless— or perhaps out of spite—this essay will praise expulsion.

Habit is like a cotton blanket. It covers up all the sharp edges, and it dampens all noises. It is unaesthetic (from *aisthesthai* = perception), because it prevents bits of information from being perceived, as edges or noises. Because habit screens perceptions, because it anaesthetizes, it is considered comfortable. As comfy. Habit makes everything nice and quiet. Every comfortable surrounding is pretty, and this prettiness is one of the sources of love of the fatherland. (Which, indeed, confuses prettiness with beauty.) If the cotton blanket of habit is pulled back, one discovers things. Everything becomes unusual, monstrous, in the true sense of the word *un-settling*. To understand this, it is quite enough to look at one's right hand with all its finger movements from the perspective of a Martian: an octupus-like monstrosity. The Greeks called this "discovering" of the covered up *aletheia,* a word that we translate as "truth."

It is not as if we could actually be expelled from our right hand, unless, of course, we let it be amputated. Thus, when we discover how monstrous our bodily condition is, it is owing to our strange ability to expel our body from our thoughts. An exile as radical as this cannot be maintained for long: we are overcome with an irresistible homesickness for our own beautiful bodies, and we reimmigrate. Yet, this example of an extreme form of exile is instructive: For the expelled, it is almost as if he has been expelled from his own body. As if he was out of his mind. Even the usual things that he takes into exile are creepy. Everything around him and in him becomes sharp and noisy. He is driven to discovery, to truth.

The transcendence in which the expelled finds himself (as much as the word *finds* describes him, for in reality he is lost) causes everything around him and in him to appear provisory, transitory. In habit, only change is perceived; in exile, everything is perceived as if in the process of change. For the expelled, everything challenges him to change his life. In exile, where the blanket of habit has been pulled back, he becomes a revolutionary, if only because it enables him to live there. Thus, the suspicion that confronts the expelled in his New Land is completely justified. His advent in the New Land breaks through the usual and threatens its prettiness.

Only for the expelled is the New Land truly new. Wherever he is driven, he discovers America. For the natives who must accept him, it is Old Land. Only the immigrant in America is truly an American, even if he should migrate to ancient lands (for example, to Jerusalem). His immigration into exile radiates an American atmosphere. Yet, from his perspective, it is something completely different: he is concerned with making the unusual livable (that is, everything). It is possible to shape a creative dialogue between the expelled and the original natives out of this reciprocal misunderstanding.

It is not inconsequential where one is driven. Certainly, for the expelled himself, all exile is New Land. But, for the original natives, every land has its own character, that is, other habits that cover up the truth. There are lands that consider themselves new out of habit (for example, America or the land of our grandchildren or the land of automatic apparatuses). Also, there are lands that consider themselves old out of habit, which is to say "sacred" (for example, Jerusalem or the land of linear texts or the land of bourgeois values). If the expelled moves into a land that considers itself new, then the original natives are forced to uncover their senility petrified by habit. And, if he moves into a land that considers itself sacred, then the original natives are forced to uncover their sacredness as habit. On the one hand, he forces the Americans, the grandchildren, and the apparatus functionaries to uncover themselves as something that has always existed. On the other hand, he forces the citizens of Jerusalem, the authors, and the defenders of eternal values to uncover themselves as lazy creatures of habit. In this manner, the creative dialogue between the expelled and the original natives can be divided into two types. The one type (such as the dialogue between an expelled and a New Yorker) will bring renewal through information; the other type (that between an expelled and a citizen of Jerusalem) will bring de-sacralization through information. This classification is important for an understanding of the present (such as the phenomenon of the so-called guest workers or the phenomenon of the critique of apparatuses, as has been advanced in Germany by the Greens).

The expelled are uprooted people who attempt to uproot everything around themselves, to establish roots. They do it spontaneously, simply because they were expelled. It is an almost vegetable process. Perhaps one can observe it when one tries to transplant trees. It can happen that the expelled becomes conscious of the vegetable, almost vegetative aspect of his exile; that he uncovers that the human being is not a tree; and that perhaps human dignity consists in not having roots—that a man first becomes a human being when he hacks off the vegetable roots that bind him. In German, there is the hateful word *Luftmensch,* a careless "man with his head in the air." The expelled may discover that *air* and *spirit* are closely related terms and that therefore *Luftmensch* essentially signifies human being.

This sort of discovery is a dialectical change in the relationship between expelled and expeller. Before this discovery, the expeller is the active pole and the expelled is the passive pole. After this discovery, the expeller is the victim and the expelled is the perpetrator. This is the discovery that history is made by the expelled, not by the expellers. The Jews are not part of Nazi history; the Nazis are part of Jewish history. The grandparents are not part of our biography; the grandchildren are part of our biography. We are not part of the history of automatic apparatuses; the apparatuses are part of our history. And, the more radically the Nazis, the grandchildren, and the apparatuses have driven us into exile, the more we make history: the better we transcend. But this is not the decisive part of the discovery that we are not trees—that the uprooted make history. Instead, the decisive part of it is to discover how tiresome it is not to establish new roots. After all, habit is not merely a cotton blanket that covers up everything. It is also a mud bath where it is nice to wallow. Homesickness is a *nostalgie de la boue,* and one can make oneself comfortable anywhere, even in exile. *Ubi bene, ibi patria.* The discovery that we are not trees challenges the expelled to struggle constantly against the seduction pleasures of the mud bath. To continue to experience expulsion, which is to say: to allow oneself to be expelled again and again.

Of course, this leads us to the question of freedom. The discovery of human dignity as uprootedness seems to reduce one's freedom to the mere right to come and go as one pleases. The right of the spirit to drift from one place to another. But, in reality, the question of freedom leads us to the question: Is it possible to allow oneself to want to be driven? Is there not a contradiction between "allowing" and "wanting"? Are we able to want our fate? A famous question. But, for the expelled, it is not a theoretical question, such as the dialectic between determination and freedom; rather, it is a practical question. The first expulsion was suffered. It has shown itself to be productive. Afterwards, exile becomes habit. Should one, like Baron von Münchhausen, try to pull oneself out of this habit by one's own bootstraps, or should one provoke a new expulsion? Thus, the question of freedom is not the question of coming and going, but rather of remaining a stranger. Different from others.

At the beginning, I said that creating is synonymous with data processing. By that I meant that the production of new information (creating) depends on the synthesis of previous information. Such a synthesis consists in the exchange of information, just as it might be stored in one singular memory or in multiple memories. Thus, with respect to creating, one can speak of a dialectical process where the dialogue is either "internal" or "external." The advent of the expelled in exile leads to "external" dialogues. This spontaneously causes an industrious creative activity in the vicinity of the expelled. He is a catalyst for the synthesis of new information. If, however, he becomes aware of his uprootedness as his dignity, then an "internal" dialogue begins within himself; which is to say, an exchange between the information he has brought with him, and an entire ocean with waves of information that toss around him in exile. The objective is the creation of meaning between the imported information and the chaos that surrounds him. If these "external" and "internal" dialogues are harmonized with each other, they transform in a creative manner not only the world, but also the original natives and the expelled. This is what I meant when I said what freedom means for the expelled: the freedom to remain a stranger, different from the others. It is the freedom to change oneself and others as well.

The expelled is the Other of others. Which is to say, he is other for the others, and the others are other for him. He himself is nothing more than the Other of others. In this manner, he is able to "identify." His advent in exile allows the original natives to uncover that they are unable to "identify" without him. Because of his advent in exile, the "self" is rent asunder, opening it up to others, to a being-with-others. This dialogic atmosphere that characterizes exile is not necessarily part of a mutual recognition, but rather, it is mostly polemical (not to mention murderous). For the expelled threatens the "particular nature" of the original natives; his strangeness calls them into question. But, even such a polemical dialogue is creative; for it leads to the synthesis of new information. Exile, no matter what form it takes, is a breeding ground for creative activity, for the new.

(1984)

A New Imagination

Man's unique ability to create images for himself and for others has been a theme of philosophical and theological speculation at least since Plato. This ability seems truly unique to man, because none of the species preceding him seem to have created anything comparable to images such as the cave paintings in Dordogne. In this tradition, speculative thinking on this human ability has been grouped around the terms *imagination* or *visualization*: it is often taken as a given, as a fact. One assumes that something like "powers of imagination" actually exists, and then one attempts to come to terms with its existence. Since Husserl, we have learned to bracket off these sorts of assumptions and to allow the phenomenon to express itself. If we do this here, then the imagination appears to be a complex, purposive ("intentional") gesture. With it, the human being adjusts to his life-world. If one examines this gesture more precisely, one realizes that images owe their existence to two diametrically opposed gestures rather than one singular gesture. The philosophical and theological tradition privileges one of these two gestures, and for good reason: the second gesture of image production has become a functional alternative only in the recent past.

Idolatry and Iconoclasm

Initially, the first gesture of image production will be considered. The pony's image on the walls of the Pech-Merle cave will serve as an example. One could say that it suffices to take a couple steps away from the pony and then to climb somewhere in the distance (for example, up a hill). However, experience tells us that this description does not hit the mark. To be able to form an image of the pony, one must somehow simultaneously retreat into oneself. The philosophical tradition describes this strange nonplace—into which one enters and out of which one draws images for oneself—with names such as "subjectivity" and "existence." For instance, "imagination" is the unique ability to step back from the objective world into one's own subjectivity, to become the subject of an objective world. It is the unique ability to "ek-sist" rather than "insist." In any case, this gesture commences with a movement of abstraction, of pulling out, of retreat.

Tradition (not only the philosophical tradition, but, above all, the theological tradition inspired by Judaism) has raised important objections against this sort of image creation. If one translates these objections into a more contemporary terminology, one is able to group them into three main arguments. First, the perspective from which the images are created is ontologically and epistemologically suspicious: it casts doubt on whether what you see is, in fact, an object. Second, the image codes are connotative out of necessity: they allow for contradictory interpretations, and, therefore, one cannot put much faith in images as models of behavior. Third, images are mediations between the subject and the objective world. As such, they are subject to an internal dialectic: they present themselves before the objects that they should be representing. The third argument in particular plays a central role in the theological tradition.

Images (like all mediation in general) have a tendency to block the path to the objects they mediate. Their ontological position is turned inside out in the following manner: Signposts become obstacles. The result is a pernicious about-face of the human being with respect to images. This about-face of the human being is called "idolatry," and the resulting behavior is called "magical." Images are to be prohibited, because they alienate the human being out of necessity, driving him into the madness of idolatry and magical behavior.

Considering these three arguments—especially the third one—we are able to represent a view that avoids the prohibition of images. One can say the following: we cannot orient ourselves in the world without first creating an image of it. (Imagination is imperative for comprehending and dealing with the world.) Nevertheless, the arguments against images are correct. Thus, it makes no sense to prohibit image creation. Instead, the created images should be critiqued. This sort of critique should enlighten us about the ontologically and epistemologically suspicious perspective of imagination (argument 1); it should transcode the image codes into denotative codes (argument 2); and, it should make images transparent for what they represent (argument 3). To do this, a critique of images must distance itself from images (thus removing itself one step further from the objective world).

The position that I have outlined has been held at least for the last 3,500 years in the West. Taken as a whole, Western civilization can be considered a progressive attempt to enlighten the imagination (to explain images). To do this, linear writing was invented. The rules for writing are relatively clear and definite, and the alphabet is relatively denotative, so that the objective world, taken as a bundle of processes, is relatively manageable by method: which is to say, the scientific and technical method. In essence, it is necessary to explain the images causally and logically, to be able to deal with the world methodically, using images that have been made transparent in this way.

Critique of Image Criticism

It has become apparent that an image criticism established by linear writing is not radical enough. Which is to say that linear rules of writing (especially causal explanations and logical thought processes) cannot always be used as models for a methodical treatment of the world. This "crisis of science," this critique of science, is essentially a critique of the Enlightenment. It does not begin with Hume and Kant but accompanies, sotto voce, the entire discourse of the West. Viewed from the perspective of the thoughts on imagination proposed here, the critique of image criticism can be formulated in the following manner: The linear gesture of writing tears the pixels from the image surface, but it then threads these selected points (bits) torn from the image into lines. This threading phase of the linear gesture negates its critical intention, in that it accepts the linear structure uncritically. This is probably a very old cultural technique that has been accepted uncritically: mussels have always been threaded together in chains. If one wants a radical critique of images, one must analyze them. Which is to say, processing the selected bits formally, instead of ordering them into preordained linear structures. One must "calculate" them. Only an imagination that has been thoroughly calculated can be considered explained.

For a long time now, we have had a useful code at our disposal, the numeric code. However, as long as the numeric code was tangled in the alphabetical code—which is to say, throughout almost the entire history of the West— its denotative power (the clarity and distinctness of its symbols) curiously made for unbridgeable difficulties. The numeric code is "empty," and the thought that is keyed into this numeric code must necessarily lose sight of the subject matter of thought. Using analytic geometry, Descartes attempted to remove this difficulty. Moreover, Newton and Leibniz attempted this task using the integration of differentials. With the benefit of their ever more complex techniques, they hoped to force the numeric code into the structure of the linear code and differential equations, to describe all processes. In spite of the abstractions attained by numerical thought, one hoped to adhere to linear and procedural ("historical") thinking.

Recently, the entire situation was radically changed. The numeric code broke out of the alphabetical code, freed itself from the pressure of linearity, and switched over from numeric to digital. In this manner, all the artificial techniques that were once considered necessities, such as differential calculus, have become superfluous: it is now possible to count with fingers, even if this means using superhuman, speedy, automatic calculating machines. The breakthrough in thinking (and acting) that comes about in this manner can still not be fully predicted. Viewed from the perspective of the thoughts on the imagination proposed here: Owing to the currently available speed of finger counting, images can now be completely and thoroughly analyzed. As a result, all of the objections that the philosophical and theological traditions have raised against images have now become groundless. We are now able to step backward from our imagination into an unsurpassable abstraction. Having arrived, we can deal with objects in a new way. We are finally able to hunt for ponies in a methodical and correct manner.

Calculated Images

The numeric code's retreat from the alphabetical code (and thus the retreat of calculating thought from linear, historical thought) has had consequences that were not foreseen by tradition. It made possible a new gesture of image creation that is diametrically opposed to the old gesture. A new imagination diametrically opposed to the old imagination was created, and the result is images that cannot be opposed by the objections of philosophy and theology. If one allows this new gesture of image creation to be expressed phenomenologically, then it reveals itself as a gesture of the gathering together of dot elements (of calculated subject matter) into images. It reveals itself as a computation. One might think that the philosophical and theological objections are groundless in the case of these images, because the imagination has been thoroughly critiqued and analyzed in advance. Even the most orthodox Talmudist could not object to these images, because they do not lend themselves to the ontological error of confusing representation with the thing represented. And even the most orthodox epistemologist could not object to these images, because they do not disguise their identity as simulacra. Even Plato could not object to these images, because they are "pure ideas." Contemplating them leads to wisdom rather than opinion. But if this is one's intention, then one has not yet given due respect to the radical nature of the reversal of imagination established in these images. It is therefore necessary that we examine this new gesture of image creation more closely.

It is a concretizing gesture: it collects zero-dimensional elements, to spread them out in a surface, thus bridging the intervals. In this manner, this gesture differentiates itself from the other gesture of image creation mentioned earlier: it neither abstracts, nor steps backwards; just the opposite, it concretizes, it projects. Certainly, both gestures lead to the creation of images (and both can therefore be called "imagination"), but then one is really dealing with a different sort of images. The images created by the traditional imagination are two-dimensional, because they have been abstracted from a four-dimensional life-world. In comparison, the images of the new imagination are two-dimensional, because they have been projected from zero-dimensional calculations. The first type of images signifies the life-world; the second type signifies calculations. The first type of images represents the life-world; the second type represents calculations. The vectors of meaning of both types of imagination point in opposite directions, so that the first type of images must be interpreted differently than the second type. This is the real reason why traditional image criticism misinterprets the new images.

If one observes the synthesizing of computer images, one will recognize how this new, concretizing, image-creating gesture operates. The computer is a calculating machine equipped with memory. Calculations can be entered into this memory, assuming that they have been translated from the numeric code into the digital code; which is to say, assuming they are taken from the alphanumeric code. One sits in front of a keyboard, taking one dot element after another out of the memory, to fit it into an image on the screen, to compute it. This step-by-step process of extraction can be automated so that it can proceed very quickly. The images appear on the screen one after another in breathtaking speed. One can follow this sequence of images, just as if the imagination had become self-sufficient; or as if it had traveled from inside (let's say from the cranium) to outside (into the computer); or as if one could observe one's own dreams from the outside. In fact, some of the appearing images can be surprising: they are unexpected images. They can be preserved on the screen (and in the computer's memory). Then, one can modify these pre-served images; one can become engaged in a sort of dialogue between one's own imagination and the imagination fed into the computer. Images modified in this manner can be transmitted to other image creators (it does not matter where they live), and these image creators can modify the images further before sending them back to their original senders. Thus, one recognizes: the new image-creating gesture assumes a different structure than the one discovered in Pech-Merle, even if certain elements can be recognized as being similar.

Two Types of Imagination

The real novelty of the situation is this: The purposes (intentionalities) of these two gestures are different. The intention behind Pech-Merle is to produce a copy of the facts. The image is to serve as a model of the future way of dealing with things. The intention behind the synthetic image can be similar: to produce a copy of a calculation (such as the calculation of an airplane). This image may serve as a model of the future way of deal-ing with things (such as the construction of airplanes by robots). How-ever, if one produces the new images with this sort of intention, then one puts the new imagination into the service of the old, and one has not yet carried out the radical change to come; for it is essential that one create new images, to bring out the unexpected from among the given possibili-ties (in a dialogue with others). The realization of the unexpected by dealing with the objective world is experienced as nothing more than a side effect. The images of the "fractal equations" offer an impressive ex-ample of this new intention: they are copies of calculations that analyze very complex and "self-identical" (let's say chaotic) systems. These calcu-lations produce extraordinarily unexpected (informative, "beautiful") images, and one can play with them almost endlessly. It is true that some of these images look like copies of facts (especially when facts, such as geological formations, clouds, or coastlines, possess a fractal structure); and it is also true that some of these images could serve as models for treatments (for example, for the production of drugs that have the dia-metrically opposed fractal structure of viruses). Nevertheless, this is a side effect of the production of these sorts of images. The real purpose is to bring out unexpected situations from among a given field of possibili-ties. The real intentionality behind the new imagination is that which the tradition called "pure aesthetics" (*l'art pour l'art*). Thus, it is possible to say: that which differentiates the new imagination from the old is the fact that "pure aesthetics," which already belonged to the old imagination, now finds expression in the new. This is possible, because the new imagination finds itself in an unsurpassable position of abstraction. At this level of abstraction, images can be designed that have been thoroughly critiqued and analyzed. To put it another way: only when one produces images of calculations instead of facts (it does not matter how "abstract" the facts) can "pure aesthetics" (the joy of playing with "pure forms") find its true expression; only then can *Homo ludens* replace *Homo faber*.

In this attempt to differentiate the two types of imagination from each other, a series of gestures has been mentioned. When they are taken in their totality, they offer a complete picture of human development. In this way: First, man took a step back from his life-world, to imagine it. Then, man stepped back from the imagination, to describe it. Then, man took a step back from the linear, written critique, to analyze it. And finally, owing to a new imagination, man projected synthetic images out of analysis. Certainly, this series of gestures should not be considered a linear sequence of events. The individual gestures neither replace each other nor cancel each other out. Instead, they overlap and mesh together. Despite the ongoing synthesis of images, people will continue to paint, write, and analyze. Moreover, these gestures will continue to coexist in unpredictable tension and cross-fertilization. But what concerns us right now in an existential sense is the burdensome, but necessary, leap out of the linear into the zero-dimensional (into the realm of "quanta") and into synthesizing (into computation). We have been challenged to leap into the new imagination.

(1990)

Mythical, Historical, and Posthistorical Existence

The Brazilian situation is extraordinarily instructive for Europeans. The European situation presents us with layers stacked on top of each other; but the Brazilian situation presents the same layers resting side by side: the layer of magic and myth, the layer of historical consciousness and action, and the layer of programmatic and systems-analytical thought and behavior. Consequently, the Brazilian situation enlightens the European about European history: There, his own history is spread out before him on a horizontal axis. Prehistoric Europe is present in Brazil. There, the historical phase of Europe is in the highest gear. At the same time, contemporary European disillusionment, especially with the idea of progress, is also palpably felt. A broad section of the Brazilian people live prehistorically, while the proletariat and bourgeoisie live historically. A small elite is aware of apparatus-like programming. Many people—perhaps most—are even conscious that their prehistorical and historical lives are at least partially programmed. Please allow me to describe these three levels of being in cursory form.

Mythical Being

This is being in a world full of "spirits" and "gods," which is to say, a world full of values. Space is "valuable," so that "above" is also "sublime," "below" is also "infernal," "right" is also "right," and "left" is also "sinister." Time has a moral and ethical function: It sets everything into its proper place in space from which it has distanced itself. It sets things right. It circulates in space and does not allow trees to grow into the heavens. Because human existence is the movement from birth to death, it generates disorder in time and space; it "goes against the world." It is justifiably punished. Time sets it back into its proper place in space. But human existence can also forgo its deserved punishment, if it takes the initiative and offers "sacrifice" in advance. Magic is the technique that allows human beings to forgo revenge through sacrifice. The attitude of mythical being is one of circulating time, the eternal recurrence within a static space full of values, its world picture being a scene.

Historical Being

This is being in a world of becoming. Time flows out of the past and into the future, taking everything with it. It is not long after something is born that it is already dying. The present is nothing more than a zero-dimensional point: nothing is a given fact; everything is the consequence of causes and the cause of consequences. The chain of causality is recognizable and can be controlled. It is ethically neutral: the "gods" have been driven from the world, and man can rule the world. Nothing repeats itself, every day is new and singular, and every lost moment is definitively a lost opportunity to comprehend the world and to intervene in it. Owing to man's ability to know the world, human existence is in the world and simultaneously transcends it. It "realizes" itself when it changes the world and thus itself. The attitude of historical being is one of engagement in world changes, of the "exploitation" of a world devoid of value, of the realization of values, its world picture being a drama.

Posthistorical Being

This is being in a world of absurd chance; in a world that has by accident realized a few possibilities out of a large, but limited number. Time and space are no longer to be considered separate from each other. "Future" corresponds to these as yet unrealized possibilities; they are coming from all sides into the present; and they "approach" each other in the spatial and temporal senses of the word. "Past" corresponds to the already realized possibilities, but the past is present: it is the present in the sense of a dam holding back already realized possibilities. The future and the past are only "real" when they are made present. Only the moment is real; it is a node in the surrounding field of possibilities. This field is structured like a game of dice: its possibilities create accidental combinations, so that, as the game continues, even the most improbable combinations become accidentally necessary. The present moment is a throw of the dice in this game of possibilities. Human existence is at the heart of this reality: where I am is where all possibilities are present, for I am always present. The structure of the field of possibilities, blind chance, makes probability analysis possible. One can figure out for oneself what is more probable and what is less probable; one can consciously participate in the global game and shoot the dice of possibility. One can reprogram the global program and remain conscious of the fact that the programming game cannot touch the heart of reality, my accidental and absurd being. The attitude of posthistorical being is one of a calculated game of chance, its world picture being a field of possibilities inscribed in a program.

These three levels of being can be grouped together under three headings: fate, causality, chance. In addition, the way of life corresponding to these three levels of being can be grouped under three headings: sacrificial magic, creative work, calculating strategy. Mythical being has been characteristic for all human societies everywhere and for all time. Historical being surfaced for the first time some three thousand years ago in the eastern Mediterranean region, and it brought Occidental civilization, where mythical being has been slowly suppressed. Posthistorical being began breaking through historical being some one hundred years ago and calling it into question. Western man lives his magical life in an unconscious and subconscious manner, but he lives his historical life in a conscious manner, concentrating on overtaking his own consciousness. The tragedy is that he becomes more and more conscious of the absurdity of historical action, of progress, and of work.

To understand why a similar tragic scenario leads to different results in Brazil, one must take the following into consideration. Brazilian society is made up of majorities and minorities. According to the categories mentioned earlier, it can be separated into two branches: the Occidental and the non-Occidental. The Occidental branch is the offspring and the spiritual heir of Western immigrants since the sixteenth century. It is inextricably linked with the West, and it dominates Brazilian society. The non-Occidental group is the offspring and spiritual heir of Africans transported to Brazil and of Indians who mixed with Europeans. It is hardly connected with the West, and it consists of the majority of those who live in the countryside or in the poverty-stricken sections of the city. In terms of sheer numbers, both branches are evenly balanced. The two branches cannot be distinguished along "racial" lines—whatever that might mean. The Occidental branch is not "white"; the non-Occidental branch is not "colored." Despite continuous mixing, each branch has preserved and developed its cultural differences. Whereas the Occidental branch tries to soak up elements of the non-Occidental branch, elements of the Occidental branch are breaking away and become immersed in the non-Occidental branch. This process of continual mixing and simultaneous separation has been covered up by ideology. Critical distance is required to take this into account.

The abyss that separates the branches is identical to the abyss that separates mythical and historical being. The mythical branch is continually being exposed to the global changes of the Occidental branch—to the streets, to radio transmissions, to "projects"—but it builds these changes into its own fundamental structures. It mythicizes them, as the serfs did in the Middle Ages. It plays a passive role in history, as its porter and victim. On the other hand, the historical branch is continually aware of the seething unrest of the mythical being under its feet. Still, it does not consider it to be an alternative form of being, but rather material to be transformed. Despite continual mixing, there is no way to a constructive dialogue between the two forms of being. Democracy in the sense of dialogue is thus made impossible.

Considering the mythical branch of society, one is impressed by its cultural poverty. Cultural poverty is just as painful as economic or social misery. Mythical societies are usually characterized by a baroque proliferation of forms, be they in Asia, in Africa, on the western coast of South America, or in Central America. In Brazil, the African myths have been reduced to a minimum, while the Indian myths have been assimilated by the African, and a mythicized Christianity of the most primitive type covers up this mixture. For lack of a better term, one has distinguished the result with the African word macumba. Despite this poverty, the Afro-Indian-Christian magic has a powerful effect. Not only does it give meaning to life, it also gives it beauty. Of course, it is important to point out that it is careless to speak of mythical life as such. We must remember that the African myths produce a different behavior than, for example, the Indian, Greek, or Germanic myths. Nevertheless, macumba is a perfect example of the similarity of all myths. It demonstrates the fact that he who lives in it is connected to the secret powers of fate, so that he serves them while they serve him. He leads an intact, a "sacred" life, whatever his particular myth may look like.

It seems unnecessary to describe the minute details of this cult or to count up its many significant rituals. After all, they would only seem confusing and complex to anyone accustomed to historical and causal thinking. At the heart of macumba, there is a technique, which enables its practitioners to summon a spirit and direct it into the human body through rhythmic drumming and rhythmic bodily movements. In this manner, the man is possessed by the external world and, in turn, possesses it. It obeys him, because he has submitted to it. This spiritual possession finds expression in a frothing epileptic seizure carried out on the floor. The seizure is contagious, so that eventually an entire mass of people is writhing on the floor at the center of the cultic scene *(terreiro)*. Every spirit has its own rhythm and its own costume, which the possessed wears, not to mention its own function (for instance, to make the possessed fertile). Every spirit is a specific aspect of the world, one of its values. The authorities of the world, the fathers and mothers of the saint *(pai e mao do santo)* lead the incantations, and the dancers (mostly elderly women) are possessed by the spirit and are changed into "horses." Not every rite is successful, for the invoked spirit must fight with other spirits before he descends. Sometimes, a spirit takes over a man's body and does damage. This is expressed by a sudden, unintentional change of the drummers' rhythm. Thus, participation in the cult is always an adventure, and it colors one's entire life. One's entire life is cultic. Every seemingly profane movement, such as walking in the street, typing, or waiting at bus stops, is possessed by this rhythm. The Carnival is an alienated form of this way of life. The non-Occidental social branch has been bathed by this all-healing rhythm. Therefore, it is not surprising that many people who suffer from the unbearably monotonous grayness of Occidental life would seek an outlet in this alternative lifestyle.

On the other hand, if one considers the branch of Brazilian society that lives historically, one should be aware that this branch has been exiled from the West and exploited by the West: these are people who are the object of history, most of whom do not make decisions themselves. Consequently, their historical consciousness is a consciousness of impotence. This experience leads to a constant attempt to escape this situation and to take control of the reins, and to make decisions; that is, to penetrate actively into history, to make Brazil into a "power." Even if they are not always aware of it, this people's engagement in each one of their activities consists in changing from historical objects into subjects, thus "emancipating" themselves. Their prerevolutionary attitude can be compared to the period of eighteenth-century Europe. This is the context in which the Catholic church's function has to be seen.

Historical consciousness, the sensation of swimming in a dramatic river of time, found a home for itself in Brazil in the form of Christianity. The world is understood as "creation," as the work of a transcendental subject, and everything in the world flows from the act of creation to the end of the world. Man, because of his soul, participates in this transcendence. He can intervene in history and change the world from this vantage point. He can act historically. The world in itself is "inanimate" (ethically neutral) and only begins to take on significance through man's intervention. Thus, the purpose of historical action is not to transform the world, but to lead man toward "salvation," to bring closer the end of time, the kingdom of God on earth. History is sacred history. Since the Renaissance, historical consciousness has worked out other forms besides Christianity. Nevertheless, they all follow the same fundamental model: that of an unambiguous flow of time and an intervention in time that comes from an external source. During the modern period, the various forms of historical consciousness have often come into conflict. The church has played an increasingly defensive and apologetic role in this struggle.

In Brazil, the branch of society that lives historically mirrors this conflict in a somewhat distorted form, even though the church's role is much different there. Vis-à-vis the mass of people who live a mythic life, the church has continued to be the emissary of historical consciousness. Its role is more or less like the role it played during the European Middle Ages. The difference is that the Brazilian church channels the prerevolutionary tendencies of the historically active. It is both a missionary to the heathens and a Jacobin. However, this description does not do justice to the ambiguity of its historical position; for, as a mirror that reflects Occidental history onto the surfaces of Brazilian society, the church also plays its European, apologetic, "reactionary" role. Consequently, the Brazilian church has three faces. As a branch of the Roman church, it defends traditional values against the onslaught of new, "godless" forms of historical consciousness. As a missionary to the heathens, it throws a redeeming light onto the darkness of their primitive blindness and educates them. As an emissary of historical consciousness, it collects all remaining prerevolutionary tendencies, beginning with the liberals, then the socialists, to the radical leftists, to emancipate man from his oppression and to free him for historical action. Of course, this brings the church into theological difficulties, though, in this respect at least, it has never been at a loss. The theology of violence ("Masses don't fill stomachs") is one of the attempts to give orthodox reasons for the threefold function of the Brazilian church.

The history of the West is reflected on the Brazilian surface not only in specific events, but also in consciousness. The Brazilian elite has not been Westernized like that of many Third World nations; rather, it is actually Western. It feels almost as strange vis-à-vis the non-Occidental social branch as a European would. Indeed, even stranger, in a way. Thus, it is not surprising if the current breakthrough of a new way of living and thinking into historical consciousness sweeps a member of the Brazilian elite away with it. Like the European or the American, he realizes that the faith in progress with respect to scientific, political, and aesthetic experiences has become increasingly untenable. Like every Occidental, he has at his disposal new critical instruments, such as cybernetics, structural analysis, and formal logic. He too repudiates as ideology any engagement for history as a "doctrine of salvation." He too attempts to intervene in history in a postideological fashion, to play with its components. Because he suffers less under the weight of historical traditions than his European brother, and, because his historical consciousness is less burdensome, he would tend to program history more generously and less responsibly. The technocracy currently developing in Brazil must be viewed in this context.

In terms of historical thinking, man is an acting subject, a "being-with-others." In terms of posthistorical thinking, he is a problem, an object to be dealt with, which is to say, one can know him—and know oneself—and transform him. Man's ability to be objectified is the new ability to transcend history. The absurdity of the new way of being consists in the fact that man no longer plays games for others. Instead, the game is played for its own sake. The game becomes independent of man; it follows its own rules determined by chance; it becomes an autopathic game of permutations, thus transforming humans into game pieces, into numbers, and into functionaries. Programmed human beings—and the game programs themselves—are becoming increasingly well programmed for the programming of the game.

Right now in Brazil we are neither making way for a more or less strict military dictatorship nor for a more or less fascistic totalitarian regime. Instead, we are making way for a programmed society. The military is only a cover-up for the coming technocracy, which will not be fascistic, but will be made up of postideological, posthistorical men: *Homines ludentes*. It would be a tragicomic error if we tried to recognize past phases of European history in the current political, social, and economic situation of Brazil. What is making its way there is the possible future of Europe: with nonideological institutes of public planning, with a programmed capital, with passports programmed for computers, with "CIC"[1] identification numbers for all citizens, with targeted subliminal programming of the mass media, with planned massification by Carnival and soccer. In Brazil, a new society of programmed and programming functionaries is making its way: the totalitarianism of apparatuses.

Of course, this futurological tendency runs up against two non-European opposing tendencies: against the active resistance of a historically aware, prerevolutionary, church-led opposition and against the passive resistance of the prehistoric, mythical, and magic-practicing class.

The futurological tendency tries to play around with both oppositional tendencies, in order to use them as "feedback" that will be entered into its programs. It uses the more active resistance as an ideology to cover up its programs: it pretends to program society, to "empower" it rather than make it functional. It uses the more passive resistance as a pretense for its programming: what is of interest is not the program itself, but that it is supposed to eliminate poverty. But both games are flimsy. The situation in Brazil demonstrates this fact. The goal of programming is not "historical freedom," for this could have been attained long ago; and, it is not the "elimination of poverty," for this has been left untouched by programming. It has become more and more obvious that the goal of programming is programming—more and more obvious for outside observers to see; it is not for the affected, the ones who are programmed not to see this goal.

Admittedly, this description of the Brazilian situation is inexact in many details and is debatable. Still, the schema captures the essential elements, and it allows us to see the tragedy of contemporary Brazilian life. The tragedy of those who belong to the mythic level, who sense how their lives are being programmed—for example, how they are being charmed by television to function better. The tragedy of those who are historically engaged, who are being denied access to the mythical level—for which they are allegedly fighting. Moreover, they recognize how the programs turn their engagement into a function. Finally, there is the tragedy of the programmers, who must recognize that the engagement of the historically conscious class is an ideological, "outdated" blindness; and yet, they must sympathize with this class—from which they themselves have come. The internal tension in Brazil has become obviously unbearable, and it has to come to an end in an unimaginable explosion.

In essence, this tension originates from an inability to engage in dialogue. There is no common language between the non-Occidental class and the Occidental class. Portuguese, which both have in common, covers up this fact. The Western class is incapable of recognizing an alternative lifestyle in the other social class, perhaps a lifestyle that in fact presents a better way of life than their own. On the other hand, the non-Occidental class is incapable of recognizing the motives behind the engagement of the other social class, because it lacks the historical categories that would explain them. The tension between the technocrats and the historically engaged is part of a different problem. It seems to resemble similar tensions in Europe, but this is an error. Historical engagement in Brazil is artificial, because it pretends to fight for the prehistoric class, while at the same time it tries to eliminate this class and absorb it. This is also the reason why its attitude toward the technological tendency is false. The technocrats are more honest with the mythical class than the historically engaged: at least they admit to manipulating the mythical class. Still, this does not earn them access to dialogue. One cannot exchange opinions with one's object. Essentially, the tragedy of Brazil is its obvious inability to dialogue, to *abertura*.

This unbearable, explosive tension is not foreign to a European: he knows it thanks to self-analysis. The classes, which are publicly opposed to each other in the political arena, without being able to communicate, are, by analogy, opposed within every one of us. This tension will explode here and there. That is why we can learn from the example that Brazil presents us.

(1981)

Note by the Editor

1. A French banking trust offering a cash-free electronic payment system.

Photography and History

We should differentiate between prehistoric, historical, and posthistorical images, and we should consider the photograph to be the first posthistorical image. Prehistoric images are those that were produced before the invention of linear writing. Historical images are those that contradict linear texts either directly or indirectly. Posthistorical images are those that set linear texts into the image. This differentiation is intended (among other things) to divide image thinking from writing thinking as clearly as possible.

Prehistoric images (from cave paintings to protohistorical wall paintings) are maps that enable their addressees to orient themselves in their environment. Their producers have stepped back from their environment and into their own subjectivity. From this vantage point, they have been able to achieve a panoramic view of their environment. They have preserved this fleeting view in a memory and encrypted it in a manner that enables others to decipher it. Prehistoric images are subjective world pictures that are stored in memories. Once there, they are codified intersubjectively. Then they can be retrieved from memory. Thus, the designing subject is himself embedded in an intersubjective tradition: to a large extent, his code is preset.

These images originate from a magical consciousness, and they produce magical behavior in their addressees. The consciousness is magical, because the environment, where things affect one another in reciprocal relations, is experienced as scenic: the eye hovers across the surface of the image and produces relations that may be reversed. The behavior of the addressees is magical, because the images are not experienced as a function of the environment, but rather the environment as a function of the images. There is a consciousness for which time circulates in space, to order space. And there is a behavior that works to obey the structures of time and space seen in the image.

Linear writing (especially the alphabet) was invented to replace magical consciousness and magical behavior with enlightened consciousness and historical action. Linear texts explain images, they roll out their scenes into processes, and they order things into irreversible chains of causality. The environment can be causally explained and progressively manipulated. Texts are instructions for a progressive way of dealing with the environment. Their goal is to explain away all images. The following is the enlightened goal of history: to identify all imagined events as historical happenings.

Historical images are manifestations by means of which the imagination defends itself against the linear conception of the world that wants to explain it away. These images penetrate texts, to illustrate them and to fill them with imagination. Even images that appear independent of texts, such as church windows, columns, or oil paintings, can be understood as illuminations of this type: they originate in historical consciousness, but oppose it with an imaginative consciousness. This dialectic, by means of which images become more conceptual and texts more and more imaginative, is the dynamic of history. This dialectic is interrupted thanks to the invention of letterpress printing. Texts get out of hand, and the images—as "art"—are expelled from everyday life. From this point on, all models of perception and behavior can be found in texts. As models of experience created for an elite, images become increasingly difficult to decode. Which is to say, culture is divided into two unequal branches. The text branch drives history forward up to the industrial revolution and beyond, and the image branch threatens to wither, despite the fact that it has been transfigured by the Benjaminian aura.

This was the cultural situation about 150 years ago. Photography was invented to bring pictures back into everyday life, to bring perceptions and the behavior depending on them back to experience. To do this, the new images had to assume certain characteristics of printed texts. Like texts, they had to become mechanically producible, reproducible, and distributable, and their value had to be contained in the information that they carried rather than in their material base. Pictures had to become pamphlets. This called not only for a change in image making, but also for apparatuses. From this point on, image makers could no longer solely produce images. Instead, image makers were required to work together with technicians. Later, owing to advances in automation, image makers became ever more superfluous, so that today fully automatic apparatuses produce, reproduce, and distribute images. Although this cannot be called "art" in the modern sense of the word, it is about powerful models of experience.

The division of culture into a scientific-technical culture and an artistic culture has been overcome thanks to photography: scientific perception and technical behavior can be experienced in the image. Nevertheless, the image has remained an image. Structurally speaking, it is antihistorical. We do not experience our environment through images as a process, but as a scene. Even when we order images into rows (as in film or video), we experience the environment not as a process, but as a sequence of scenes. For we are able to cut and paste the rows; not acting historically, but magically. Certainly, the photograph has succeeded in carrying the image into history; but, in doing so, it has interrupted the stream of history. Photographs are dams placed in the way of the stream of history, jamming historical happenings. Thus, the photograph can be considered to be the first posthistorical image.

Photographs are technical images: they are produced, reproduced, and distributed by apparatuses, and technicians design these apparatuses. Technicians are people who apply scientific statements to the environment. If one observes these statements, one discovers that they are coded in numbers rather than alphabetically. Photo apparatuses are based on equations of mechanics, chemistry, and optics. However, the carrier of historical consciousness is the linear code of the alphabet rather than the code of numbers. In the numeric code, an unhistorical, calculating, formal consciousness articulates itself. It is meaningless to say that one and one is four at around six o'clock. Consequently, photographs are posthistorical images, not only because they stand in the way of the stream of history like dams, but also because their generation depends on unhistorical, posthistorical, which is to say calculating, formal thought.

The historic-procedural (progressive) consciousness had begun to exhaust itself long before the invention of the photograph. Which is to say, since the time it became clear that the environment is indescribable but calculable. Since then (thus, at least since Descartes), numbers began splitting off from the alphanumeric code and asserting their independence (for example, as analytic geometry and as differential calculus). Since this time, most of the models of perception and behavior have been coded numerically, and we owe the photographic apparatus to the behavior coded this way. Numeric thought is timeless, because it perceives the environment as a mass of particles in which clusters form, either accidentally or intentionally. The order in the environment (if there is one) can only be formulated statistically. Of course, there is a fundamental tendency toward becoming continually formless, and this tendency toward entropy can be used as a measure of time. Photographs are intentionally produced, negatively entropic clusters. Negative entropy can be called "information." From the perspective of formal consciousness, photographs are information intentionally produced from a swarm of isolated possibilities. Thus, photographs differ in principle from prehistoric images. Prehistoric images are worldviews (copies of the environment). Photographs are computed possibilities (models, projections onto the environment). This is the real reason why photographs should be considered posthistorical images.

Photographs are only the first of these posthistorical images. In more recent examples of these images (for example, in synthetic images), the computation aspect is more clearly recognizable. But, it is also apparent in photographs. In photographs, the calculation of dot elements (such as molecules in silver compounds) and the computation of these elements into images are also apparent. They are not actually surfaces (like the prehistoric and historical surfaces), but rather mosaics. Thus, to be more exact in speaking about photographs, we should not say imagination, but rather visualization. For imagination is the ability to step back from the environment and to create an image of it. In comparison, visualization refers to the ability to turn a swarm of possibilities into an image. Imagination is the consequence of an abstraction from the environment. Visualization is the power to concretize an image from possibilities. Photographs are posthistorical, because they concretize rather than abstract. Often, they have the appearance of copies (and are thus confused with them), but, structurally speaking, they are actually projects.

However, the level of consciousness (that is, the calculating, formal level of consciousness) thanks to which photo apparatuses came into being has not yet become common. Most of us (including most photographers) are still caught up in historical, progressive, enlightened consciousness. Thus, photographs are received with a different consciousness from the one that produces photo apparatuses. (In the field of synthetic images, this discrepancy is less dramatic than in that of photographs.) Most of what is said and written with respect to photos can be attributed to this discrepancy. Photos are not received as projections, that is, as images of the future, but rather as copies of scenes, that is, as images of the past. And, it is generally assumed that photographs illustrate (document) happenings, as if they were historical images. The consequence of this misunderstanding between the programmers of photo-production and photo-distribution apparatuses and the addressees of the photographs is absolutely characteristic of the present cultural situation.

Photographs are programmed to model the future behavior of their addressees. Yet, they are not only models of behavior, but also models of perception and experience. The programmers of photographs (from their perspective, photographers—as long as they are not replaceable— are nothing more than human factors built into the apparatus) hover above history, and they project a potentially alternative future. To the addressees, however, photos are not the starting points of programs to be developed in the future, but rather end points of history. For addressees of photographs, linear history moves in the direction of photographs where it is taken. (The term *to take* deserves to be examined more closely in a different context.) For the addressees, it is as if the stream of history had to flow into photographs where (thanks to reproducibility) it can turn around, thus repeating its path for eternity. As if the goal of all linear texts were its transcoding into photolike images, and as if these texts were "reconciled" in this sort of images. The behavior of the addressees of photos expresses their understanding of them: being photographed is the goal of everything they do. For these sorts of addressees, the image is not a model of the future. Rather, they (and their environment) will be immortalized in the image.

This misunderstanding is convenient to the programmers. Because the addressees behave according to the function of the images, they become functionaries of the modeling programs. As mentioned earlier, this misunderstanding is based on a false interpretation of photographs: they are understood to be the transcoding of linear texts (of linear history) rather than the realization of algorithms. In this manner, the addressees of photographs are blind to the new level of consciousness where the photographs have been programmed. In this manner, the programmers become a cultural elite of technocrats, media operators, and opinion makers who manipulate an unconscious society.

There are parallels to this present cultural situation. When linear writing was invented (around the middle of the third millennium B.C.), the historical-causal consciousness of the scribes was similarly reserved for a small elite only. Meanwhile, the masses continued to live on a magical level. Thus, a ruling class of literati built itself up (from the Egyptian dynasties unto the medieval church fathers), and the illiterate masses were forced to obey the texts without being able to decode them. With respect to posthistorical images, we too are illiterate. We too are incapable of decoding the "software" generating these images. The hegemony of the literati was breached thanks to the invention of the printing press: everyone became a literatus. The same is possible today: everyone can become a programmer.

Photographs are simply the first among the posthistorical images. In the case of photographs, the acquisition of the codes, in which the new consciousness articulates itself, is a more difficult task than in the case of more developed images, such as synthetic images. Two aspects of the photograph make it more difficult. First, photos resemble copies more than projections. At first glance, a photo of an airplane does not reveal that, just like a synthetic computer image, it signifies a possible airplane rather than a given one. Second, the photograph seems to be made by a photographer operating the apparatus, rather than by a software specialist programming the apparatus. The projecting and computing nature of the photograph is less evident than in synthetic images. Yet this is precisely why learning to photograph in the sense of a posthistorical projection would be extraordinarily emancipatory. Because photographs are in the process of departing from paper and chemicals in favor of electromagnetic fields, there are already numerous approaches to learning how to photograph. Thus, the universe of images that surrounds us and whizzes us around will be changed from the bottom up. No more will we have to follow these models blindly. Instead, we will be actively engaged in the production of these models. It will be a universe through which we will project ourselves out of the present and into the future.

Photography was invented 150 years ago. Not until now, however, have the dormant utopic virtualities of photography been revealed to us. Therefore, our meeting today[1] is important for numerous cultural and political reasons: not only to look back on the past 150 years (on the so-called history of photography), but also as an opportunity to look toward the horizon opening up before our eyes (on the posthistory that articulates itself in the photograph and its successors).

(1989)

Note by the Editor

1. The colloquium on Document and Invention at the Obere Galerie im Haus am Lützowplatz, Berlin, May 24, 1989.

A Historiography Revised

Narrative is no longer the model for historical events. That is film. From this point on, one can speed up events, watch them in slow motion, and work them into flashbacks. Most important, however, one can cut the tape of Western history and splice it back together. I propose cutting out the twelve hundred years between A.D. 200 and A.D. 1400, then replacing the cuttings with two hundred newly composed years. Then, I would show the remastered film in the theaters of the cultural elite—with the hope of constructing a more lucid and entertaining plot for the film.

Indeed, the cuttings that will be thrown away contain a number of confusing scenes and subplots that unnecessarily detract from the film's central theme. Undeniably, the film also contains beautiful scenes that the film critics will miss. The film critics will miss characters, such as Charlemagne and Dante, and they will regret the fact that scenarios, such as Córdoba and Cluny, were cut out. Nevertheless, creative activity consists in cutting out superfluous material. Ockham (one of the characters who did not make the cut) cleverly made this point: "entia non sunt multiplicanda praeter necessitatem."

If one looks at the film from the perspective of focusing, one recognizes the following structure: Until the year A.D. 200, the camera follows certain converging story lines: Egypt, Mesopotamia, Palestine, Greece, Italy. Then, it focuses on the point where the story lines meet: Alexandria. After A.D. 200, it begins to move around erratically: Rome, Byzantium, Ravenna, Córdoba, Aachen, Palermo, Provence, Burgundy, Flanders, without giving away any clues about the filmmaker's intentions. Around 1400, the camera continues from Alexandria. It focuses attention on Florence and then slowly pans in the direction of the northwest. I propose that we cut out this unnecessary traveling.

The plot is based on the structure outlined here. Heterogeneous themes can be wrapped up in Alexandria in one central theme. This central theme will be enriched by supporting resources. It goes from the eastern Mediterranean to the North Atlantic, where it achieves the domination of the world, and in the final scenes this domination is challenged. The intention of the proposed revision is to make the central theme more lucid and to help the film critics understand the final scenes.

Unfortunately, it is impossible simply to cut out the superfluous twelve hundred years and then paste the markers "200" and "1,200" back together. A gap would appear between Alexandria and Florence. Two hundred years would be sufficient to bridge this cultural and geographical gap, thus making an organic transition from the Alexandrian library to the Uffizi. Therefore, these two hundred years must be composed. Two questions arise: Which of the elements of these twelve hundred years will make the cut and which will not? Second: On which particular scene should the new film track be focused?

In response to the first question, I propose the following: The Christian dialectic between Athanasianism and Aryanism should be preserved, because it is important for our understanding of the Reformation. On the other hand, Islam should not be allowed to penetrate into the Mediterranean or to occupy Jerusalem and Alexandria. The Alexandrian Jews should be maintained as a viable alternative to Christianity. On the other hand, the Spanish Jews have become superfluous: their cultural function as translators has become irrelevant. The Alexandrian library should be preserved: medieval Aristotelianism is pointless and confusing owing to the loss of literature. Alexandrian mysticism and Gnosticism should be preserved, because they are important for our understanding of the Baroque persecution of witches and, in part, the arithmetization of the modern sciences. On the other hand, the decline of Alexandrian art into academicism should be cut, so that we no longer need explanations for pre-Carolingian primitive art. The Roman Empire should be preserved, so that we can comprehend the Latinization of the West. On the other hand, the division of the empire can be eliminated: because Constantinople is never built, Byzantine culture has become superfluous.

In response to the second question, I propose the following: The film should be shot in Palermo. For our purposes, this particular scene is favorably situated between Alexandria and Florence. Of course, I do not mean the city of Frederick the Pious. Despite our fascination with this character, he will not show up in this film. Our Palermo is the heir of *Magna Graecia*. Our Palermo speaks Italian and contains a sizable Jewish population. It should be ruled by German kaisers—whether they are Vandals or Normans.

The planned film of two hundred years should contain the following plotline: At the beginning of the third century, the Arabs have conquered Persia, and the Islamic nation threatens the empire from the East. Meanwhile, the German tribes invade, take the empire over, and defend it against Islam. Arabia Felix and Asia Minor are lost, while Syria and Egypt are preserved. This is the origin of the Limes in the East. It will be fought over for the entire two hundred years, and impoverish the empire. This leads first to the Christianization of the poor and, second, the entire civilization. Around A.D. 280, Caesar Constantinus Carolus makes Christianity into the state religion. However, he must continually fight with the Athanasian pope in Rome and the Aryan patriarch in Alexandria. Caesar Fredericus Pius transfers the capital seat to Palermo, to avoid splitting the empire. The Alexandrian library, the cloister schools, and the Talmud schools are also moved there. Continuous technological progress leads to the creation of a middle class in the cities who, in turn, revolt against the weakened centralized government of the empire. Around A.D. 380, the empire falls apart into truly independent nations and cities only nominally subject to imperial rule, Florence being the most important city among them. We have now reached A.D. 400 (ex-A.D. 1400). At this point, the regular film can be restarted.

These are an eventful two hundred years. Only with great difficulty are Celtic and Germanic elements assimilated into the Western synthesis. Country folk and Germanic nobility continue to live a pagan way of life until the end of the film. A well-populated Egypt threatens the West internally with conversion to the Coptic faith. The califate spreading to India and Turkestan threatens the West externally with conversion to Islam. The epoch's great "synthetisator," Thomasius Augustinus, writes a *Summa* in which he attempts the unification of all these influences under the aegis of Christianity. He fails owing to the resistance of the scientific tendencies at the University of Palermo.

The empire recognizes two official languages: Latin and Koine, a Greek dialect. But, in reality, the language situation is much more complex. Theological texts are written in Aramaic, esoteric texts in Coptic, philosophical and scientific texts in Greek, political and juridical texts in Latin. The masses speak vulgar Latin and Germanic, and these languages are also used in poetry, the novel, and theater. The Babel of languages contributes to the empire's decline and provides a partial explanation for the establishment of individual nations.

The official ideology is a Christianity divided between Athanasianism and Aryanism, while an underground surge of Manichaeanism and Hermeticism calls this ideology into question. Thomasius Augustinus, the Carthage German whom we mentioned earlier, tries in vain to declare war on Manichaeanism. The results are internal crusades, religious fanaticism, and pogroms against the Jews. Two hundred years later, during the sixth (ex-sixteenth) century, Luther and Calvin will take up Thomasius Augustinius's theme, during the califate toward the end of fourth and fifth (ex-fifteenth) centuries. The Turkish invasions into the califate toward the end of fourth and fifth (ex-fifteenth) centuries give these religious wars a new slant, and Aryanism is absorbed by Protestantism. In the fourth century, Manichaeanism surfaces as part of the Catharist movement, but it is suppressed. In the tenth (ex-twentieth), it will reappear again in the guise of Existentialism. The modern sciences (Paracelsus, Bruno) assimilate Hermeticism, thus contributing to the appearance of gnosis at Princeton in the tenth (ex-twentieth) century.

The official philosophy is Neoplatonism, as taught by Abaelardus Plotinus in Palermo. Because this brand of Neoplatonism is partially indebted to Philo, there are rumors of heresy and Jewish influence. Meanwhile, the scientistic school of Duns Maimonides is challenging it. In this manner, a controversy between theology and science breaks out behind the back of the official philosophy.

Science is divided into two branches: "pure" and "applied." Among the "pure" sciences," we find Euclidean geometry, despite objections to its third postulate. We also find Aristotelian logic, despite objections to its "excluded third element." On the other hand, proponents of a heliocentric system hotly debate the Ptolemaic system. Consequently, there is increasing belief among the scholars of Palermo in the notion of a circumnavigable earth. From the port of Carthage, the exploration of the western coast of Africa proceeds apace. Toward the end of our period that we have composed, the navigational center of Carthage will be transferred to Sagres. Also, the medical world continues to make progress. Medical research is the core of studies at the University of Palermo. In physics, a battle between atomism and dynamism (Democritus and Heraclitus) rages on. Ever more complex machines, most of them hydraulic, are being designed. Nevertheless, the real scientific breakthrough is expected in the realm of chemistry. Scientists are in search of the fountain of youth and the philosopher's stone. Preparations are being made for a scientific revolution.

The "pure" sciences are Greek and theoretical, the "applied" are mostly Hermetic. The writings of Hermes Trismegistos, the Egyptian god Toth—who purified himself while wading through Greek and Judeo-Christian writings—serve as the basis for the "applied" sciences, along with Aristotle and the Bible. They combine alchemy, astrology, and cabala. Modern science is born in the fifth (ex-fifteenth) century out of the Gnostic character of the "applied" sciences and the theoretical character of the "pure" sciences.

The art scene of the period to be composed begins with the technical perfection of naturalistic Hellenism. The contradiction between rationalism and mysticism under the aegis of Christianity amounts to a breakthrough of the Hellenistic style toward a transcendentalization without the loss of artificial technique. From this point on, it moves in the direction of a transcendentalization without the loss of artificial technique. An example of this change in style is Monreale (A.D. 290), from which, however, all Islamic elements have to be removed carefully. An important step forward is the use of the canvas as a medium for oil-based paints, for this enables the Euclidean idea of perspective to be utilized in artistic technique. The artist Simonius Martinius (283–344) deserves mentioning. In vulgar poetry, the alexandrine is replaced by the *trova*, a new vernacular mode of expression native to Palermo. The music of this period continues to be based on the Jewish liturgy, even though it begins to take on a different, more mathematical form in the *ars nova*. Important for this period is the Milanese poet-composer Ambrosius Macaldus, a k a Machaut (300–377). Generally speaking, Alexandrian art, after its Christianization in Palermo, organically leads to the Renaissance.

The proposed substitution of the medieval film with a brand-new two hundred years allows us to clear up many of the formerly unfathomable connections of the plot. Not only with respect to the special case of the Renaissance, which no longer appears as the rebirth of a mystified Rome and Athens, but also with respect to the necessary continuation of the Alexandrian synthesis. Now many other modern phenomena can be acknowledged in their proper context. For example, the Reformation as the continuation of the internal dialectic that has characterized Christianity since its foundation. Or the Baroque as the continuation of the Alexandrian tension between rationalism and mysticism. Modern science no longer appears as "spontaneous generation," but rather as the revolutionary consequence of Alexandrian science. In particular, the final scenes of the film make much more sense: now, at the end of the tenth century, we anticipate the Millennium and the end of the film plot.

Thanks to our revision, the film *Western History* has become consistent, intellectually satisfying, and aesthetically pleasing. Inconsistent, illogical, and unpleasant elements have been edited. Still, the question remains whether the inconsistent, the illogical, and the unpleasant, in short, the absurd, are not in fact essential to the film. Or whether the absurdity of history is not in fact a reason for hope: the hope that all rational "prospectives" must fail. Now that we are at the end of the twentieth century and not the tenth, is it possible that, despite everything, we are not approaching the Millennium?

(1982)

The Vanity of History

Few of the things that surround us are inherited. Few have been delivered to us by the stream of generations, carrying their stamp. Instead, most carry the stamp of novelty. The novelty of things that surround us differentiates our surroundings from previous surroundings in a characteristic manner. In earlier times (and by this I mean all epochs that I know of), things were handed down from the father to the son, they were amassed in family chests and in the attics of homes in villages and towns, and they filled living rooms and bedrooms. The farmer stepped across fields tilled by his father. His ancestors wrested these fields from nature. The son inherited his craft from his father. With the father's craft also came the necessary tools. When there was a wedding, a young woman searched the family chest for a wedding dress preserved by her mother. The majestic stream of history left behind things that some considered treasures and some considered prisons. Yet, they shaped lives. Our own epoch wiped the slate clean. Our own epoch disinherited itself.

A number of the causes for this transformation can be pointed out. The industrial revolution of the nineteenth century swept a large part of the population from the European countryside and huddled them together in the new cities. The old workshops were lost in the hurly-burly of this process. The agrarian revolution of the twentieth century transformed European soil into mechanized plots of land. A part of the population emigrated to America, and, while crossing the Atlantic, they lost many of the things that they had inherited. The demographic explosion of the last 150 years scattered the collected treasures among the great mass of heirs. But all these and other causes are trivial and meaningless in comparison to the following cause: inherited things no longer have any place in our milieu. The new things that surround us reject the presence of the old things, because they are of a different kind. The topic of this essay is the specific difference between things that surround us and the inherited things, which is to say, the specific difference between the present and the past. The thesis will be that the past no longer matters to us. The argument will be made that contemporary historiography—for the first time in history—has ceased to be an activity that explains the present. The assertion will be made that the chain of history has finally broken. The entire nineteenth century helped prepare this break, but only the twentieth century realized it during the 1940s. Therefore, it is asserted that our situation differs qualitatively from previous ones and that an abyss divides them.

Consider the following three examples: atomic energy, the computer, and rockets. Other examples could be chosen, but these three will suffice. Atomic energy can be considered a historical development of the energy derived from beasts of burden, from coal, from petroleum, and electricity. There is a straight line along the stock of energy increases. The computer can be considered a historical phenomenon in which a tendency beginning with the Roman abacus finds fruition. Rockets can be considered a perfection of the technology inherent in oxcarts, automobiles, and jet aircraft. Nevertheless, this historical method of "explaining" the three instruments provided as examples is inconsequential, because it does not "explain" their quality. Atomic energy has done away with physical work in the traditional sense. The computer has done away with planning and administration in the traditional sense. Rockets have done away with the concept of distance in the traditional sense. The enormous quantity has resulted in a qualitative leap. The three instruments under consideration are historical phenomena in the sense that they resulted from efforts to solve specific problems. However, they are ahistorical phenomena because they have finally solved these problems. The notion that history is an attempt to solve these problems does not speak to us anymore. Problems of history are not our problems. The study of history does not shed any light on our problems, because they are qualitatively different. The entire philosophical, political, and social historicity is an anachronism. All attempts to explain or find motivations for our historical conduct—whether through historical dialectics, or through psychoanalysis, or whatever historical criterion one chooses—fail to come to terms with the break in the chain of events. I will attempt to describe this break in more detail.

The history of humankind is the sum of actions by means of which the human species has imposed itself on nature. It is a short history in comparison to the enormous epochs of life on earth and, indeed, in comparison to the history of vertebrates. A mere five thousand generations separates us from the origin of mankind and a negligible two hundred generations from the origin of our culture, the origin of history in the actual sense of the word. The family tree of humankind has many branches, but its trunk is short. Our history is short; but because we consider it our history, we assume that its themes are eternal. In reality, there is only one theme: nature. Man is a being who has manipulated the nature that surrounds him throughout history. He tames animals and plants. He builds canals for rivers. He builds roads and bridges, fights diseases, floods, and drought. He cuts down forests and makes deserts arable, dams up waterfalls and tunnels through mountains. He forces himself upon nature. The rest of history is nothing more than a complicated commentary on this process of conversion. This entire complicated commentary, all the wars and revolutions, all the travels and conquests, all the religions, philosophies, arts, and sciences have the same fundamental theme: nature. In the Western tradition, this theme is known by the name "paradise on earth." It refers to man's domination of nature, the humanization of nature. It refers to the messianic epoch as the goal of history, and it refers to the objectification of the spirit of nature. This topic has been exhausted. Nature is not a problem anymore. Paradise on earth, the humanization of nature, the messianic epoch, the objectification of spirit are all within reach. The goal of history will be realized automatically without further human intervention. History in the traditional sense is about to reach its goal, and it does not mean anything to us anymore.

The new things that surround us, all these apparatuses and all these institutions, are forerunners of the Millennium rather than descendants of this search. The spirit of history was stifled by the voice that proclaimed the Good News. Yet, the same cannot be said of our thoughts. Our thoughts continue to participate in the historical process; we continue to think historically. There is a contradiction between our mentality and the things that surround us. The things that surround us are descending rapidly in the direction of the end of time, carrying us along with them. In our thoughts, we continue to grab onto categories, values, and terms that belong to an irrevocably out-of-date past. This contradiction between our thoughts and our "reality" prevents us from experiencing this "reality" as "real." There is something unreal about the speed of rockets, the memory capacity of computers, and the power of the

H-bomb, even though we know very well that we have to conform to this unreality. We are still historical beings, and, as such, we are running the risk of becoming outdated. This is our problem, and it is novel. Historiography does not teach us anything in this respect.

The new problem that originated from the break in the chain of history is hidden. There are still large areas of land to be conquered. Tropical rain forests, endemic disease, hunger, and lack of housing seem to be challenges for humankind. A large portion of humankind continues to vegetate in a prehistoric stage of history. It seems almost cynical for us to say that the goal of history has already been reached. Yet this is an error. The instruments already exist that will destroy these "underdeveloped" regions and transform them into "developed" regions automatically. This process is lightning fast, such that the changes currently taking place in Western Europe seem to pale in comparison. The disparity between the developed and underdeveloped regions is now increasing thanks to the rapid progress of the developed economies. Yet this is a transitional phenomenon. No matter how much progressive alliances and independence movements disrupt the automatic mechanism of technological progress, it will triumph and eventually win out over what is left of nature. The present transitional phase merely covers up the new problem, because it points out the old problems of history to the superficial observer. Still, these are false problems, because we already have the means and the methods to catch up with them.

A thorough examination of our milieu reveals the new problem. The human spirit hesitates to face up to this problem, because, in its search for a solution, it feels that it has been abandoned by history. The collected wisdom of generations of men is silent in the face of this new problem. The great thinkers of the past, the founders of religions, the lawmakers and the philosophers, the visionaries and prophets have never looked beyond the civitas dei. We, however, are this city's citizens. Our ancestors swam in the stream of history; it fed and informed them. But we have overtaken history, and the inheritance from our grandparents means nothing to us anymore. It is as if they have thrown us here and left us at the edge of the abyss. We feel betrayed. Alone and forsaken, we have been tossed into the middle of new things, and we must find a solution within ourselves, so that we will have a future.

If we hope to find solutions for the problems that plague us today, the study of history as the history of actions during the last two hundred (or five thousand) generations is in vain. Moreover, the historical lessons that have resulted from various studies, these diverse historicisms, only confuse our thoughts with their anachronisms. What other kinds of study are we left with? Is there anything more passionate, more heartwarming and inspiring than reports about famous deeds and the agony of defeat, about the fulfillment of dreams and the suffering of our ancestors? The vanity of historiography, even though we are all secretly aware of it, does not take away its charm. In this manner, a new attitude toward history is born, and one does well to describe it with the phrase "wallowing in desire." For hundreds of years, during the entire modern period, a belief in progress was dominant. Now the climate of the "good old times" arises. In developed countries, functional chairs make room for Baroque chairs, Gothic statues decorate the offices of industrial magnates, and medieval castles are transported—stone for stone, to preserve their authenticity—to the banks of the Hudson River. This "wallowing in desire" is an attempt to consume history and to annex it to the present. These tendencies do not want to accept the fact that we have been disinherited. Various historicisms, which have been poured into books in order to manipulate our present conduct, seem to me like Baroque doors in a modern home. I do not believe that history can be resuscitated in this manner.

Rilke writes in a frightening poem: "Every dull turn of the world gives us these disinherited." Has any turning back ever been as shameful as ours? Never in the history of humankind, that is, if my thesis is correct. Perhaps we find ourselves at the same point as at the origin of the first human being? In the messianic era, the prophet says the following about the goal of history: "You shall be changed." This is one of the few sayings that originate from the lap of history and direct our gaze beyond the horizon. Shall we perhaps find ourselves changed? The trumpets will sound on the day of wrath, and we shall find ourselves changed. And perhaps the trumpets have already sounded, and the world has already dissolved into ashes without anyone having noticed. Perhaps our sense of unreality is a sign of this change. Perhaps we have already been changed. Perhaps the transformation has already occurred and we did not notice, because it was not a biological transformation. These are thoughts provoked by the experience of the vanity of history.

(1969)

On the End of History

Whoever speaks of the end of history should be able to explain what he means when he is speaking about history. But, this is fundamentally impossible. It is unfair to expect a clear definition of the concept of history from historians and posthistorians. The explanation for this is the double meaning of the concept and the difficulty involved in disentangling these two meanings. In the first sense, the word means a process, a course of events. In the second sense, it means a narrative. On the surface, these appear to be completely different meanings; yet, has there ever been a process about which no one told a story? This is a metaphysical question. On the other hand, are there any stories that are not based on processes? This is a rhetorical question. To express this in a more radical manner: For a process to be recognized, it must be narrated. And, for a narrative to be a narrative, something must happen. Every attempt to separate history in the first sense definitively from history in the second sense, which is to say, history from historiography, *history* from *story*, necessarily creates more confusion instead of eliminating confusion altogether. Added to this is the fact that storytelling itself is a part of the history being narrated; in other words, narratives make history. The Trojan War is a part of history, and it has *The Iliad* to thank for this. Moreover, *The Iliad* is part of history, and it has the Trojan War to thank for this. Neither Schliemann's archaeological research nor the philological research of Homer interpreters can alter this fact. Still, both camps are able to place the double meaning of the concept of "history" before our eyes.

Posthistorians, people who tell a story about the end of history, are necessarily storytellers. When they tell a story about the end of history,

they make history. It seems as if they are caught up in a sophistic paradox, like someone who speaks about the end of philosophy and then, with
this philosophical pronouncement, drives philosophy forward. Nevertheless, to speak about the end of history is not contradictory. For stories
are not endless; they have an ending. One can divide stories into short
and long stories. Consequently, posthistorians believe that all narratives
approach their endings, that no one tells a story any longer. From now
on, one either counts up or portrays in pictures: from now on, either statistics or electromagnetic image recordings. Moreover, when nothing
more is narrated, then nothing more will happen. The posthistorians believe that the question "What comes after the end of history?" is absurd.
Similarly, it would be absurd to ask Scheherazade the question "What
comes after the thousand-and-first night?"

Let us be naive for a moment and pretend that we know what we
mean when we speak about "history": namely, a process. Then there is
only one history. For every process is the continuation of something preceding it and something leading to a continuation. Every process is embedded in one large process. Let us call this one, singular history "natural
history," and let us pretend not to know that there is an academic discipline that tells the story of natural history, namely, natural sciences. Let
us pretend not to know that there is no natural history without natural
sciences, and vice versa. This pretense, this doing-as-if, is not difficult for
us, because we do not actually know if we know it.

There is a relatively simple equation, namely, the second law of thermodynamics. It tells the complete, huge story of natural history. This law encompasses all past, present, and future processes. It is a marvelous narrative. Short and compact, it narrates all the short and long stories. It is
possible to formulate this short algorithm in different ways. For example,
one method is to use the German language. Of course, this makes the
story a little longer, but it continues to give us an overall picture. It goes
like this:

Roughly sixteen billion years ago, there was a big bang whose echo we
still hear today if we listen the right way. Since that time, particles have
been tearing through the universe almost at the speed of light. During
this process, they bump into each other by accident and form clusters.
Despite these accidents, the entire process moves in the direction of a
uniform distribution of particles. When this goal is reached, history
comes to an end—because then there will be no more time, for time signifies the distribution of particles. This "short story," which narrates the
long, wide-ranging story of natural history, will also come to an end.

Then, all past, present, and future processes will have run their course. In the meantime, however—that is, during the narrative process—they continue to run their course. And the temporary process sounds something like this:

The diameter of the natural universe is presently sixteen billion years wide, because it is sixteen billion years old. One is roughly aware of its size. It is fundamentally empty space through which the particles travel as they approach their uniform distribution, entropy. However, in this empty space there are clusters formed by chance, and between these are powerful forces. Some of these clusters do not look as if they were formed by chance—our nervous systems, for example. Their complexity is so great that the thought of chance creating something so complex is completely beyond our imagination. In a similar manner, the number of particles that have been spinning around and crashing into each other for sixteen billion years is beyond our imagination. These unimaginable numbers persisting for unimaginable lengths of time make the origin of unimaginable complexities like our nervous systems a necessary coincidence. From among these absurd, improbable clusters, the simple, short algorithm of the second law of thermodynamics was pieced together (and the one gigantic natural history), so that they can tell their stories.

The posthistorians believe that these sorts of narratives can no longer be spread. People no longer allow themselves to be convinced by this sort of explanation. Stories as short as this, telling of the one and only long history, can no longer be told. Moreover, if they have lost their narratability, then absolutely nothing can be narrated anymore. For the one singular, large, narrated history, which is the subject matter of the short story, already contains all the stories that have been narrated, those currently being narrated, and those still to be narrated. But, if this one short story of the one large story can no longer be told, then one can no longer tell stories in general. This is the meaning of posthistory.

Why is it that one can no longer tell such stories? Because they turn in circles, like a dog chasing its own tail. This can be explained in the following manner: the algorithm that formulates the second law of thermodynamics is an idea for a film. The German translation for this algorithm is the screenplay. The story of natural history is the film itself. The natural sciences are the film criticism. What do they critique? The film? The screenplay? The film idea? The idea (the algorithm) comes from the film criticism itself, from the natural sciences, which is to say, from thermodynamics. However, thermodynamics believes that the algorithm has been taken from the film. Someone has an idea. The idea is derived from a film that he will shoot. People can no longer be persuaded of this. Posthistory.

This vertigo, this whirlwind in which our thought must move when it tries to think about the relationship between natural sciences and natural history, is a symptom of the end of history. The dizziness that has seized us is the screw by means of which we unscrew ourselves from historical consciousness, to drill ourselves into another hole. The turns of the screw are processes, and our thought must move along these turns. Yet, the screw itself is not a process, but rather a form. Thus, we proceed from the process to the form, from the historical into the formal. This is not only vertiginous, but also comprehensible.

The central nervous system is a cluster created by chance. At least this is how it tells its own story, thus developing all other history from this self-narration. But the reverse is also true: history in its entirety is told by the central nervous system, and, in the course of this, the system discovers that it has narrated itself. In this manner, we arrive at what seems to be another sophistic paradox: How can the world be part of the brain when the brain is part of the world? It turns out that this paradox is resolved once the dog stops chasing his own tail. Then, one needs no longer speak of brain-ness in the world and the brain's being-in-the-world, because the brain narrates the world, and the world is narrated by the brain. Then the brain is to the world what Homer is to Achilles or K. is to Kafka. Because it makes little sense to ask if Achilles is in Homer or Homer in Achilles, it also makes little sense to ask if the world is to be sought in the brain or the brain in the world. The world and the brain are related to each other like process and narrative: the process creates the narrative and the narrative creates the process (the brain makes the world and the world makes the brain). It makes one dizzy when one thinks about this historically, but not when one thinks about it formally. The apparent paradox is one of the turns of the screw, out of the historical into the formal.

But now, another turn of the screw: Like the history of every species, the history of the human species is part of natural history. Like the origin of trilobites, great dinosaurs, or the woolly mammoth, the origin of the human species can be explained by what preceded it. Because the extinction of these three species was predictable, the same can be said about the extinction of our own species. Like all other biological species, our species is a transitional excrescence in the accidental, ever-changing, and mutating stream of genetic information. Still, the history of humankind is different in kind than other species. Indeed, it is different in kind than all other natural history. This difference in kind can be formulated in the following manner: All of history—except for human history—concerns processes that have become necessary by chance. The shell of a trilobite, a dinosaur bone, and a mammoth tusk are the products of chance. It is impertinent to ask why they are so and not so. On the other hand, the history of the human species is full of things that demand a different set of questions. Whoever does not ask for what purpose a hand ax, a pitcher, an automobile, or even a word, a song, or a philosophical thought, has been created has not yet begun to tell the story of human history. The difference between natural history and human history is that natural processes can be explained by the question "why?" and cultural processes by an additional question, "for what purpose?" But wait, now we have to start over from the beginning. Our ancestors—as well as the myths through which they still speak to us—approached all processes with the question "for what purpose?" "For what purpose does the sun shine? So that we can see our way." "For what purpose is the Christmas tree always green? A symbol for the faithful." "What purpose does the cow fulfill? To give us blue cheese." If natural processes do not allow questions of purpose, then our ancestors (and their myths) did not have nature. Everything was human history, and man was on a first-name basis with the animals, plants, stones, and stars.

Then, much later—but certainly not before the pre-Socratics—certain processes were no longer questioned about their purpose. Nature came into being in this manner. First, stars and stones; second, plants and animals; and, finally, people themselves were approached from the perspective of the natural sciences, which is to say, as accidental phenomena devoid of intention. And, now we have to follow another thought process:

On the one hand, it is correct to say—as we have done—that the human species is a biological species, that is, a natural-historical process. On the other hand, it is equally correct to say that natural-historical processes are the processes that were narrated for the first time around 2,500 years ago. On the one hand, the history of the human species is one of the final chapters in natural history. On the other hand, natural history is a late chapter of human history. On the one hand, man is a recent accidental result of nature. On the other hand, nature is a late product of man. He created it with the intention of explaining the world and himself without reference to intention. On the other hand, nature is a consequence of value judgments, like every other product of the history of the human species. Whoever thinks historically is hopelessly confused by this method of argumentation. For how can culture originate from nature and nature from culture? But this confusion is nothing more than a turning of the screw out of history and into posthistory. In posthistorical thinking, the dog no longer chases its own tail. Natural history is one of the narratives of cultural history. Thus, cultural history is one part of the natural history it narrates to itself.

The one large natural history is measured with scales whose unit of measure is billions of years. One can divide this unit of measure further, but this division is still not precise enough to make centuries visible—not to say, minutes. In fact, it would probably make for a completely uninteresting story, because our life-world is touched by natural history only in seconds flat. Surprisingly, however, it is an extremely fascinating story. It is much more interesting to tell a story about the origin of life on earth two billion years ago than to talk about last year's weather. It is much more interesting to tell a story about the first lemurs—our ancestral primates who roamed the earth two hundred to four hundred million years ago, similar to modern-day squirrels—than to talk, with permission, about our grandmothers. The modified, logarithmic eyeglasses that we put on during storytelling provide an explanation for this. The first billion years may then appear shorter than the last half hour. Like binoculars or reading glasses, we can turn these modified eyeglasses around. If we make this adjustment, history becomes much more interesting. The playful lemurs that roam a forest incomprehensible to us in its details are much closer to us, existentially speaking, than our great-grandmother (out of politeness we should not mention our grandmother). These focal adjustments to our lenses result in what we call history. It is not a somber, plodding litany, in which a monotone voice indifferently recounts one trivial event after another. Instead, it is an exciting, rhythmically orchestrated epic poem, in which fabulous heroic figures, such as trilobites, giant dinosaurs, woolly mammoths, and lemurs, gallop toward us and make our hearts beat a little faster. Moreover, what is good enough for natural history is good enough a fortiori for the history of the human species. It does not tell us of the plight of Homer's or Hegel's chambermaid (pardon me, cleaning person).

Third turn of the screw: some people are antiquarians. These are people who collect curiosities, for example, trilobite fossils, giant dinosaur bones, woolly mammoth tusks, and lemur teeth. Other antiquarians collect monstrosities, such as photographs of five-legged calves, doubtful signatures from Dante, and even more doubtful fountain pens from Kafka. Tourists usually shop at cheap antique shops, while expensive shops deliver to museums. But, serious historiographers despise all kinds of antique shops. Unfairly. For antiquarians are the ones who make history. Historiographers are satisfied with putting their collected curiosities into a row, to make them into processes. But, it is not as if something actually happens in cultural history or the history of the human species. Instead, antiquarians belatedly thread their collected curiosities into processes, like pearls on pearl necklaces. It is not as if lemurs originated from dinosaurs, but rather some natural scientist pulled some threads between lemurs and dinosaurs together, so that it appears that lemurs originated from dinosaurs. Moreover, it is not as if the Baroque originated from the Renaissance, but rather historians visited antiquarian shops, collected some curiosities there, then divided them up into two piles. One pile they labeled "Renaissance" and the other "Baroque." Ultimately, they connected these two piles together diachronically. And this is all very questionable.

At this point, the sophistic paradox reenters our discussion. Does the world consist of grains of sand, which amass themselves into dunes and resemble waves? Or does it consist of waves, which break against cliffs and then resemble dewdrops? Is a wave a mass of particles, or is a particle a frozen wave? In historical thinking, this is an insoluble ontological problem: Heraclitus on one side, Democritus on the other. In posthistorical consciousness, the problem is solved. History is a suspenseful narrative, because historiographers have processed the particles, the curiosities collected by antiquarians, into waves, into processes. Thus, history only narrates matters of suspense, because banalities are never taken up. Even apparently banal tales of everyday life are really curiosities that have been processed into processes. In comparison, antiquarians put their hands into the foaming waves of processes, to pick out curiosities. Trilobite fossils from banal rock, five-legged calves from a banal cowshed. In posthistorical consciousness, the question whether history (and reality in general) possesses either a particle structure or a wave structure is a nonquestion. It depends on the manner in which one reflects on history (and the world), whether in an antiquarian manner or in a historical manner. Finally, this insight is a further turn of the screw out of historical consciousness into posthistorical consciousness.

(1991)

Waiting for Kafka

A literary work is the expression of an intellect. It is the linguistic form an intellect takes. Through this realization, an intellect participates in a general discussion. Thus, a literary work participates in the great conversation that we—roughly put—call "civilization." As an essential part of this conversation, the literary work has two fundamental aspects: it puts an end to previous conversation and calls the next one into existence.

In the first case, it is an answer; in the second case, a provocation. There are two fundamental possibilities in the evaluation of a literary work: we can try to understand it as an answer or approach it as a provocation. In the first case, we analyze the work; in the second case, we enter into a dialogue with it. Criticism is the sphere of the first attempt. In this sphere, the work is the synthesis of provocations to which the intellect that generated the work had been exposed. Speculation is the sphere of the second attempt. In this sphere, we experience the work as a message of the intellect that generated the work, as a message coming in our direction.

The two spheres cannot be completely separated from one another. The critical investigation is a spontaneous experience of the work's message in our intellect. Speculation about the message spontaneously awakens our curiosity about the elements that have made the work possible. Yet, the two spheres correspond to two different "attitudes." The sphere of criticism corresponds to the attitude of curiosity, whereas the sphere of speculation corresponds to the attitude of sympathy—in the Greek sense of the word, "vibration-with." The word *sympathy* sprouts from the humus of music. Consider, for a moment, the viola d'amore: in the viola, particular strings vibrate in sympathy with the strings being played by the bow. As we approach Kafka's work, I plead with the reader to focus on the attitude of sympathy—the reader should transform his own intellect into strings, to vibrate in sympathy with Kafka's strings. This takes tremendous effort. Kafka's work is not "sympathetic" in the common sense of the word. Nevertheless, it demands our sympathy, in more than a musical sense. Not by accident do I ask you to consider the viola d'amore.

The moment our spirit tries to become open to the message of Kafka's work we are immediately confronted with two difficulties. The first difficulty is concerned with the form taken by the message, which is to say, the language of the work. The second difficulty is concerned with the overwhelming timely immediacy of Kafka's work, an immediacy that makes critical distance impossible. Because these two difficulties characterize the message of the work, they should be looked at even before we actually consider the message itself.

Kafka's work is written in German. This is not by accident. Rather, it is fundamental to his work. The thoughts that make up his work are sentences written in German. As such, Kafka's thoughts are determined by the structure of German grammar. Kafka had German thoughts, and everything he thought was structured a priori by the grammar of this language. When they are translated into other languages, Kafka's thoughts are structurally distorted. Thus, any alleged sympathy with these translated thoughts may actually be based on errors. In the case of Kafka's work, the difficulty inherent to all translation takes on extraordinary significance. Written German, "High German," is less of a unified language than the majority of other civilized languages. In truth, written German is a "lingua franca" positioned between dialects, and it subtly reflects the author's regional dialect. Kafka writes the language of Prague, and this language is a High German sui generis. It is a literary language that does not belong to any authentic sort of dialect, because the group that uses this language consists of intellectuals or pseudointellectuals and is completely isolated within a Slavic milieu. This official and artificial language originated in the chancellery offices of the Emperor Charles IV of Prague. It sparked the creation of modern "High German." In this sense, Prague German is the "purest," which is to say the driest and most sterile, German. On the other hand, this language experiences the uninterrupted influence of the Czech language, whose structure is completely alien to the German language. In part, Prague German takes up this structure without ever being able to assimilate it. The result is a language that combines official-sounding sterility with an eccentric mix of languages in the most grotesque manner. Here I offer two examples, the first to show the artificiality, and the other to show the language mix: "Einrücken gemacht" ("einrücken")[1] and "Was ist dir in das hinein?" ("Misch dich nicht ein").[2] Kafka's work is peppered with this sort of idiom.

Because of this idiom, Kafka's message possesses the aura of the ridiculously absurd pedantry so characteristic to him. The language of Prague oscillates between the poles of pedantic artificiality (historically embodied by the Austro-Hungarian bureaucracy) and ridiculous language mixes (for example, historically embodied in the Czech, semi-German Officer Schweik). Because this language structures Kafka's thoughts a priori, they automatically oscillate within this dialectical tension. The overcoming of this tension leads directly to a malicious irony, which we usually call Kafka's irony.

Although this irony is typical for the German thinking of Prague, it reaches its highest point in Kafka's work. With an almost morbid clarity, Kafka drives to the core of his own thinking, to the core that was imposed on him by the character of his language. Kafka uses this formerly unconscious, yet fundamental irony to articulate his message. He uses the climate of inauthenticity that the language of his thoughts imposes upon him authentically, to deconstruct this inauthenticity by deconstructing himself in the process. This is an ironic situation in the highest degree. The fundamental inauthenticity of Kafka's thinking is the source of his purest authenticity. It is therefore self-destructive.

The method used by Kafka to reach this high point of irony consists in the shift of his language onto levels of meaning where its inauthenticity cries to the heavens. Language has many levels of meaning, and normally each one fits within its own climate. I offer three examples: the levels of conversation, science, and poetry. Language has a different "reality" on each of these levels. The level chosen by Kafka to formulate his message is normally called the "theological" level. Which is to say, its sentences represent a "reality" normally addressed by religions. However, the climate of Kafka's language is incompatible with its level of meaning. In *The Castle* or *The Trial*, it is the dry and sterile climate of bureaucratic language, or, in *The Metamorphosis*, the familiar, bourgeois climate. Thus, Kafka opens up an abyss between the form and the meaning of his sentences that cannot be bridged by aesthetics. The message automatically takes on the character of a code. It is encoded. Whereas the message—as we will see later—is almost unbearably tragic, the code is ridiculous and grotesque. The experience of Kafka's absurd originates from the incompatibility between code and message.

The code Kafka uses helps to disguise the level of meaning of his message. Although it is not difficult to decode this code, there is a certain doubt with respect to the validity of the decoded message as a consequence of the absurd incompatibility of both. Certainly, it was Kafka's intention to elicit this existential doubt in the reader's mind. Moreover, it is very possible that he nurtured the same doubt. I believe this is an instance of self-irony seldom repeated in the history of human thought. A prophet (because Kafka is a prophet, a heterodox prophet with respect to the Jewish tradition) who quietly confesses the inauthenticity of his encoded message, thus making the message doubly authentic. If I wanted to conjure up an image, I would say that Kafka does not try to hide the key to his code. Instead, he secretly admits the possibility that he has provided the false key.

Let us summarize the first difficulty, the linguistic difficulty of gaining access to Kafka's work: the message has been submerged in the bureaucratic and familiar Prague German, which is incompatible with its meaning. Ironically, however, this incompatible language is the real source of the message, because it has structured all Kafka's thoughts in advance. After presenting this absurd proposal, so typical of Kafka's world, I now proceed to the second difficulty.

An intellect may project a message in the direction of a general conversation. Then the message is handed over to intellectuals who participate in this conversation. Through a process of wear and tear, they eventually talk this message to death. It is a complicated process, demanding a difficult analysis. On the one hand, we are tempted to see it as a process that cleans up the message and makes it more lucid. For example, an Orthodox Jew might assume that the message of the Bible becomes more clear as the commentaries pile up. On the other hand, we suspect that this process represents a distortion of the message. In their effort to cleanse the Bible of the impurities of subsequent commentaries, the Protestants of the Reformation sought the pure message of the Bible. We might also consider this process to be an uninterrupted transformation of the message itself. The message comes alive according to the ancient phrase "habent fata libelli." For example, the message of Aristotle in antiquity meant one thing in the Middle Ages and something else in Renaissance humanism or the Romantic period. Whatever our opinion of the process a message undergoes during a debate, one thing is certain: the message has, according to its own nature, its own addressee, its own fate. It is not complete, it has not realized itself, until it reaches its addressee, and has suffered its particular fate. What I am trying to say is that the message, which Kafka throws at us, has not yet completely reached us. From our perspective, from the perspective of Kafka's partner in dialogue, his message is premature. My reasons for this assertion are the following:

Kafka lived in a world whose problematic had little or nothing to do with that of his contemporaries, which is why he was not "understood" during his lifetime. The problems that persecuted and plagued him meant nothing to those who lived with him. Only today do some of these problems begin to take on significance—for example, the situation of parents who flee from an impersonal persecution executed by insignificant functionaries. Instead of survival, they seek a sure death and hand their children over to their persecutors. Another example is the situation of a man who has lost his individuality and has become a cog in the apparatus. However, Kafka's work contains several situations where we cannot imagine ourselves as participants or where we simply cannot relate authentically, even though we can understand them on an intellectual level. These situations are all gathered around a central problem: around a single man who has been forgotten by an all-powerful, yet careless and incompetent bureaucratic apparatus and who—without the least capacity for anger—seeks in vain to have himself recognized. Today, it does not take much to imagine that a similar situation could be a fundamental problem in the near future. Nevertheless, there is a difference between imagining a situation and actually experiencing it. Kafka is not a utopian writer. He does not write "science fiction." He experiences the situations that he articulates, and he suffers through them in an authentic manner. They are timely for him, but not for us. In this sense, Kafka is a prophet. And, in this manner, Kafka's message is premature, like Jeremiah's message to the citizens of Jerusalem. Despite being threatened, Jerusalem was not yet destroyed.

But now I hasten to add the following: the prophetic situations that we discover in Kafka's work are part of Kafka's codes. Thus, they mask the message's true meaning. Although they retain their validity when taken literally (this is another aspect of Kafka's irony), they preserve their final impact for the moment of decoding. Perhaps we experience the decoded message even if we do not experience the message in the code itself? With this question that I leave unanswered, I venture closer to the true message of Kafka's work.

As it passes through the prism of the two difficulties that I have mentioned, this message of the work seems distorted and unconvincing. It is concerned with man's situation in relation to the powers that rule over him, with the situations of these powers opposite man, and with the powers themselves. If we tried to reduce this message to a few sentences, something that Kafka would not allow, we would eventually arrive at the subsequent result: man lives in continual guilt vis-à-vis the higher powers. He knows of the guilt, and he recognizes the justice of all punishments randomly carried out by the higher powers. Yet, he is unaware of the nature of the guilt. He tries to come into contact with these powers. He does not seek forgiveness; instead, he seeks to find out about his guilt. The possibilities for success in this search seem very high, because the higher powers seem so close.

However, a successful conclusion to the search is continually thwarted by trivial and absurd motives. Inside himself, man is always aware of the trivial nature of his efforts to find the higher powers, and he is aware of the fact despite all evidence to the contrary. Yet, he insists on his search, because he would rather listen to what the evidence has to say than listen to his deepest conviction. The powers, so close in proximity and yet so unreachable, maintain an attitude of indifference and contempt toward man. They consider man guilty (in this, at least, they are in agreement with him), but it is not worth the effort to punish him. He provokes the punishment himself through his determination to know his guilt. The temporary deferral of divine punishment (why should this word not be used?) is not a result of his compassion, but rather, his overorganization. Divine power functions slowly and poorly, because it is much too complicated and is managed in a much too unsuitable routine. Assuming the total indifference of divine power toward man, this mismanagement does not have the slightest meaning. Yet, man's singular hope for avoiding the just punishment that awaits him is based precisely on this mismanagement. Although man is aware of it, he absurdly tries to speed up the divine apparatus. This vain effort becomes the goal of human life. Thus, we are able to understand Kafka's most important doctrine: "I have spent my entire life fighting the desire to put an end to it."

The theology unveiled before our petrified eyes by this message has several points of contact with the theologies of our traditional religions, but its climate is what makes it different. The climate of human existence is anxiety, unrelieved by hope; and the climate of the divine flock is nausea. Human anxiety is not a new concept, although, except for Kafka, others seldom use it so vehemently. What seems to me revolutionary and "epochal" (in the proper sense of the word) is the concept of divine nausea. Vis-à-vis divine nausea, our anxiety truly assumes gigantic proportions, incomparably greater than anxiety vis-à-vis divine wrath or divine jealousy. If we want to delve into Kafka's theology, we must completely absorb this nausea. It is not the nausea that God feels for his creation. The ancient prophets were well aware of this nausea ("We are like worms before you"). It is the nausea that God feels for himself. This theology goes so far in its blasphemy that we begin to sympathize with Kafka's efforts to find codes for it.

There are several different obvious points of contact with the traditional theologies. For this reason, we can consider Kafka a Jewish, yet heterodox, prophet. The concept of original sin is one example. Everyone is guilty. However, original sin is the primitive, "natural" state of man, not the result of human action. In reality, we have yet to eat the fruit of the tree of knowledge. Our efforts to commit this crime are always and absurdly in vain. Properly said (and, I believe, the utmost irony consists in this), we are still living in Paradise. Of course, it is Kafka's Paradise. In this sort of theology where the fall has not yet occurred, there is obviously no place for salvation or a savior. In the context of Kafka's work, the actual concept of "salvation" has no meaning whatsoever.

Even if it is fascinating to count up the many points of contact between the message of Kafka's work and traditional theology, it would be a useless exercise. The persuasiveness of this message has nothing to do with such exercises. Kafka is persuasive (even though we hold back just as he himself, again and again, held back), because the perspective unveiled by him coincides with our most intimate experience. This experience is so painful that we repress it, and it continues to be dormant in our spirit. Kafka has come to awaken it. Let us comment on the fury of this experience.

Kafka teaches us that human existence is a vain search for knowledge. It is neither a search that makes us proud nor one that empowers us. It has nothing to do with the hubris of the Greeks. There is nothing heroic about human existence. Man is not a rebel. The search that consumes his life is more like a quiet, humble reaching out, and the knowledge that he searches for is the knowledge of his own damnation and nothingness. This order of ideas does not agree with the picture of man that we are used to drawing. Instead, it agrees with the intimate experience of ourselves that we have in moments of introspection. Kafka teaches us that the higher powers are apathetic and disinterested in our fate. This is not the apathy and the disinterestedness of blind nature, which the naive nonbelievers of the nineteenth century substituted for God. This is apathy full of contempt. Moreover, the apathetic higher powers show their indifference toward us when they play with our lives absurdly and regardless of rules—or, we might say, idiotically. This order of ideas agrees neither with the traditional theological concept of divine providence nor with the scientific concept of natural laws. It only agrees with our deep personal experiences of the idiocy and absurdity of our misfortunes. Kafka teaches that the higher powers are an administrative, hierarchically overorganized machine, a pedantic machine, corrupt, poorly functioning, and repugnant. This idea of God is repulsive and grotesque for believers and nonbelievers alike. However, it responds to our intimate experience with the higher powers ruling over us. Why else do we pray, if not to bribe the petty authorities in the heavenly hierarchy? Why do we make promises to ourselves, if not to deceive a heavenly corporal, who, in charge of our case, finds it annoying and much too boring to really become interested in it? Why do we perform good deeds, if not to have good credit for our heavenly bank account, even though we are afraid an incompetent bookkeeper will make a bad entry? Our individual mind associates with Kafka's concept of God. Moreover, even the traditional religions nurture this concept. What other meaning could the prayer "Ora pro nobis" have if not: "Forget not to pray for us, since thou art so able to forget"? In short, the persuasiveness of Kafka's message originates neither from reason nor from faith, but rather from direct experience.

If Kafka's message could be reduced to the thoughts just formulated, we could flee from the unsentimental, authentic analysis of human existence into religious belief. The message cannot be reduced to these thoughts. Instead, it contains an unarticulated and inarticulable dimension, which does not allow a flight into religious belief in the traditional sense, because it includes and overtakes belief. Kafka's message is not antireligious. It moves through religion and overtakes it without abandoning it. If I try to articulate this region where language ceases to function, then I must use the method of approach. This dimension of Kafka's message cannot be authentically thought, but rather only intuited.

Kafka's message takes our thinking to a level that the mystics call "Unio mystica." According to the eyewitness accounts of the mystics, it is a level at which thought and the object of thought, at which "soul" and "God," merge. In contrast, Kafka bears witness to the inauthenticity and absurdity of this fusion. With respect to the meaning of life, Kafka's experience is similar to that of the mystics: it is the search for God. With respect to the final situation of this search, they differ from each other: after being discovered, God discloses himself as nothingness. At the place where belief assumes God, Kafka's experience uncovers the abyss of nothingness. In its procession toward God, thought reaches a point where it succumbs to vertigo, for it suddenly realizes that God is nothing more than a reflection of one's own thought on the silent and bottomless surface of nothingness on whose shores it now finds itself. In this verti-go, "vis-à-vis nothingness," the intellect is exposed to both the destruc-tive experience of the total nothingness of the meaning of life and its re-flection, the total nothingness of "God." For Kafka, this is the authentic experience of the "Unio mystica." Shortly after this experience, the intel-lect absurdly enough puts itself on the same path, and (despite its op-posite conviction) it once more carries its mirror image for God, thus beginning its Sisyphean task from the beginning—the difference being that it now takes the "new" God as a power hierarchically higher than the first one. Thus, the progress of thought is a way into the hierarchy of nothingness.

In my opinion, this is Kafka's message *in nuce*: The pedantic, over-organized, ridiculously incompetent God sick and tired of himself is nothing other than the increasing accumulation of man's reflection on nothingness. The progress of thought, the progress of human existence is progress in the direction of nothingness. It leads through a hierarchically organized range of experiences of nothingness. Nausea and boredom are the other side of anxiety. Similarly, God is the other side of thought. The "Unio mystica" is the meeting of nausea with anxiety. This meeting is the authentic experience of the simultaneous thinking of Nietzsche's two principles: "everything is will to power" and "the eternal recurrence of the same." Kafka is the existentialization of Nietzsche.

We understand finally the deep reason of the code in which Kafka's message is bathed. Kafka is concerned with articulating the inarticulable, because he thinks the unthinkable. Obviously, this is an absurd effort. In its ridiculous inconsistency with the message, in its absurd incompatibili-ty with the task it sets itself, the code ironically makes the effort possible. The inarticulable is not articulated, the unthinkable is not thought. Instead, something completely, ridiculously different is articulated and thought. In the reader, it brings something unthinkable and inarticulable back to life—as a contradiction. Kafka's message is a parable similar to the message of the prophets of Israel. In this sense, Kafka is a link in the chain of the Jewish tradition. However, it is an absurd parable. This is precisely why it is successful in calling forth the oscillation and the expe-rience of the absurd in the "sympathetic" reader.

Although we are speaking about an author who could still be alive, his message does not reach us directly. Instead, it reaches us via his student, perhaps via an exegete, via Max Brod. Even this apparently accidental cir-cumstance is absurd. It heightens our doubt concerning the authenticity of the message. The message has been delivered in a doubtful, ironic, and absurd manner, so that we can respond to it as best as possible. One cannot say that our attempts at an answer have been brilliant. These attempts cover up a series of excuses that usually come under the heading of Existentialism. It represents so many different sorts of answers from Sartre to Buber. For the most part, they have not been directed expressly at Kafka. But, the climate where they have originated is Kafka's climate, and the categories of thought are Kafka's categories. Nevertheless, it seems to me that all the answers that have so far been given have been attempts to return to a traditional religiosity—or else to atheism. Certainly, this is an impossible recourse for anyone who has made Kafka's message his own. They are fundamentally inauthentic; they are excuses. Kafka's challenge must be accepted authentically, even at the risk that the great discussion of civilization may get lost in total nothingness. Waiting for an authentic answer to Kafka, we also continue to wait for the complete realization of his message. Waiting for Kafka.

(1967)

Notes by the Editor

1. "to be drafted" ; from the Czech "být odveden."

2. "Don't butt in!" or "This is none of your business"; from the Czech "Co je ti do toho?"

Orders of Magnitude and Humanism

Translated by Elizabeth Wilson and Andreas Ströhl

"Man is the measure of all things." That was easy for the ancients to say. Then everything in the world could indeed be measured in centimeters, hours, dollars (or the contemporary equivalents thereof). What was not measurable thus was unmeasurable. For example, the sea was wide without measure and the grain of sand small without measure because it was uncomfortable to apply the above-mentioned units of measurement to them. They were outstanding things; they stood outside of the human norm. Things that were big without measure had to be worshiped; things that were small without measure could be held in contempt.

We cannot afford this anymore. We can no longer pray reverentially to things that explode in megatons. We have to measure them. We can no longer disdainfully neglect things that explode in microseconds or flash on screens. We have to measure them. If somebody tells us that Allah is great, then we must ask that person how great he is; and if somebody tells us that we are nitpicking, then we have to ask him what order of magnitude he has in mind. We are forced to differentiate between orders of magnitude. In this, the human order is one among many. Humanism is inappropriate to the present.

The lens is to blame. It made visible small things on the surface of the moon, so that it became difficult to admire the size of the moon. It made visible great things in human semen, so that it became uncomfortable to hold it in disgust and contempt. The present apparatuses, with the machines and instruments that are based on them, are descendants of the lens. However, the lens alone does not bear the blame for the penetration of inhuman orders of magnitude into concrete everyday life. If the church

160

had managed to burn the writings of Galileo and the remaining humanists in order to save humanism, the penetration would not have been
avoided. For the world has not only expanded into space in order to bend
at one of its horizons and to fray into quarks at the other, it has also expanded into time, in order to creep into the big bang on the one hand,
and into the quantum leap on the other. It would have been necessary to
burn the stopwatches too. Besides, the world has also expanded with respect to values, thereby assuming inhuman dimensions, in gross net products on the one hand, and calculations of cost on the other. The slide
rules would have had to be burned too. In short: man has advanced into
the inhuman, the inhuman strikes back at him, and under these blows,
humanism breaks down.

At the time of the ancients, the island of centimeters, hours, and dollars that was inhabited by human beings was surrounded by the immea-
surable world. An ocean of enormous sizes and eternal values then
washed around the beaches of this settlement that provided measures.
Then there were fishermen indeed who fetched food out of the ocean and
adventurers who dared to sail out on it in boats, as well as divers who
risked their lives in order to bring pearls to the light of day; but most
people were farmers who dug measured furrows in order to fill calibrated
measures of quantity with the fruit of measuredness. At present, hardly
anything of this measured Mediterranean landscape can be noticed anymore. We are somewhere in the interior of a *matrjoschka* (Russian doll), a
hierarchy of orders of magnitude in which each contains all smaller ones
while being contained by all bigger ones. We ourselves are such containing and contained dolls. The transformation of our region from a Mediterranean island into the Russian doll is called—not to put too fine a
point on it—the "Copernican revolution."

But we have to put a fine point on it, for it is just what is pointy about
it that hits us in our glands, guts, and heart, deep in our marrow and
brain. It is not in question whether the earth spins around the sun or—to
put it in a more modern way—whether mental processes can be reduced
to quantum leaps of particles between nerve synapses. It is in question
what we are actually doing when we jump from doll to doll, from measure to measure, from scale of values to scale of values.

Without a doubt, we must differentiate between orders of magnitude.
If we do not, we cause nonsense and mischief. One example of nonsense:
a person who wanted to apply Einsteinian equations to the production of
ink pens would be stupid, because, for the order of magnitude of ink
pens, Newtonian equations are valid. One example of mischief: a person

who brings up the term *race* in political discourse commits a criminal act and has to account for millions of deaths because the order of magnitude of race is measured in hundreds of thousands of years and political phenomena in decades. Although necessary, it is not easy to tell orders of magnitude from each other. There is no exact point at which Newton stops being valid and Einstein becomes valid. There is no exact point at which political thinking would have to resign in favor of biological thinking. The dolls not only contain one another; they are also each permeable by the other. It is especially these gray zones between the orders of magnitude that set our teeth on edge—in case we stay long enough in that doll inside of which we have teeth, marrow, and bone.

For we only have marrow and bone in the margin between 10^{-5} and 10^5 cm and between decades and seconds, that is, in that order of magnitude which we can perceive with our senses but which we leave more and more often. Because neurophysiology has taught us that our perceptions take place in the order of magnitude of particles of atom nuclei, we emigrate there more and more frequently. For it is there that our fantasies, notions, wishes, feelings, decisions take place—in short, what earlier was called "mind." And from there we can project the spiritual processes on intelligent tools in order to program them from the outside. Thus released from the skullcap, the mind can develop even if it has lost much of its former glitter.

In the order of magnitude of spiritual processes, the point is not marrow and bone, but rather the computation of quantum leaps. However, at present, we are slipping into another doll; and there, marrow and bone are spoken of in a way that makes the flesh of many of us creep, that is, in the order of magnitude of molecules. In it, processes take place for which chemistry is competent. Among these processes are also the processes of life. We are beginning to understand the processes by which life emerges from the inanimate in order to turn back into the inanimate. This insight allows interference in the processes of living and dying. We are beginning to produce marrow and bone at will so that, in the near future, we can populate the world perceptible through the senses with living beings (including artificial supermen). Compared with this "genetic revolution" of molecules, even the "informatic" one of particles of nuclei fades. For one day it will be nonsense to want to differentiate not just artificial from natural bacteria, but also artificial from natural human beings. Then the question concerning life and death will put itself forward in the even-tempered mood of the production programmer.

The three orders of magnitude considered here, that is, "perceptible by the senses," "quantum," and "molecular," show what thrills us to the core: the gray zones between the three orders and the jumping from order to order. Both tear apart our deep respect for mind, life, and death.

The indifference to mind, life, and death is antihumanist (barbarian). It identifies, for instance, the Nazis. But it is advisable to distinguish the new technical barbarism from the preceding one if we want to overcome it and find a new humanism. The preceding barbarism despises without measure, it was measureless, it could not measure mind, life, and death. Precisely because they measure, the emerging technologies despise mind, life, and death. This is why traditional humanism cannot get at the new barbarism. The new barbarism is more enlightened than traditional humanism. The new barbarism, and not traditional humanism, is ultimate enlightenment. With it, enlightenment has left traditional humanism far behind, as an obscurantist ideology. The new humanism would have to criticize the gray zones between the orders of magnitude, that is, the zones in which dwell artificial intelligence, artificial life, and artificial immortality.

Let us illustrate what a new humanism would have to provide by looking at the example of immortality: the "I" is a diffuse term, if it is a term at all. It is enshrouded with theological, philosophical, and psychological fogs. The new technologies start to define the "I" clearly, that is, as a complex system of electromagnetic and chemical brain processes. Brains or parts of brains can be transplanted, for instance, from dying bodies to fetuses—for the time being, only in the case of rats. Nevertheless, the immortality of the "I" in the sense of its repeated transfer to new bodies has thus entered the realm of the technically doable. A new humanism would have to show that in this entanglement of the order of magnitude perceptible by the senses with that of particles and that of molecules, a decisive aspect of the "I" slips away, that is, the one from which the "I" is seen as the "you" of a different "you."

Such a new humanism would have no intention of making the *matrjoschka* a Mediterranean island again. The new barbarism cannot be attacked from behind; and lenses, stopwatches, slide rules, computers, or genetically manipulated tomatoes cannot be assaulted. The raging bull of progress can only be taken by the horns. The new humanism cannot want to deny that different orders of measurement overlap each other and interpenetrate. On the contrary, it has to emphasize that, for each order of magnitude, there is a typical epistemology, ethics, and aesthetics that is effective, and that, in spite of the gray zones, abysses gape between the orders of magnitude. Thus, it is mischief to apply the geometry of what is perceptible by the senses to the astronomical order of magnitude or causal thinking to the order of magnitude of particles of atom nuclei. The specificity of each order of magnitude would have to enable the new humanism to call attention to the priority of the human order of magnitude. A Ptolemaic counterrevolution is required.

The accomplishment of this task is inconvenient. If a person says to a starving Brazilian child that it has no beans because the national debt is several billions of dollars, this is an enlightened and enlightening explanation that can contribute to putting "right" the problem of beans and bring it closer to a solution. The new humanism, however, would have to show that it is inhuman, barbarian, to speak like this to a child, because in this way inhuman orders of magnitude are introduced into the human relation to the child.

This example shows that the extreme rationalism of the new technical barbarism turns into the irrational. Of course, every humanism has the task of fighting the irrational, and so does the new one. But at the present, the irrationalism manifests itself as extreme rationalism. The Enlightenment has overshot its mark. The position that must be taken in the struggle against this extremism is extraordinarily uncomfortable because it is—where humanism and barbarism seem to change sides—always in danger of falling into irrationalism itself.

In order to be able to maintain the priority of the human order of magnitude, the new humanism has to refer to something nameless. It must circle it and beat around the bush. This may serve as an explanation (and apology) for the rather intricate argument of this essay.

By the way, some people affirm that God writes in winding lines in order to hit his goal. The new humanism is forced to break out of the linearity of technical progress into the winding.

(1990)

Celebrating

In the Platonic model, the main emphasis was leisure *(schole)*: it is the goal of life, the seat of wisdom. Moreover, it appears that we are making great strides toward reaching this goal. Unemployment is gaining ground, because automatic machines are taking charge of the transformative gestures that were previously carried out by humans. The division of labor is increasingly a question that must be addressed to those who program these robots. It is becoming less a political question and more a question of calculating. In this manner, the question of life during leisure time has become a very pressing one. Currently, this question is being carelessly belittled as "leisure-time management." There is no doubt that the question of leisure should be the focus of this entire essay.

It is not only a question of quantities, or of how the increasing amount of "leisure time" should be managed. Certainly, what the politically organized craftsman once referred to as closing time has now become a holiday, vacation, and retirement of the economically organized industry worker. In addition, this has turned into the cybernetic life of the information-consuming functionary whose life is only periodically interrupted by the performance of his services. The relationship between work and leisure has been quantitatively reversed. We should speak of a service morning instead of closing time. In a telematic society, we should only speak of celebrating. Yet, it is not only a matter of dividing leisure into hours, days, or years. We must also take into account the experience of leisure, the celebration. If the power of imagination is to develop in a telematic society, it must live life as a celebration.

We will come closer to celebration if we forget Plato's notion of leisure as the seat of wisdom and of theoretical life, and if we give recognition to the other root of our culture, Judaism. There, we run up against the Sabbath. It is "holy," and it alone is holy—except for God himself. The commandment says: "Thou shalt keep holy the Sabbath." It is a matter of holiness, which would be incomprehensible to Plato. For him, as for all of our Greek tradition, holiness is a sector that has been excised and given protection from the *polis*: a *temenos*, a temple. It is a sector for contemplation, for leisure. It is a school. It is a preserve sheltered by a god (for example, the god Akademos) where one walks around exchanging ideas with others who enjoy their leisure. In comparison, the Sabbath is a sector extracted from and raised above the flow of events. It is a temple made of time rather than marble. It is holy only if one extracts it from history, if one celebrates it.

If one raises the Sabbath out of linear time (out of the "week"), then history is broken through. Then, the six days of the "week" grow into the Sabbath, to be subsumed in it. History takes place during the six days of the "week" (for example, God creates the world) only to dissolve into nothingness on the Sabbath (nothing happens on this day; for example, God rests on the Sabbath). The six days of the week pursue a goal, they are motivated, and they have something in sight. Their goal, their motive, their intention (the goal, the motive, the intention of history in general) is the Sabbath. The Sabbath itself finds rest in nothingness; it has no goal, no motive, and no intention, because it is itself the goal and the motive. The six days of the week are meaning-"full." Their meaning is the Sabbath. Yet, the Sabbath itself is meaningless. The six days of the week are value-"full." Their value is the Sabbath. Yet, the Sabbath itself is valueless, because it is its own value. Thus, the Sabbath—when it is observed—is holy. It is the "transcendence" of history. According to a cabalistic interpretation of messianic time, it is the moment when two Sabbaths directly follow one another. For Christianity, the holy moment is the Sabbath between Good Friday and Easter Sunday. This moment negates history. It is the celebratory moment of salvation from suffering.

Not that this Judeo-Christian notion of celebrating, of holy observance, is opposed to the Greek notion of theory, of contemplation, of philosophy. Both stand for the transcendence of happening, for "posthistory." In both cases, in the Academy as in the Sabbath celebration, one turns one's back on politics and economics, and one surfaces in the realm known as the "Mothers" in Goethe's *Faust*. Still, there is a powerful difference between an academic and a celebratory life. For, in the Academy one looks (one sees ideas there), whereas in the celebration one hears (one is called there). The Academy is an extraction from space, and one sees forms there. The Sabbath celebration is an extraction from time, and one gains callings there. Thus, Greek leisure is contemplation, whereas the celebratory leisure of the Judeo-Christian tradition is "responsibility" (response to calls). Greek leisure is "essential": one sees being. Celebratory leisure is "existential": one faces the other. In Greek leisure, one discovers the holy (*aletheia* = discovery = truth). In celebratory leisure, the holy reveals itself, it "comes into the word." Only when school and celebration meet, when Academy and Sabbath merge, when space and time negate each other, can one expect the Western tradition to be complete. This is the religious aspect of telematics.

We have forgotten how to celebrate ever since the bourgeois revolution of the fifteenth century. This forgetting is what history books often refer to as the "secularization of modern life." According to the Platonic model, the bourgeois revolution brought about the submission of theory under the yoke of praxis; since then, theoretical leisure has been in the service of the progressive transformation of the world. Viewed from the Judeo-Christian perspective, the bourgeois revolution sought the submission of celebrating in favor of utility; since then, holiday leisure was designed to provide rest for future useful activities. The Academy and the Sabbath were subordinated to work (to technology, to the workday). The industrial revolution of the nineteenth century completed the disenchantment of school and celebrating. Theory itself became technology. It became an undertaking carried out at specially constructed and specially financed institutions. Similarly, celebrating became the weekend, the summer vacation, and the ski trip, organized by specially designed institutions. Thus, the bourgeois revolution—in both the Greek and Judeo-Christian sense—built leisure into work. In turn, the industrial revolution built this type of work powered by leisure into the economic engine.

The current revolution in automation reveals this building of leisure into work and the subsequent engineering of work into economy in a peculiar way. In fact, it appears that the degraded and disenchanted leisure bloats up in the abdomen of work, and, following the economy's digestion of work, the entire economic engine swells up like a soap bubble. Thus, the current problem of idleness, of joblessness, and of free time appears as an economic problem: it calls the economic engine and industriousness into question. When viewed from the perspective of work, the problem of increasing idleness presents itself as a political problem. For, owing to automation, idleness is not the source of vice, but rather virtue's reward. The domination of leisure time is, first, an antithesis to business and, second, an antithesis to bourgeois values. But both the economic and the political perspectives concerning the suppression of work through leisure distort the view of the actual problem: that we degenerate in leisure once we become incapable of celebrating.

Our inability to celebrate can be seen in the current use of the term *idleness*. We use it dismissively, with a dismissive gesture—for instance, it is idle to bust our heads over something. Clearly, "idle" means "useless." However, the ancient Greeks knew that "useless" was a synonym for "pure." They knew that philosophy only comes about when heads are busted idly over something. Moreover, the old Jews kept the Sabbath holy precisely in order to separate it from workdays and to bust their heads idly over sacred texts on this day. Both of our prebourgeois traditions used *idle* as an expression for the human capacity to raise ourselves above usefulness. It is a ceremonial expression. As long as we do not remind ourselves of this meaning of the word, we continue to be incapable of recognizing a blessing in unemployment.

One method for helping us to remember is to observe human gestures versus animal gestures. Certainly, purposive (economic) motions can be ascertained in the human being: like the animals, he reaches for something to eat or something to copulate with, and he too distances himself from danger. But we also recognize purposeless, useless, antieconomic, celebratory gestures in the human being. For example, children play with inedible, nonsexual, and harmless pebbles; they play "theoretically." It is characteristic for our current forgetting of the holiness of leisure that we are now providing a utilitarian interpretation of these games. For example, we say that the useful stone knife and useful culture originated from these sorts of pebble games during the Stone Age. Thus, we do not acknowledge that the useless and idle things in culture, the celebratory and the theoretical, which is to say art and the theoretical sciences, are the core of culture. A phenomenology of human gestures helps us to remember that man is a celebratory being. He is religious in the Judeo-Christian sense of the term.

In essence, this is the message of the traditional religions: to remind us of the uselessness, the celebratory nature of human life. But, we have become deaf to this message. With the possible exception that it came to us through the filter of a more accessible discourse, for example, through Kierkegaard. In his work, we recognize to a certain degree the overcoming of "ethical life" (the purposive life in politics and economics) through "religious life" (the purposeless life before God). It is one of the fundamental theses of this essay that we now have a completely new and unexpected method for recovering the Kierkegaardian view of religious life. We now possess telematics, which allows us to recognize ourselves in others through images in a purposeless, idle, and celebratory manner. Telematics is a school where we learn to celebrate.

In my opinion, it seems completely wrong to ask the question for what purpose future generations of men will manufacture images. This is a typical pretelematic line of questioning, which is to say, it is born from purposive historical thinking. The idleness of the manufacture of images, this above and beyond all "for what purpose," this motivelessness—if my prediction is correct—is, precisely, the existential attitude of the future man. He will live life problem-free, not running into objects and obstacles, but rather, living in "pure" imagination, in leisure. Everything he will do will be done in leisure. He will live in celebration. One giant Sabbath will stretch itself across the sky of future humankind. And, if this all seems much too boring to us, it is because we have forgotten what "celebrating" signifies, despite all our festivals (or precisely because of all our festivals).

In the chapter "Playing,"[1] I attempted to make a similar argument. However, I attempted there to consider the problem from a profane perspective. "Playing" and "celebrating" are, in fact, related ideas. This is demonstrated, as I mentioned, by the celebratory gestures of playing children. Except, there are games where one wins or loses, whereas in celebrating, there is nothing to be won. In contrast to all previous societies, there will be no profit in a society playing "telematics." Certainly, new information will continually be produced and the sum of accessible information will continually be increased. But this flood of information will not be made useful, and it will not become profit. One will "only" celebrate it.

The religious attitude, which is the attitude of this essay, helps us to ask the question about programming anew. What exactly do I mean when I say that telematics allows a dialogic programming of image-producing apparatuses? First, I mean that it will no longer be the centralized senders but everyone sitting in front of an image-producing terminal who will be able to dictate his own programs to the apparatus. Second, I mean that all these "own programs" will be compatible, feeding and correcting each other. That in this manner a continuous dialogic programming of all apparatuses will be generated by all participants. That in this manner the future man will be different from the contemporary functionary. Unlike the functionary, he will not judge according to a program. Rather, he will judge by programming. But, in light of celebrating and the solemnity, I mean something much more fundamental with the phrase "dialogical programming." I mean approximately what Buber called "dialogic life."

In the term "own program," which is being discussed here, the emphasis is on "own." It is *my* program and not that of another. I want to have my own program, so that no one else can throw his own on me. I want to possess, in order not to be owned. Elsewhere, this essay tried to make the point that the categories of "property" and "ownership" can no longer be used in an information society. Accordingly, the notion "own program" would be meaningless in an information society. Yet, our experiences in the emergent information society teach us otherwise. We are experiencing it as imperialism of information. The senders possess the programs, and we are possessed by them. Thus, telematization would be a technique for tearing the programs from the hands of the senders, to make them the property of all participants. In the current stage, "own program" signifies "dispossession," the socialization of imperialistic programs. It is a socializing slogan.

This meaning of the term "own program" cannot be maintained once the telematic society has finally been installed. Once the central senders have been taken down, one can no longer speak of "dispossession." Then one can only speak of dialogic programming. And then, it is not a matter of having one's own program, so that no one can throw his own down on me, but to have other programs (the programs of others) and to be able to change them (to recommend them to others). Thus, once the telematic society is finally here, one will no longer speak of "own program," but rather of "other program" (to me, a neologism characteristic of the telematic society).

These speculations bring us now to the pair of terms "own-other." A heavily burdened pair of terms. If one attempts to carry this burden away (as Heidegger did in "Identity and Difference" and as the debate between Sartre and Foucault has tried to do), then one will recognize the reversibility of this pair. "Own" is the other of "other." "Original" is what is different from the other. Identification ($a = a$) means defining difference in relation to the other ($a = \sim[\sim a]$). If one comprehends this, and not only logically, but also existentially, then the shell breaks open where ownness, property, and the ego have been encapsulated, and the view is open for the completely other. Thus, "I" is the other of the completely other.

Judaism forbids image making, and Christianity and Islam have taken up this view (in their own way). Because man-made images cover up the "true image." The "true image" is every human face. It is the image of the completely other: the "image of God." Every human is "for me" the image of God, and "I" am the image of God for every human. Thus, every human is the other for me, and I am the other for all humans. As the image of the "completely other" (God). Because for me every human is the true image of the "completely other," he is the only image (the only idea) that I can make of God for myself and have to make. All other images that I make of God for myself (and of everything else) are false images and therefore forbidden. Every single human is my only "medium" to God, and I can only arrive at God if I go to him "through" the other (every single other). All other "media" (all other images, representations, ideas) that I make for myself are false "media." They are idolatrous. The one true love of God is love of the other. It is love of man. "Thou shalt love thy God (the completely other) with all your heart, all your soul, and all else that remains" is therefore synonymous with "Love thy neighbor (other)."

All pretelematic images from Lascaux to video are discursive images, broadcast, designed against the other, and covering his face. They are forbidden. They are dead-end streets leading away from God. On the other hand, dialogically synthesized telematic images are the "media" from one human to another through which I see the face of the other. And through this face, I see God once more. Thus, the dialogical programming of images (the "dialogical life") can be a celebrating of God (the "completely other"), of everyone with all others and "by means of" all others. It can be a "prayer." In essence, this is what I meant by "other program."

Perhaps we are about to remember again the forgotten celebrating. Perhaps we are about to find our way back through the strange detour through telematics to "authentic" being human, which is to say, to celebratory existence for the other, to purposeless play with others and for others. Thus, the pretelematic existence, dependent on purpose and motive, this existence that insists on what is one's own, has already begun to repulse us as a brutally serious, noncelebratory, and thus profane way of living. A new, completely unorthodox religiosity begins to surface out of the buried corners of our consciousness. But, surprisingly, in the form of a dreamlike universe of technical images.

(1985)

Note by the Editor

1. This essay is chapter 18 of *Ins Universum der technischen Bilder* (Into the universe of technical images). In chapter 11, "Spielen" (Playing), Flusser argues that the coming telematic society will enable humankind to playfully produce new information in a systematic manner and thus to resist entropy.

Designing Cities

Meant here is not the glistening city of Le Corbusier, for which Brazil is the strikingly gray and terrible counterargument. Meant here is the rejection of civilized life in favor of another, an alternative. We were thrown into civilization: we are bourgeois *(citoyens)*, civilians, without anyone asking us for our permission. But, as soon as we become conscious of the fact that we are not individuals (not civil subjects), with one stroke we are no longer bourgeois identifiable by a passport. As a result of this situation of being expatriates, we are able to design alternative cities. That is what is meant here.

Marketplace and Temple Mount

First, a genetic question: How did we come to a civilization into which we could be thrown? This is a fundamental question that archaeology should be made to answer. The answer is: civilization originated out of culture, approximately six thousand years ago. If there had not been a culture (had the people not eaten grass), then we would not be civilians today. Why people began eating grass in spite of their digestive apparatus, and why they went for each other's throats in defense of their grasses, is a follow-up question (not addressed here). If one asks about the origin of culture in the narrower sense of "agriculture," then one runs the danger of wanting to hunt and gather. And for this we are much too civilized. The Paleolithic paradise of those who waded through the abundant intestines of the woolly mammoth and sucked up bird's eggs is not an alternative to civilization: we cannot design these sorts of utopias.

If one eats grass, one has to eat a lot of it not to starve, even if one limits oneself to eating grass seeds only. This circumstance demands that one sow the seeds and sit down and wait until they ripen. It demands a sedentary life. If one sows and then leaves (as in the Mesolithic period), then others can come. This patient sitting and waiting (this guarding) is the cultivated attitude toward life. One still lies in wait (as when hunting), but no longer for something edible (for animals), but for eaters (humans). This is culture in its narrower sense: *homo homini lupus.* In short, the village. The people who write Culture with a big C, these village wolves, represent patience and tolerance. But, these vegetarian wolves do not describe lying in wait. Only those who write culture with a little c describe lupine lurking. They are not hunters, but civilians. They describe culture from the perspective of the city, even if they want to reinstate paradise.

Approximately six thousand years ago, canalization of some riverbanks was begun, to regulate and increase the harvests (for example, in Mesopotamia or along the Nile). This required not only geometry (thus, an intellectual class), but also forced labor (thus, slaves) and supervision (thus, an executive class). The "Big Man" sitting on the hill is in charge of supervision. He also has to raise his hill ("rampart") to a certain artificial height ("tower") to have a full view of the area and to make sure his commands are being heard. Thus, civilization is called into life: The individual villages lengthen their streets, so that they converge at the bottom of the hill. Harvests and commands are transported up and down. The city that originated in this manner consists of three spaces: the homes, the marketplace situated at the bottom of the hill, and the hill. The home dwellers farm the grasses according to commands from on high (according to statutes and laws). Geometers (intellectuals) stand in the marketplace, to formulate the commands, and the "Big Man" on the hill evolves from a guard into legislator, king, high priest, and finally God. This is the political structure of civilization into which we were thrown.

A number of circumstances have changed during the last six thousand years, but the structure has essentially remained the same up to the beginning of the modern period. Modern civilization, which came into being as a result of this revolution, is characterized by the suppression of theory by politics, and of the contemplative life by the active life. The result of the marketplace's dominance over the temple mount is modern science and technology, as well as the industrial revolution and the expansion of Western civilization across the rest of the globe where temples have not yet been overthrown.

From Masquerade to Relational Field

The city and the village are tools for the production of anthropologies, to achieve social identification among the residents. For example, I become "I" in the village thanks to a medicine bag and in the city thanks to an official identity card. For example, I identify myself in the village as a howling goat and in the city as a taxpayer. Village and city are structures through which people identify with something or identify themselves as something. Put another way, culture and civilization are strategies for the generation of human individuals, and these strategies are constantly improving.

This is a truism: village and city are factories for the masks with which people identify themselves. In the village, the masks are still material. In the city, they become increasingly immaterial and thus increasingly numerous. But this truism stops being one once it is recognized that nothing is hidden behind the masks, and that they are really the dancers. That culture and civilization are a masquerade, a *danse macabre*. That there is no one who lays on a mask to identify himself, but rather, that these masks secrete those wearing them out of themselves. This is another way of formulating the assertion that culture and civilization generate anthropologies, which claim to serve as their foundation. This sounds ghostly: these abstractions, culture and civilization, secrete concrete, individual humans. This essay is concerned with formulating this situation the other way around and with bringing an end to this ghostly talk. To demonstrate that culture and civilization are concrete, and that the individual is abstract. The concrete is to be seen as a network of relations, and the threads of this network become tangled without connecting anything concrete. The only concrete thing is the relations themselves, whereas everything related or in relation (all objects and subjects of relations) are abstractions. The network of relationships is to be seen as an intersection of different relational fields, one of these being the field of intersubjective relationships. The field of dialogical intrahuman relationships is networked with other fields in a way that is almost too complex to understand (for example, with the electromagnetic, with the psychological or the ecological). Nevertheless, it possesses its own unique structure: it functions negentropically. It is a relational field where information is generated, stored, and distributed. When viewed from this perspective, the terms *culture* and *civilization* can be formulated: they are two forms of connecting to the intersubjective relational field, two strategies for the generation, storage, and distribution of information by means of the threads of intrahuman relations.

Such a perspective is rather simple to reach—we already possess models, for example, electrical connections or the telephone network—but it is difficult to maintain. It is barely possible to experience every day the products of culture and civilization (for example, Stone Age knives, airplanes, or ministries) as abstractions from a negentropic relational network or to recognize ourselves and our neighbors as products of such a network. This is what is meant here by a change into a sincere life. If, however, one maintains this perspective (and even if it is only for brief moments of insight), then horizons will be opened for possible reconnections of intrahuman relational fields, for alternative civilizations. Then it is possible to design cities.

Cities, Not Villages

First, one asks: Why cities and not villages? Why not, as some alternative thinkers are suggesting, discard civilized life in favor of a cultivated life? Why not focus, for example, on McLuhan's cosmic village? Short and sweet, because the village does not open up theoretical space. Because, despite appearances, the cultivated and cultivating village life does not offer leisure in the civilized sense. Villages cannot have temple mounts. This is not because they turn into cities *(suburbia)* when situated under a temple mount. Put another way, as soon as villagers theorize, village life becomes citified. This is an assumption, and it must be taken into consideration. It does not suffice to give historical proof: as soon as geometry is practiced, villages become cities. The question to ask is why this is so.

The cultivated and cultivating life is a connection plan. Intrahuman relationships are so tangled thanks to this plan that the knots behind the mask of vegetarian wolves can be identified. This blanket description of village life does not only depend on the Roman model with its *colere, cultura,* and its *lupa* (even though it is impossible for the Occident to forget this Roman model). It is also a matter of trying to get a handle on lying in wait for the harvest. In terms of their attitude toward life, cultivated and cultivating people are vegetarian wolves. They are wolves to each other, because the harvests must be distributed. And they are a pack of wolves to others, because the others lie in wait for their harvests. And they are vegetarian, even when they eat an occasional grazing cud chewer, because they sit around and wait for the grain to ripen. Certainly, different masks may be used in the village dance, but they all possess this wolfish mien. All dances are *lupernalia,* even when they honor a different, but equally clever and bloodthirsty totem animal (such as the boar). Lurking anticipation of this kind is an attitude toward life that is opposed to theoretical leisure (the Greek *schole,* the Jewish Sabbath). Village "free time" is great, but antiacademic.

It is not as if the city had "ennobled" the vegetarian wolves or bred them into sheep. On the contrary, it has opened a political space where the wolves are able to let off steam. And, it offers an economic space that places herds of sheep at their disposal. The city resounds with the cry of the wolf and the bleating of the sheep (one need only think of car horns and walkie-talkies). In the city, the wolf occasionally wears sheep's clothing and the sheep mask themselves in wolf's clothing. But this transformation of vegetarian wolves into cannibalistic wolves and this taming of the city dweller into sheep (something that Christianity aided) allow the city to cut out a space for silence and to raise it above the din. There below, the wolves and sheep eat one another, and precisely for this reason a few academics are able to theorize up high (granted, they have gained entrance owing to their mathematical and musical skills). Even this blanket description of the city, similar to the description of the village, has its own inescapable model, namely, Athens. But, similar to the description of village life, this description arose from the desire to get a handle on the city dweller's attitude toward life.

It needs to be asked: Why is it desirable to open up a theoretical space, and why should cities be designed instead of villages? The Platonic answer that the city is justifiable because it allows for theory, and that theory leads to the true, the beautiful, and the good, is no longer satisfying. From the relational perspective, which has been proposed, another answer can be offered: because theory is the connecting force of intrahuman relationships, to which we owe the production of information. The political wolves shred this information into pieces, and the economic sheep consume it, but in a theoretical space they will always be dialogically threaded anew. Therefore, if the intrahuman network has the tendency (is thus "engaged") to produce information in spite of universal entropy, then the theoretical space is its alpha and omega. Thus, one sees how Plato can be stood with his feet on the earth in a sort of Copernican revolution (one more time). In short, the designing of alternative cities must be concentrated on the designing of theoretical spaces, which do not look into the heavens, but drag them down.

Granted that the future projection of cities will be concentrated on theoretical spaces, the following question needs to be asked: Will not the political and economic foundation, on which the ivory tower is built, be neglected? Brutally stated: If the future builders of cities become satisfied with the building of temples and should thus elegantly forget the marketplace and private residences, will one not be justified in accusing them of a pharaonic, elite oligarchy, an aristocratic fascism? The answer is that since the time of the pharaohs (and since Plato) a few things have changed, and this above all: it has become minimally possible to think that the marketplace and private residences could be handed over to simulacra of humans, and that all human citizens could be settled on the temple mount. It has become minimally possible to think that politics could be handed over to artificial intelligence and economics to robots, and that humans would be concentrated on programming these robots.

In this way, the following alternative city for the sincere human life begins to take shape on the horizon: There, where sheep consume and chew their cud in private residences, herds of ever more operative automatons will be working day and night. There, where currently bloodthirsty wolves shred themselves into pieces in the marketplace, and lie in wait for sheep, packs of ever more intelligent computers will be governing the automatons. And there on the temple mount—where currently an elite of programmers and set designers, mostly unnoticed, pull the invisible threads of the marketplace and private residences—the entire citizenry will produce information in a setting of leisurely dialogue without friction, to program the marketplace and private residences to take care of the temple mount.

A New City Model

In order to conceive of this new city model, one must surrender the intellectual categories of geography in favor of topology. This task is not to be underestimated. One should not conceive of the city to be designed as a geographical place (such as a hill near a river), but rather as a fold in the intersubjective relational field. This is what is meant by the assertion that the future civilization must become "immaterial." This change is not to be underestimated, even if we are getting used to seeing folds in fields in synthetic images of equations on the computer screen. One must only think how difficult it was to see the geographic surface as a body surface rather than as a plane. Strangely, a rethinking in terms of topology rather than geography will not make the city to be designed "utopic." It is "utopic" (placeless) as long as we continue to think geographically, because it cannot be localized within a geographical place. But, as soon as we are able to think topologically—that is, in terms of networked concrete relationships—the city to be designed allows not only localization, but also localization everywhere in the network. It comes into being forever and everywhere, where intersubjective relationships accumulate according to a connection plan to be designed. To state this "astronomically": what a heavenly body is to the gravitational field, the city to be designed is to the intrahuman relational field, which is to say, a fold that "attracts" the relations.

If one sticks to this (somewhat awkward) metaphor, then it becomes more understandable what is meant here by the designing of a theoretical space. It has to be a space where intrahuman relationships are "somehow" soaked up. It must be "attractive."

What sort of alternative civilization can we design right here and right now? Let us draw up only one. It can be modified without difficulty (with or without a computer) into endless others, and recomputed to the point where the original version would no longer be recognizable. The city to be designed would be a result of the following connection plan for intrahuman relationships: All humans are to be connected in such a way that the currently available information must be subsumed in more and more new fields and entered into the computations. It is assumed that some of the information produced this way can be used for the programming of artificial intelligence. This, in turn, would be able to generate and control automatic machines for the production of necessary foodstuffs for humans, so that the theoretical space can remove the political and the economic from itself and relegate these two spheres to the subhuman. This sort of model for the city can be seen as a reversal of the Platonic utopia: Certainly, as in the Platonic utopia, the theoretical space moves into the highest position, but it is no longer based on politics and economics, but rather, it designs and generates these two spaces. The big difference between this city to be designed and utopia consists in the fact that this city becomes a sort of unavoidable appendix of the theoretical space, whereas the city's task in the utopia is to open up a theoretical space. The intention of this projected space is neither to create politics and business nor to lead them. Instead, it is to give meaning to the intersubjective network in the face of universal entropy—in the face of death and the fall into ever-increasing probability. In short, to understand theory no longer as the discovery of truth, but rather as the projection of meaning.

When designing the theoretical space, the city builders will take current science (and its technology) as a starting point, but not as their base. They will spin out a network of material and immaterial reversible cables (which they have already begun to do). They will allow information to run through this cable, so that it is simultaneously and completely accessible in each place in the network (which they have already begun to do). They will build raster screens and memory into the network (which they have already begun to do). And they will encode this information with an ever-increasing operability of codes (and even here the first steps have already been taken). From a geographical perspective, the city will encompass the entire globe, but, from a topological perspective, it will initially be a barely perceptible fold in the all-encompassing intrahuman relational field: most of the intrahuman relationships will lie outside of this network (in existing civilizations). The fundamental problem facing the designing of the city will be the question concerning the broadening and deepening of the theoretical fold. One solution that will be proposed is "open Confucianism." "Schools" will be everywhere built into the intrahuman network where competencies for the processing of information will be developed. In addition, these schools will create a series of grade levels moving in the direction of theoretical space. The more numerous the "mandarins" become (the more intrahuman relationships become competent in theory), the more the theoretical space will expand and the more attractive it will become. During the transitional period from the current to the future civilization, intrahuman relationships will fall into two networks: one will already be connected theoretically; the other will still be connected economically and politically. But, in time, the second network will be subsumed by the first (this process is already under way). This "open Confucianism"—everyone can become a mandarin as long as he acquires competencies—has one passing and one permanent consequence. Temporarily, the division into mandarin and layperson will be understood as mandarin totalitarianism by the laypeople (this is the opinion of the cultural pessimists). Over an extended period of time, the theoretical space will be proven to be a "fuzzy set" of interconnected and reciprocally beneficial competencies (thus, the intention of the city designers).

This also shows why science will be a starting point, but not a base. Taken as a whole and as individual disciplines, science will be only one of many competencies that mesh together in theoretical space and overlap one another. Other competencies (art and other critical disciplines, for example, will also be a starting point, but not a base) will enter into the realm of science and change it from the inside, thus losing their original character. In the long term, this gray zone of overlapping competencies will find a synthesis in a universal competency that is difficult to imagine today. This universal competency may spread itself out into many other branches. The current categories, "knowledge," "judgment," and "experience," will no longer be operative and will be replaced by others. The first signs of this decadence—of this "death" of science, art, and ethics, as the pessimists say—are already visible.

The theoretical space to be designed in this manner is a school (a place of leisure), because all work (all transformation of relational fields) is mechanized and relegated to the subhuman. But it is not a classical school of contemplation. It is much more a laboratory for formal experiments, for *sperimentazione mentale*; for it is a space for the processing of intrahuman relationships, for the concretization of possibilities inherent in these relationships. The new civilization should no longer identify humans as individuals with masks or in masks. Instead, using creative accumulation, it should project the specifically human out of these intrahuman relationships. Thus, we can talk about the "death" of science, politics, and the human subject, but only in the way we talk about the butterfly in terms of the death of larvae. A city designed in this manner is that place where the sincere human breaks out of the subject.

Contradictory Tendencies

If one considers the proposed, hastily thrown out, and not very thorough (rough) sketch of a city to be designed, one is impressed with two contradictory aspects. On the one hand, the sketch appears to be a completely unrealizable fantastic dream of someone who hovers outside the social fabric. On the other hand, it appears to be a projection of tendencies that can already be observed in this fabric. This contradiction is characteristic of the current situation. If we extend these contemporary tendencies into the immediate future, then very different scenarios play themselves out and all of them are fantastic. But, whoever does not dream, and instead wants to keep both feet planted firmly on the ground (whoever has no desire to project himself) is doomed to minimizing or misreading the majority of these apparent tendencies. Closing one's eyes is not the recommended attitude for realists. On the other hand, whoever is prepared to accept these apparent tendencies will be led into a world of fantasy. The proposed sketch for a city to be designed is a fantastic dream. It was born from a desire to be engaged in creativity and for others. And thus, it is more realistic than the scenarios provided by pessimists—among other things, for the curious reason that reality is now becoming recognizable as fantasy.

(1988)

Humanizations

The fact that today the human genus ("Homo") is represented by only one human species ("Homo sapiens sapiens") is curious. It is worthy of attention, and it should be kept in mind while we consider everything that concerns the human. So important is this fact that we should dedicate an essay to it. You might object that there is a second human species (the Abominable Snowman, whose taxonomic classification I unfortunately do not know). I will throw your objection back at you, because this species has not been scientifically verified ("yeti" is not a recognized zoological classification). We do not recognize the Snowman as one of us (do not recognize him at all), because we abhor him, and, supposing he exists, his feelings are probably mutual. Perhaps you will not willingly accept my objection to your objection, because you will correctly acknowledge that two species of the same genus necessarily abhor each other. How else would it be possible to explain that they would perform sexual intercourse only out of perversity and that, in case they did follow through with it, they would only produce sterile crossbreeds? So, you see, my dear Volker, that with our little squabble, which is really rather harmless, we have already arrived at the issue at hand.[1]

In order to show you how to approach this issue, allow me to present an example that suggests itself, the "dog." According to what I know, people are arguing over the question whether the family dog ("canis familiaris") is indeed a unique species, or whether he is not rather another breed of the species "canis lupus" (wolf), or whether there is perhaps something of the "canis aureus" (northern jackal) in the mix. This is a serious argument, because, on the one hand, the Paleolithic drawings

181

representing dogs show some similarity to jackals and, on the other hand, the jackal's jaw is differentiated so much from the wolf's jaw that we are required to consider wolves and jackals as separate species. The position of the family dog in the zoological hierarchy (dog dignity) is problematic, because it questions the criteria according to which this hierarchy is built. Thus, cannot the same be said about the position of the family man (about human dignity)? But, for now, I beg you to consider the dog.

As you see, there are breeds of dogs. Actually, this is not a zoological matter, because all the breeds are members of the same genotype. They enjoy mating with one another and, unfortunately, they produce fertile offspring. But dog breeds are very different from one another: The Tibetan bloodhound does not at all look like it would be able to mate with a Chihuahua. But, believe me, it can do it. And, supposing the little Chihuahua-hound (the word itself howls) survives, she will produce more offspring. According to some unreliable biological laws (namely, Mendel's), one should be able to tell from these canine offspring whether wolves, jackals, or merely dogs are in the mix. For, according to statistical principles, these sorts of wild crossings would have to make the genetic makeup (the genotype) apparent (through phenotyping). Unfortunately, this is not always the case: one does not know in advance what the result of this sort of miscegenation will be. Most likely, a mutt. But, perhaps, a superdog with a super Chihuahua sister. That is just how it is with statistical principles: one has to be ready for surprises. But please do not jump to conclusions—this alone does not explain racism among people. It is not true that Aryans do not want to mate with Zulus because they are afraid that a superman, a stupid, Greek-speaking beast will be the result. It is also not true that Aryans do not want to mate with Zulus. On the contrary, racism can only be explained when one takes for granted that both Aryans and Zulus want to mate with each other. But, continue to consider the dog.

There is a large superfamily of canoids. It is comparable (if, for dubious reasons, you are keen on hearing about humans) to the family of anthropoids. In this superfamily, there are several families, among them the canids. This is comparable, if it pleases you, to the hominids. Within this family, the one that interests us is the genus "canis," just as among the hominids, it is the genus "Homo." This genus "canis" is currently represented by many different species, for example, wolves and jackals, which I already mentioned, but also foxes, the foxlike Otocyons and the wolflike Lycaons. There is archaeological evidence of entire series of other species, but they are extinct. If you are searching for an analogy to humans, you will hopefully become a little dizzy. Currently, the genus "Homo" has only "Homo sapiens sapiens" as its representative, and all the other species (whether there is archaeological evidence or not) are extinct. This seems simple enough: with us the whole issue is a lot less complex than with dogs. If, however, we look at the issue at hand a little more closely, this turns out to be wrong.

"Homo sapiens sapiens" is most likely younger than "canis familiaris." Long before there were houses, previous human species must have kept family dogs. Thus, we could assume that such a young species (a mere forty thousand years old) can provide evidence whether it is real or just a fake, and whether this pompous "sapiens sapiens" is not rather a mix of different varieties. There are researchers who believe that they are able to point to Neanderthal characteristics in our ancestors and in ourselves (and others who consider the Abominable Snowman, whom I mentioned earlier, to be a variation of the Neanderthals), but, of course, none of this is dependable. The uniqueness of the human species is questionable precisely because there is only one species in the human genus.

But this cannot be the reason why your head turns. You have tried to imagine how you would react if you were suddenly confronted by someone who was a different species than you. If "Homo sapiens sapiens" is analogous to "canis familiaris," what would happen if you were confronted by someone analogous to "canis aureus" (about "canis vulpes" a little later). Would you be able to recognize in "Aureus"-Man a different way of being human, or would your humanism turn out to be sapientism? According to the researchers I mentioned, you share some similarities with Aureus. For example, Aureus-Man would most likely possess one or a few sound-based languages, but the sounds would be shaped differently than ours. The vocal sounds would be even more radically different from our vowels than the clicking sounds of the African languages, and even these are sapient sounds. If you had heard these Aureus sounds, would you try to decipher them, or would it not even dawn on you to look for a semantic dimension behind them? In any case, it is a dizzying proposition, for it shows just how irrational it is to look for "intelligent life in the universe." The intelligence of Aureus-Man, who is so closely related to you, is already inaccessible to you. What we call "intelligence" is something that we can decipher (*inter-legere* = reading between the lines). To us, there is no intelligence other than our own (the "sapiens"), because we only decipher our own a bit, and all other forms of intelligence are nothing but approaches to ours. I must admit that this makes me sad.

Now, to "canis vulpes." The fox finds itself in a different relation to this problem than does the wolf, and not only because one cannot say "man is a fox to man," but most of all, because its nasal passages do not lead to a sinus cavity. If they did, foxes would, without question, be like dogs. Thus, one has to put them aside and really say "vulpes vulpes" instead of "canis vulpes." Considering this, if you, my dear Volker, were confronted by Vulpes-Man, then not only his vocal sounds, but perhaps even the vocal cords that articulate these sounds would be different from your own. It is enough to turn one's head, because this is not only a question of language, but also of different systems of communication. Let us put it this way (in order to be decent): if you were confronted by a female Aureus, then you would be able to have intercourse with her without a problem, but it might not work out with a female Vulpes on account of her vulva. But, with a little mutual effort, which goes without saying, it might still work out. In any case, the experience would, as they say in Chinese mythology, not be something that could be denied.

Enough of dogs. It has now become clear why I have tried to convince you of the importance of an essay concerning humanizations. It can neither be assumed nor completely accepted that there is only one human species. Or, that a whole range of possibilities will not open up to us, to become human and thus to become ever more specialized. I have been entertaining you with a lot of ridiculous zoological nonsense, to take the sting of pathos out of the whole issue. This is exactly what is so sad about this issue: that there is something about humanization that seems to lead us directly into pathos. Do we want to remove the pathos from humanization? Do we want to attempt it without pathos? Do we want to go from family dog to family man and, from there, to somewhere else? We shall find out where.

First Warm-up Exercise

One can do gymnastic exercises with perspective. For example, just imagine Darwin inviting Heraclitus to dinner. Having learned from him, Darwin would most likely demonstrate how to look through being, to get a view of becoming. Darwin would show that every animal can be seen as the representative of a species. Viewed from this perspective, the specific is revealed by means of the characteristic. Then he would show that behind the specific there are ever more general forms that become visible (such as genera, families, classes, and phyla) and that this chain, where every category contains the one that came before and will be contained by those that come after, ultimately disappears in the fog of an originary moment that dates back billions of years. Lastly, he would show that a tendency toward growth, toward branching, and toward becoming will emerge from the fog of this originary moment and that this tendency points to every single animal to come. Darwin would probably say that, by practicing this perspective, one recognizes that every animal is a transitional, transitory, and vague extraction from a stream, which flows out of the original molecular cell, to form an unimaginable ocean of life in the future. With a guilty smile, Darwin would perhaps add to this that he unfortunately has only a human eye. Thus, the stream that he sees seems to move in the direction of man and then beyond him in the direction of superman. Darwin would probably say that we are dealing with the kind of perspective where all animal life is seen in terms of humanization.

At this point in the conversation, a misanthropic Heraclitus would most likely wave off these Darwinian gymnastic exercises. In response, Darwin could retreat from his original position a little out of respect for his teacher and master: certainly, the human perspective is just one among the many possible (perhaps infinite) perspectives concerning the becoming of life. With the human perspective, the animal kingdom is considered to be a branching stream whose goal is to produce men and, beyond them, supermen. Yet, every other animal can (or must) recognize the goal of evolution in its own species, even though, according to a human perspective, evolution has passed this animal by and left it in the dust. Viewed from the human perspective, all animals are either precursors of man (assuming they occupy a position in the stream before it branches off toward mankind) or a cul-de-sac (assuming they occupy a position where the stream has branched away from mankind). For example, worms and reptiles show similarities to human embryos in the different, preliminary stages of their development, whereas insects and mollusks are seen as deviant, degenerate humans. From the worm's perspective, the human is a degenerate worm. From the insect's perspective, the human would be recognized as a monstrous deviation from insect development. And, perhaps, from the chimpanzee's perspective, the human would be considered to be a chimpanzee embryo, an underdeveloped chimpanzee who still lacks certain specializations.

Still, Heraclitus would not let himself be convinced by this. He would probably say that the Darwinian perspective is not Heraclitean at all. It does not see becoming, but rather a diverse branching out of forms that leaves the single concrete animal untouched. What does it matter to the worm if it originates from a single-cell organism and that vertebrates and insects will later develop from it? It only matters to the worm that, as a concrete thing, it is a becoming in the direction of dust. Moreover, this dust, which the worm will become, itself is a becoming in the direction of something else. When Heraclitus looks at a man, he does not see the (or an) evolutionary peak, but rather a becoming without an end, a changing from one thing into another. On one stretch of this road of becoming, it is possible to speak of humanization, but only in the sense that it is also possible to speak in the next breath about the dustification of man. All in all, Heraclitus does not completely understand these gymnastic exercises of the Darwinian perspective. How is it possible that Darwin recognizes such strongly differentiated forms as species and such a rigid hierarchy of larger and emptier forms in the swiftly moving stream of the becoming of life? Are the forms not rather phantoms, which Darwin projects behind the animals, in order to veil this becoming and its shapeless weaving? If one considers the worm to be a preliminary step in the direction of humanization, does one do this in order to hide the wormification of man, his death?

Now that we have reached this point in the conversation, it is polite to let these two esteemed men take their dinners and direct their gaze elsewhere; that is, where beings attempt to become other than what they are, including becoming human. For example, there is the story of the prince who becomes a frog to become a prince again, or a god who becomes a swan to seduce a woman. We require a different sort of gymnastic exercises with perspective than those provided by Darwin or Heraclitus. Thus, we will be able to see the prince-to-be behind the frog and the degenerate God behind the swan. But we are so unpracticed in this way of seeing that we are unable to recognize this sort of becoming. If, however, someone speaks about humanization, then we will have to practice it. And not only because the Jewish God became man, to change man, and because this humanization—in comparison to numerous others, especially the Hindu—significantly influences our Western being, but also because the desire to become different (to become a "new" man) in one or another form has since typified Western history. Viewed from this perspective, "humanization" is an inconclusive process and, perhaps, an unending one. Thus, "man" is not the name of a situation (like a species of mammal), but rather, a horizon that cannot be reached, a limit.

In Darwin's view, this gymnastic exercise with perspective is a somersault, but, in Heraclitus's view, it is something less acrobatic. On Darwin's side, it is hard to see how someone can want to become something else, or even how someone can want to become at all. Everything is becoming, and there is nothing to want. Becoming is a spontaneous, aleatory process pieced together by trial and error: everything became something by chance, and it will also become something else by chance. On Heraclitus's side, the exercise of identifying desire is simpler to carry out. It is possible to see that becoming and wanting something are synonymous (just as the English "it will" is synonymous with the German "es wird"). Thus, becoming is synonymous with the will (for example, the will to power). Moreover, this somersault from Heraclitus to Nietzsche can be directed back to Darwin by taking a detour through Schopenhauer. But, one has to view it from this perspective: Behind every animal, one sees a will; "It" wants behind all animals and through all animals, and one calls this desiring "It" life. On the human being's side, this "It" wants to be human, and inside a man it wants to be something else (a superman).

However, this trick to simplify the somersault of perspective cannot be recommended. In doing so, one does not necessarily arrive at a Christian or Marxist view of humanization, where it does not matter that "It" wants to be human, but that "someone" (God or man himself) wants this. In comparison, the somersault of perspective from Heraclitus via Schopenhauer, Nietzsche, and Darwin to this particular essay distances the observer from the Christian and Marxist perspective instead of bringing him closer. If one wants insight into this desire for becoming human, one should direct one's gaze inward. If such a transition is successful, a completely new landscape becomes visible to the observer, which is to say, one where it is apparent what "being human" has meant. A view of this landscape reveals that one cannot desire anything other than wanting to be different. Moreover, it reveals that "being human" means wanting to become human in the first place. This view of mankind must have been ingrained in a misanthrope such as Heraclitus, and it enabled him to first see the becoming. Thus, it is appropriate that he—the one who saw the becoming of fire—is called the "Dark One."

The inwardly directed gaze makes apparent why the Jewish God became man: out of pity for man who can no longer be what he is. It makes apparent why, according to the Marxist perspective, man changes the world to change himself: out of disgust for himself and his own actions. In addition, this inwardly directed gaze, which is forced to see what being human implies, is able to see in humanization nothing other than the justified suicide of being human. After Auschwitz and its consequences, nothing else is possible. It is a dark gaze that foresees this humanization, but it is a perspective where the light of a completely different being human shimmers as a distant possibility on the horizon. The attitude represented by this perspective is not "death and becoming," and also not "death, becoming, death, becoming," but rather, "becoming in the consciousness of dying." This sort of experiment commences with this perspective, even though it is questionable whether this perspective can be maintained, or whether anything at all will be maintained, particularly when it is not a matter of maintaining anything but of throwing everything into becoming. It is a matter of rejecting our present being human and of projecting into humanization(s).

Second Warm-up Exercise

In case "human" is defined as the mammal who, despite biological rules, stores and distributes acquired information—that is, in case "human" is defined as a no-more-animal—then humanization is the storage and distribution of acquired information. In this manner, one could say about humanization that it is the method of progressively making a mammal into a no-more-animal. The more someone is human and the less someone is animal, the more acquired information he stores and distributes; and, thus, "animal" and "human" are the two horizons between which humanization happens. This is a more radical statement than it seems at first glance, for it means that both "animal" and "human" are located outside the process of humanization. The animal organism with the genus "Homo" must possess the proper organizational structure, especially the proper central nervous system, and must also already be somewhat of a no-more-animal, so that the storage and transmission of acquired information in the sense of humanization can commence. For example, the organs necessary for speech must already be in place and connected to the brain in such a way that some kind of language can be acquired, stored, and distributed. On the other hand, a human should be considered an absolute no-more-animal only when all animal functions have been crossed out and his being has begun to concentrate on nothing other than the acquisition, storage, and distribution of information. Certainly, this line of reasoning leads to absurd conclusions. For example, all animals in general (including the protozoa) are to be considered somewhat of a no-more-animal, because the stirrings of humanization must be present in them. This is absurd, because then *animal* is synonymous with "somewhat of a no-more-animal," and it would then be better to give up the word *animal* in favor of "capacity for humanization." This can be thought about in the context of the abortion debate: if it should be forbidden to abort human embryos, because they are somewhat of a no-more-animal, then the eating of red meat and the purification of water with the goal of eliminating amoebas should also be forbidden.

The opposite line of reasoning leads to even more absurd conclusions.

If "human" is defined as the result of humanization and no longer as an animal caught up in humanization, then everything that we have previously called "human" is a hybrid at best. And, the systems for the processing of information, which have become increasingly immaterial, are then more human than the humans who built them. Thus, the question is not (as the free spirits suggest) the extent to which such systems threaten being human—because they mechanically simulate it—but, on the contrary, to what degree half-baked man-animals simulate these systems, to advance just a little in the direction of the "human."

After all, both of these absurd conclusions are not so new as they seem. In Hinduism, the first one is seriously accepted, whereas in Angelology it is the second. Nevertheless, the respective conclusions make clear that we are dutifully bound to animals and immaterial spirits in an absurd fashion, because neither animals nor immaterial spirits can exist; rather, only extrapolations of our being human can exist. This can be seen in the present text, which is itself an attempt at humanization.

Third Warm-up Exercise

It was not so long ago that one spoke of the "missing link." This was the circumstance where the seamless transition from anthropoids into hominoids and from these into humans lacked satisfactory evidence. The circumstance was in itself not very interesting, because seamless transitions from one genus into another often lack satisfactory evidence, not only because they depend on fossils, but in particular because species (and therefore genera) originate in punctuated moments, through mutations. This circumstance garnered interest because of the hope that research would be falsified, the missing link would not be discovered, and thus the theory that there is an abyss (even a small one) separating man from the animal kingdom would continue to be tenable. Currently, no one speaks anymore of the missing link, not because it was found, but because the problem of man's position inside or outside the animal kingdom is no longer interesting. Meanwhile, belief in the fact that we "evolved from apes" has become part of a healthy mind, which says little about either healthy minds or apes. Instead, we should begin busting our heads over the next missing link, which is to say, the one from contemporary into future humans. For we are seeing the new man of the future surface in different places (even if our view may be hazy), but we are not gaining insight into the thing that binds us to him, or whether there is anything at all that binds us to him.

There is the so-called little Brain Man.[2] It is an attempt to represent in images how the brain perceives its body and how it directs it on the basis of this perception. This is a curious and ridiculous and terrible little man. One recognizes in him everything that makes up a human body, but in completely distorted proportions. Above all, one recognizes the grotesquely exaggerated size of the tongue, the penis, and the right thumb— as if the rest of the body served as a support for these three organs. If one thinks this thing over, however, one realizes that the brain actually sees the body better than the mirror; for it almost directly experiences the body and it serves the body and makes use of it with the utmost attention to detail. If the little Brain Man has been drawn properly, then one must assume that his proportions are more correct than those we see in the mirror. This is how we appear "functionally" (that is, factually): equipped with such tongues, penises, and thumbs. Indeed, all anthropologies should begin with this image of man.

Reflection gives us an idea of the little Brain Man belonging to the new man of the future, just as he is beginning to surface in different places. It is possible that his body is visible in a mirror similar to ours (this is the reason why we do not always recognize him as the new man). Yet, his little Brain Man must look completely different than ours. For example, his tongue will be noticeably smaller than ours, for he will not have the need to speak as much (he will instead communicate digitally). No doubt his right thumb will be negligible in comparison to ours, because everything will be immaterial and he will not manipulate material objects as much. As far as his penis is concerned, the whole issue of cybersex and chemically induced orgasms is difficult to make out. Perhaps other organs will replace most of the functionality of the penis, and they will therefore be more prominent in the little Brain Man of the future. The biggest difference will be in the fingertips. The fingertips, which will touch the keyboard, will doubtless be the most important organs, and it will become apparent that the purpose of the Brain Man's entire body will be to support the fingertips.

If one compares both of these little men, ours with the men of the future, one finds oneself before a tremendous abyss, wider and deeper than the one that separated our fathers from chimpanzees or the one that separated our medieval fathers from angels. How does someone like us, Tongue-Thumb Man, associate with Fingertip Man—and that he must do, for is he not his father? He cannot speak to him, because his tongue would move in a manner disgusting to Fingertip Men with their fine fingertip feeling. He also cannot point his thumb or index finger at him, because the new man of the future would consider such brutal gestures to be subhuman. On the other hand, Tongue-Thumb Man cannot decipher the tripping along of fingertips on the keys of the new man's future apparatuses. And, where this is possible—such as when the tripping along appears as an image on the screen—he is still incapable of properly responding to the messages sent to him by Fingertip Man. This is played down as "generational incommunicability" to give the impression that it has always been like this.

Until recently, there was the hope that we would not find the missing link between us and our past, so that we would be able to worship an unhistorical image of man. Now there is the hope that we will not find the missing link between us and the future, so that we will not have to deal with what is to come. Both hopes are absolutely justified, and yet, the first one has been dropped from the table. Eventually, the second one will also be dropped, because the cute little Brain Man of the future is already here. As we sit in our recliners with our legs outstretched, he crawls across our television screens like a little buffoon. We should begin busting our heads over the "missing link" between him and us.

(1990)

Notes by the Editor

1. Volker Rapsch, Vilém Flusser's German editor for many years, to whom this text is dedicated.

2. The "little Brain Man" is a virtual map of the human body as perceived by the brain. Neurologists have drawn it to demonstrate the different intensities of various body functions.

Essays

Translated by Josiah Blackmore

The problem I want to discuss is one that is certainly experienced by everyone whose goal is to write about an "erudite" topic. And it is this: Should I formulate my thoughts in an academic style (that is, depersonalized), or should I make use of a lively style (that is, my own)? The decision will profoundly affect the work to be done. And it is not a decision with regard to form only. It also has to do with content. There does not exist one idea that can be articulated in two ways. Two different sentences are two different thoughts. The decision to treat an erudite topic in an academic or lively way is the decision to treat that topic from two different angles. The arguments presented will be different, the conclusions reached will be different, and only the topic itself will apparently remain the same. The style will inform the work.

The problem does not apply to a nonerudite theme. Academic style does not present itself as an alternative, but is a special kind of style. It unites intellectual honesty with existential dishonesty, because the person who has recourse to it commits the intellect and withdraws the body. Academic style characteristically avoids use of the pronoun "I." It substitutes "I" with the bombastic (although apparently modest) "we," or by "one," a pronoun that makes no commitments. I will not deny it has its own beauty. It is the beauty of rigor, which is not necessarily rigor mortis. And that beauty, so resplendent in mathematics and formal logic, is, to a certain degree, characteristic of the intellect. But I declare that style is a pose. No one thinks academically. People just pretend they do. They force themselves to think like that. Academic style is a result of effort (or, if you prefer, of mental discipline), so it is therefore a result of a first thought.

The academic is a second thought, because it is a translation of a first thought. It is not spontaneous, but deliberate. The choice between the academic style and my own is therefore a half-choice: I will speak spontaneously, or I will choose "academicism."

Like all choices, this one also involves the problem of responsibility. Academicism assumes a responsibility for rigor (validity) of the argument and minimizes the responsibility for the author as a person of flesh and blood (as Unamuno would say).[1] A lively style assumes the latter responsibility and subordinates the former. The validity of the argument about validity (value) depends on this style, on that which it argues. They are two different ways of engaging oneself. It is conceivable that the strategy depends on the topic. It seems difficult to imagine a nonacademic treatment of the topic "anatomy of cockroaches" (although there is Kafka's *Metamorphosis*). But I should confess that, in my opinion, it is difficult to imagine a strategy at all, even an academic one, regarding this anatomy. A treatise on the anatomy of cockroaches—when it is an authentic one—always has a broader dimension. The treatise is to be inserted at a future date in a more significant context. And, if this is so, the problem of style also arises. The example, however, is extreme. I think that choice, in the case of the anatomy (or similar topics), will fall on academicism in a "natural" way. The problem will appear in full force if the topic is from the social sciences or from philosophy. And these are the topics I wish to consider.

I will call the writings on these subjects "treatises" when written in the academic style and "essays" when in the subjective one. I would also add that the choice between writing a treatise and an essay is an existential decision in the strict sense of the term. It will determine my attitude about my topic, and about those who will read my text, "my others." In a treatise, I will think about my subject and I will discuss it with my others. In an essay, I will live my subject and I will have a dialogue with my others. In the first case, I will seek to explain my topic; in the second, I will seek to implicate myself in it. In the first case, I will seek to inform my others; in the second, I will seek to change them. My decision, therefore, will depend on how I face my topic and my others. It will depend on my identity. In the treatise, I do not take on myself, I take on the topic for my others. In the essay, I submerge myself in the topic and in my others. In the essay, I and my others are the topic within the topic. In the treatise, the topic is of interest; in the essay, I and we are within the topic. The decision to opt for the treatise is de-existentializing. It is the decision on behalf of "one," of the public, of the objective. Making a decision in favor of the essay is what should be contemplated.

If I decide on the essay, on my style, and on implicating myself in my topic, I run a risk. It is a dialectical risk: that of losing myself in the topic, and that of losing the topic. These are the two dangers of my identification with the theme. Let us suppose I want to write an essay on translation and translatability. It is an erudite topic, so I could choose the treatise form. In this case, I could base my argumentation on authors I have read, citing these authors in a bibliography as well as in the text in order to reduce my responsibility, although I still could add some of my own thoughts. The topic would be rendered explicit, and my readers would be informed. But I choose the essay. The problem of translation and translatability takes on the cosmic dimensions of all existential issues: it encompasses everything. For example, it encompasses the problem of knowing, which is an aspect of translatability. It includes value, which can be considered an aspect of the validity of the translated sentences. It encompasses the problem of meaning and of the absurd, part of the limits of translatability. In sum: I begin to lose my topic by having identified myself with it. And I simultaneously begin to lose myself in it, because I start to identify with its different aspects. For example, I find that I myself am a translation problem, that is, a multiplicity of systems to be translated among themselves into a metasystem. And the style of my essay will begin to reflect, to articulate, to formulate my project of body and soul.

This is the danger of the essay–but it is also its beauty. The essay is not merely the articulation of a thought, but of a thought as a point of departure for a committed existence. The essay vibrates with the tension of the fight between thought and life, and between life and death, that Unamuno called "agony." Because of this the essay does not resolve its topic as the treatise does. It does not explain its topic, so in this sense it does not inform its readers. On the contrary, it transforms its topic into an enigma. It implicates itself in the topic and in its reader. This is what makes it attractive.

Philosophy and the sciences oscillate between the treatise and the essay. And because of this we can speak of academic philosophy and science and of essayistic philosophy and science. This oscillation constitutes, perhaps, an aspect of the "classic romantic" pendulum, or of the "Apollonian Dionysian" (in Nietzsche's terms) one. Some examples: Renaissance physics is essayistic (Leonardo da Vinci, Galileo), and Baroque physics is academic. Bruno dies for physics, something unimaginable in the case of Volta. Nineteenth-century biology is essayistic (Darwin), twentieth-century biology is academic. Analytic psychology is essayistic, and behaviorism, academic. But let it not be said (as these examples seem to suggest) that every discipline begins with the essay and ends with the treatise. We can find examples of the inverse trend. At the moment, one of those examples seems to me to be sociology. But the most significant case of the oscillation I mentioned is, obviously, philosophy.

There exist two philosophies and the dialogue between them is much like a dialogue of the deaf. Essayistic philosophy includes Plato, Augustine, Eckhart, Pascal, Kierkegaard, Nietzsche, Camus, Unamuno. Academic philosophy has the likes of Aristotle, Saint Thomas Aquinas, Descartes, Spinoza, Hegel, Mach, Carnap. Both philosophies deal with the same issues, but only apparently so. This is what makes the dialogue between them so difficult. Because, if I invalidate the thinking of an academic philosopher, I have invalidated his treatise. Consequently, it is not enough to invalidate a way of thinking to shoot down an essay. In order to do this, it is necessary to "deauthenticate" its attitude. The vulnerability of academicism is different from that of essayism. So it is more difficult to topple an Unamuno than it is to topple a Carnap. If I toppled Carnap, all I did was topple his way of thinking. If I toppled Unamuno, nothing remains of him.

The reader may argue that I have greatly exaggerated the "treatise–essay" antimony, that Hume's essays, for instance, are really treatises, and that Wittgenstein's *Tractatus* is really an essay. I disagree. I will not deny that there are inspired moments in great treatises when they change character. I will not deny that there are islands in great essays where topics are treated academically. But I insist that the decision comes before the writing and that it definitively influences the climate. All you need to do is open an "erudite" book to feel that climate. And it is enough to live that moment of liberty which precedes the decision about style that will inform my work.

Academicism reigns in Brazilian universities, perhaps as a reaction against the essayism that dominated Brazilian thought almost up to our own time. But universities–as the word implies–should not be unilateral if they strive for erudition in the widest sense of the term. They should be balanced spaces in which academicism's disdain for essayism and essayism's contempt for academicism cancel out each other mutually. And this is especially true during a time when, in my view, the pendulum of philosophy (as well as of certain sciences) swings toward essayism. To provoke this consideration is the goal of this article—an article that certainly falls into the category of "essay."

(1967)

Note by the Editor

1. Miguel de Unamuno (1864–1936), Spanish philosophical writer and existentialist. His major work is *The Tragic Sense of Life in Men and Nations.*

In Search of Meaning (Philosophical Self-portrait)

(1) *Curriculum vitae.* I was born on May 12, 1920, in Prague. I studied philosophy at Charles University Prague and the London School of Economics. I am a visiting professor of the philosophy of science at the Polytechnical School of the University of São Paulo and full professor of the theory of communication and art communication at the Communications and Humanities School of the Armando Àlvarez Foundation. I am a member of the Brazilian Institute of Philosophy, where I am the director of lectures. I contribute to a number of Brazilian and foreign periodicals, such as *O Estado de São Paulo, Revista Brasileira de Filosofia,* and *Frankfurter Allgemeine Zeitung.* I represented Brazil at various events abroad and here.

(2) *Genesis of my thought.* I must confess, as a start, that the challenge of a self-criticism is ambiguous. Its motive is vanity, implied in exhibitionism (as this essay will be published). And who ignores the seduction of being able to speak about himself in public? But, at the same time, it is an invitation to take honest stock of what I am and do. And who ignores the danger of facing oneself? I accept the challenge, to both vanity and honesty.

To live is to accept oneself in order to change oneself. He who does not assume himself does not live his own life, but the life of people. He who assumes himself and accepts himself without at least trying to change does not live actively, but just functions in the function of what determines him. Because the attempt to change myself implies the attempt to change the surroundings in which I find myself. In short, to live

197

is to discover who I am and to try and start from there in order to "be better" (or "more"), thus changing not merely oneself but also the world. In fact, this task which is life is a task that renews itself at every instant. The question "Who am I?" is new whenever I ask it, and the decision to start from its answer is painful and radical whenever taken. Thus I shall ask the question "Who am I?" as if it were for the first time, in order to make (who knows?) a decision.

I come from well-to-do intellectual Prague Jewish parents. I spent my youth in the spiritually and artistically inebriating atmosphere of the between-wars Prague. I survived, groggily, the bestial and stupid earthquake of Nazism, which devoured my world (i.e., my others and my things), but also the scales of values that had structured that world. I was vomited, by the fury of events, upon Brazil, which is a greatly amorphous situation, greedy in every sense, and also in an ontic one. I was vomited upon Brazil at a plastic and assimilable age, and I spent the last thirty years of my life in search of myself in Brazil, and in search of Brazil within myself. If to live is to search one's way, I lived intensely, that is, philosophically. But if to live is to have found one's way, I did not even begin to live, that is, to have committed myself. I spent my life in availability, and I am still available. Is this a confession of failure? Is it a confession in that I failed to find myself in Brazil and Brazil within myself, and therefore that I failed to even assume myself? But what does "Brazil" mean in this context? It means the scene into which I was thrown. If I did not find myself in Brazil and did not find Brazil within myself, it means that I did not find the ground of my being in the world. Taken thus, my failure has a religious taste to it. Mine was a life without religion and in search of religion, and is this not, after all, a definition of philosophy? At least of one type of philosophy? I am a failure, because I live philosophy. Which is to say that philosophy is my life. And this seems to me to be a first approach to answer the question "Who am I?" which is the subject of this tortured argument.

No doubt, when I was thrown here, not everything "Prague" was destroyed. It was, however, radically questioned. My German culture persisted, but gained a new coloring: he who dwelled within the nucleus of myself was my enemy. My Czech culture persisted too, but as if condemned to smothering by amputation of the umbilical cord that had linked me to it. My Jewish tradition (weak and anemic to begin with, because of Jewish culture I have almost nothing) acquired a much greater importance than before, and at the same time was put to a severe test that it hardly stood. I did not recognize myself in Brazilian Jewry, mostly of

Eastern European origin, which is totally foreign to me. And the appeals of Zionism, though reinforced by the sufferings of my people in Europe and by the beauty of social experiment and heroism in Palestine, did not reach me sufficiently to commit me. They were held in check by the appeals of my Brazilian surroundings. I shall speak of the appeal of Jewish religion for me a little later. But the thing that persisted mostly was my philosophical formation, though it too suffered a crisis.

Like most who share with me my cultural and historical background, I have a solid Marxist basis. However, it must be said that it was not exactly the same Marxism as that of my Brazilian contemporaries. It is more vital in the sense of being closer to true Marxist movements (my father was an active member of the Socialist Party), and in the sense of its antifascism. But it was less vital in the sense of being decadently bourgeois. This possibly explains why my Marxism did not, as a commitment, survive the Moscow Trials, the Communist–Nazi alliance in Germany, and the German–Russian alliance during the first war years, but why, as a utopia and anthropological model, it stubbornly persists in the very center of my thought. A true Marxist will be right in saying that I never was truly a Marxist. But so will be he who, ignorant of the persuasive power and internal beauty of Marxism, says that I always have been and still am a Marxist. This illustrates the difficulty in accepting oneself: I agree with both arguments.

But very soon I suffered a second influence, less vital perhaps, but much more solid intellectually: the Prague School, the Vienna Circle, and above all Wittgenstein. I did not know then, but now know clearly: the attraction of formalism (now called, in its more mature development, "structuralism") does not dwell in the beauty of its rigor, nor in its break with historicism, but in its inherent mysticism. This is most clear in Wittgenstein: intellectual rigor cuts through itself in search of the unutterable. At the time of phony mystical shouting and bleating, of pseudo-Romantic, pseudo-Greek, and pseudo-Germanic poses, be they uniformed or not, that filled the air between the two wars, this way opened by (mostly linguistic) analysis toward the unutterable was like a breath of true religiosity, and, without realizing it consciously, I tried to hold on to it. I tried to synthesize within myself transcendental formalism and Marxist dialectic. The meta-Marxists of today seem to succeed in this, but I do not think I have been very successful.

A third influence on me during the formative period in Prague was Ortega's *Revolt of the Masses*. By the Ortegan way I discovered that vast world vaguely called "Existentialism." For so many years, it marked my thoughts, and possibly my acts. Because of Ortega, I reread Nietzsche, who had taken hold of me earlier, mostly through the beauty of his language. Now, sensing the approach of the rising tide of brown vulgarity, I believed I had found myself in Nietzsche. I think that my encounter with Nietzsche marked me forever and kept me from dissolving into banality in shipwreck and exile.

Of course, I read many other authors in Prague. But to read does not mean to vitally assimilate. The genesis of my thought must be placed within the three incongruous coordinates I mentioned.

(3) *Development of my thought.* During the war, having the extermination camps for background and a foreign society for surroundings, I fell into the loneliness of mysticism, prefigured for me in the *Tractatus* and in Nietzsche. I studied Oriental thought, Saint John of the Cross, Eckhart, I read and reread Angelus Silesius, rediscovered German Romantics and Dostoevsky. I took up Buber and Protestant theology, and discovered Jaspers. The first writings of Heidegger reached me in full and filled me with enthusiasm and hatred in a hardly sustainable tension. In that period, I began to feel the call of Catholicism for the first time and in despair, as a promise of salvation and comfort. But I always knew within a corner of my being (perhaps the Marxist corner) that all this was nothing but alienation, a running away, that I was committing treason of the mind, not sacrifice.

The end of the war and advent of Communism in Prague meant the impossibility of ever returning, an impossibility owing in part to egotistical and opportunistic considerations, but also in part to more noble considerations. I started to open myself up ever more to the Brazilian situation. My first contact with things Brazilian on a more serious level was a shock. The mysticism I found seemed to be a caricature of my own, and reinforced my misgivings. The many forms of voodoo, spiritism, irresponsible lofty talk, and attitudes copied thirdhand were for me like a mirror. A memento mori. And simultaneously, the Brazilian scene showed, in the way of a caricature, the other side of the medal: formalistic sterility. The Positivisms, scholasticisms, Marxisms, academisms, and formalistic preciosities *à la brésilienne* that to me were the 1940s and early 1950s, were not only ridiculous, but a sign of danger. I took as a symptom the interest vested by Brazilian thinkers in such things as the Portuguese grammar (unrelated to the Viennese analysis), or the history of the Brazilian empire, or minute analyses of texts by Farias Brito.[1] Adoration of fleas. Between the Scylla of idle talk and the Charybdis of phony erudition, in which I was myself as in distorted mirrors, I fell into a crisis, this time a more internal than external one. I considered suicide for years and survived only with this ever-present possibility. I devoured Kafka, Camus, the art of the absurd. This was when I painfully learned that faith cannot be provoked and that if God had died, he is dead. I went back again to Nietzsche, to the pre-Socratics, refused with disgust everything non-Occidental, and began to understand the late Husserl, radical phenomenology. I then wrote my first book, *A história do diabo* (The history of the devil). I wrote it in German, and translated it into Portuguese much later.

My salvation was Kant, my catharsis in every crisis. This is not the place to sing praise to his crystalline dignity. I read Cassirer, Cohen, Hartmann, the entire Marburg School.[2] The outlines of my future way began to appear: my central problem was going to be language. First, and obviously, because I love language. I love its beauty, its richness, its mystery, and its charm. I am truly myself only when I speak or write or read or when it murmurs within myself to be articulated. But also because it is symbolic form, the dwelling of being that veils and reveals, the channel that links me to others, the field of immortality *aere perennius,* the matter and instrument of art. It is my repertoire and my structure, the game I play, the model of all my models. It is open and opens up the unutterable. It is my commitment, in it I become real, and through it I float toward its horizon and its foundation, which is the silence of the unspeakable. It is the form of my religiosity. And possibly the form of my perdition.

(4) *First productive phase.* I began to read systematically about language. In part to regain contact lost with Prague, the Viennese, Russell, and Wittgenstein over again. In part, as a development of the themes of the 1930s, the Americans based on the Viennese; in part, under new aspects resulting from my Heidegger readings *(Unterwegs zur Sprache).* But I discovered aspects I had ignored, especially French ones. My lack of contact with French civilization is one of my most serious shortcomings. Saussure did not impress me.

But my concept of "language" required a more varied reading. My interest began to expand. I read linguists, philologists, psychologists, biologists. I tried to penetrate a little symbolic logic and mathematics, and I struggled not to fall victim to etymology. I never could explain the attraction of etymology, not only for me, but also for many others. This formal reading was, of course, nothing but the arsenal for the attack on the linguistic problem. The problem itself lies somewhere else, namely, within art. I discovered and rediscovered the great masters of language: Joyce,

Pound, Eliot, the Maudits, Morgenstern (who is an unending pleasure). And I returned to the ancients. Goethe is always with me, perhaps for being everything I cannot be, but at that moment he became my bridge to Thomas Mann, who marked me profoundly. *Joseph and His Brothers* and *Doctor Faustus,* the two great victories of German language become self-conscious, the two great feasts of the spirit, became two inexhaustible wells for my thirst for language. Hermann Hesse had a much less intense effect on me. I am not in sympathy with his language, which tends to become kitsch, and I am not in sympathy with his Orientalizing. Obviously, I was not indifferent to *Steppenwolf,* for I recognized myself in part in him, and I recognized even more a close friend of mine, a partner in my searching. *The Glass Bead Game* had a retarded effect on me. I understand that effect better now than during the reading, as I rediscover Hesse at the bottom of my efforts with games and with translation qua "sense giving." But I must dedicate a short paragraph to the two most important influences of that period, Kafka and Rilke.

In some ways they are opposites; in others they are inseparable brothers. They are opposites on the level of language. Kafka, the ascetic, and Rilke, the orgy of language. Kafka, like Wittgenstein, the relentless revealer of the phoniness of language, in order to clear the way toward the sacred purity of the fundamental silence of language. Rilke, like Heidegger, the prophet revealing the mystery that dwells in language. Two opposed beauties, one purifying, the other inebriating. And nonetheless, the same beauty at bottom, namely, the beauty of poetry as the mouth of the unspeakable. The two Praguers travel in two different vehicles toward the same goal, which is also mine. And I bow before the two giants who are, taken as one, my model.

Following that model, I dove, as if spontaneously, into the ocean of music, the world of records. For reasons I cannot explain, Mozart took hold of me violently. I felt his almost superhuman perfection in the effort to overcome human despair. And this dive of mine into music returned me to Schopenhauer, so anti-Mozart and yet so language become music and music become language. "Was er sagte ist vertan, was er war, das bleibt bestahn. Seht ihn nur an! Niemand war er Untertan" (Whatever he said is gone, whatever he was remains. Just look at him! He was inferior to nobody) (Nietzsche). I wrote *Lingua e realidade* (Language and reality) trying to say all this.

(5) *Second productive phase.* The publication of that book by Herder was my true opening up to things Brazilian. And Brazil opened itself to me

through two gigantic windows: Guimarães Rosa and Vincente Ferreira da Silva. My two great Brazilian masters and (dare I say it myself?) my two friends—dead, both of them. What does that mean? But I learned with Husserl that to live is not to discover meaning, but to give meaning.

Nonetheless, it cannot be a mere coincidence that I recognized in Guimarães Rosa all my linguistic commitment on a grandiose level. *Sagarana* and *Corps du Ballet,* and especially *The Devil to Pay in the Backlands,* are like demonstrations *in fieri* of my theses in *Lingua e realidade.* The intermittent dialogue I maintained with Guimarães Rosa until his death occurred as if in a dream. I had to pinch myself to know that Guimarães Rosa was not a fiction of my fancy and that he existed in a reality different from that of Riobaldo.[3] His linguistic religiosity, his fanaticism in speaking and writing, his ludic attitude in handling vocals and words, his irony and his humor (see *First Stories,* on which I hope to have had a more than extraneous influence), together with his iron discipline, were, taken as one, the picture I had made of the True Poet. Yet, Guimarães Rosa existed in flesh and blood. I shall say no more about him except that he became for me an imperative, no longer a revelation.

To think that Vicente Ferreira da Silva[4] lived in my next neighborhood during the terrible war period and during the years of anxiety that followed it, and that I did not meet him is a nightmare. Had I known Vicente in 1940, my way would have been different. And had he known me, this I believe with all my heart, he, and with him Brazilian culture, would have changed at least a little. Vicente's big misunderstanding by projecting his own beauty and dignity on the disgusting indignity of the furious fascist petit bourgeois in Europe would have been avoided. But that game called destiny had it so that we met very late, in the last hour. For me it was the discovery of an "alter ego," though certainly in greater proportions. A mirror, though, in which the same ingredients made up an entirely different structure. The same Wittgenstein and the same Heidegger, the same Rilke and the same Kafka, the same thirst and the same search. Yet everything different. I stopped everything. I fought him almost daily. Him and his writings. His vision of Christianity. Fichte and Hegel, whom he had provoked in me and whom he gave me. His Nietzsche, my third one. German Romanticism, seen now not from within, which was my vision, but from outside: his vision. I learned, I changed in a way difficult to say, I opened myself up to him. But I always felt a barrier made of tragic misunderstandings—all, I believe, coming from him. I tried to break it. I started succeeding. Death intervened. But he goes on challenging all I do. Under the impact of his presence and absence I wrote a series of articles and essays, in part collected under the title *Da religiosidade* (On religiosity), published by Comissão Estadual de Cultura, São Paulo.

(6) *Third productive phase.* I rewrote *A história do diabo* in Portuguese to reply to Guimarães Rosa and Vincente Ferreira da Silva. It was published by Livraria Martins Editora and received without echo. And I began to be attacked by the so-called left, wrongly so called, I think. On the other hand, my (not entirely negligible) influence on certain segments of Brazilian culture grew, mostly on the Paulista new generation. I gave numerous lectures and courses. I became conscious that my problem, language, was too vast, at the stage of my development, to be attacked "in toto." I had to discipline myself and refrain myself. I returned to logic, to those aspects of the Vienna Circle I had suppressed, to Quine, Chomsky, and epistemology. For a time, the philosophy of science occupied a large part of my horizon, certainly in part owing to Vincente with his apocalyptic vision of technology, but in part, too, as catharsis. I returned to Kant, always. Science as language—and how avoid Kant in that context? This type of interest led me to Leonidas Hegenberg,[5] who taught me not only logic, but even more the virtue of refrainment. The virtue of an intellect that does not think itself omnipotent but knows how to relegate the transintellectual to the horizon, ever present, but far off.

I then wrote "A filosofia da linguagem" (The philosophy of language), to be published by ITA, São José dos Campos,[6] and my essay "Da dúvida" (On doubt), which to me is a decisive stage on my future way. And I met Milton Vargas.[7] Friendship is, I believe, a result of an interplay between points of contact and friction. His mobile spirit, his vast culture, his way of violently defending unsustainable positions that he himself does not sustain, his deep veracity, are for me like a constant whipping that propels me. If I may make a prophecy: much will be said about him in the history of Brazilian culture. Anyhow, I would not do what I do without him.

For example, I doubt that I would have taken an interest in the theory of communications without him. But I did, and it began to absorb me. It opened up an entirely new avenue of access to the problem of language. I relearned everything. Not only French and Italian literature, and not only Bense.[8] I reread the books I had read. And I took up contact with concrete poetry. Certainly, one reason for this was Guimarães Rosa. But another, equally potent, was that curious marriage between sciences and religion which is Milton Vargas.

Although absorbed by the new field of interest, I cannot say I was sat-

isfied in it. I felt a stranger in the desert land of formulas, of computations, and of the excessively reasonable. I felt admiration, but also a deep
divergence, for engineers in poetry such as Haroldo de Campos.[9] I had
lost myself. In order to find myself again, I wrote "Até a terceira e quarta
geração" (Unto the third and fourth generation), influenced by Foucault,
but still and ever looking for a way out into nonlanguage within the
loops of the tissue of language. The manuscript is held by Miguel Reale.[10]
This is a symptom: in him combine, who knows how, in a way for me in-
comprehensibly admirable, spiritual mobility and decisive action. I owe
him much: a large part of my integration into Brazilian culture. And a
new vision of ethics, though I have not yet succeeded in embodying it
within my thinking. How to have values without religiosity? Reale has
them, and I cannot understand this. Reale may be part of my future more
than my present.

I went on writing much during that phase. I published and gave lectures and lessons. But, looking back on it, I do not feel satisfied.

(7) *Present phase.* The theory of communication implies the theory of
decision and the theory of games. And the theory of games implies art in
a new sense. This discovery was like a rupture of dams. Suddenly, I saw a
whole new field of action extending before me: the field of critique and
translation between games; the field of freedom. In fact, critique as transcendence of games, that is, critique as metalanguage. The problem thus
stated made the odd pieces of my previous phases fall into a pattern that,
with discipline and imagination, might form a whole in the future.

What is a religious motive if not the one that makes me know that I
play? The motive of critique is religiosity. I went over, fully conscious of
what I was doing, to critique as translation and as philosophy. "Critique,"
as always, in a Kantian sense, but "critique" also in the etymological sense
of *kriein, kriterion, krisis.* I began to understand, and to experience, my
surroundings as a set of games, as conventional and gratuitous, but also
as veiling and revealing of what is unconventional and unplayable. As
channels that cross, recross, and establish passing and reversible hierarchies. But as systems, too, that point not merely at each other, but outside themselves. In short, as languages that not only talk, but say. They
say what Eco called "the absent structure."

To see the world as a set of games, and to see it as a player who knows
he is playing, is to see aesthetically. But this is not Kierkegaardian aesthetics, as it reveals not only the fortuitous and absurd, but also the meaningful. And it is not enough to see, the world must be experienced. It must

be experienced that art is better than truth. That theory of translation is epistemology. That, as Camus knew, the actor, being a translator, is the one who knows. In other words, it must be experienced that everything is art, language, including that utmost game: *ars moriendi*. It must be translated between games, including the game of death. And this is where, again and surprisingly, rite reappears. Rite as the repertoire of the game of death. The appeal of Judaism as a religion and as religiosity, an appeal too definite to be followed at the hour of the inebriating discovery of games.

I threw myself into games. In the sense of the Magister Ludi of Hermann Hesse. "Homo ludens" became to me synonymous with "the New Man" in Marx, the "Superman" in Nietzsche. The man who plays not to win but to play, fortuitously, and in this absurdity offers himself up to what is no game. Commitment, being fortuitous, remains available. And, as a matter of course, I threw myself into the game of plastic arts, because they are more clearly games than science, ideologies, or the diachronic arts such as music and literature. I took up the Brazilian plastic arts in their major and minor manifestations, their tendencies and their inner conflicts. But I took them up as a player, that is, as one who takes them for pretexts. They are pieces in my translation game, of a critique that tries to give them meaning. They are open to me. They are my way to play my *ars moriendi*. Of course, this hierarchy may be inverted. To them, I play for them. And in the infinite regression of these invertible hierarchies lies the great question mark, which recedes as translation advances. The work I am doing now is dedicated to it: *Reflexões sobre a traduzibilidade* (Reflections on translatabilty). Is this dedication a new calling, or is it still the old one? Is the New Man, after all, still the same agony of the old one? Questions have meaning only if there is no answer to them.

(8) *Summary.* I am disoriented. In part, because I have been dramatically uprooted at a critical and vulnerable age. In part, because I lost faith in the grounding set of values, which in my case were Marxist and which are no less fundamental for my having been an inauthentic Marxist, but at bottom, because man is a disoriented being. I tried all my life to find myself in order to commit myself, and I am still trying; that is, I philosophized all my life, and still philosophize. The two perils of definite perdition are for me empty oratory on the one hand (represented by the excesses of easy religiosity and easy mysticism), and scholarly erudition on the other hand (represented by the sterility of academic philosophy and snobbery). I am a writer by calling, and therefore, by calling, language is my field of search. Although I cannot say what "calling" means, I know

what it means. Language offers itself to me as a game, and I try to find its meaning. I did not find it, and I cannot even imagine or have a presentiment of finding it. It would be the end of the game.

By the way, and this by accident, I produce. I publish, that is, I try to change the world in which I find myself. I do it with many doubts and many reservations. At the same time, this publishing is my only justification to the others and to myself. And it is my only hope of not having lived in vain. Of having transmitted to others, as disoriented as myself, my search and the example of my failings. And, perhaps, some vague horizons as well. By this, I have perhaps contributed, though certainly in a problematic way, to my Brazilian surroundings. And who knows, this production of mine may paradoxically be a way to orient myself in others.

I am not dead yet and this summary is therefore no conclusion. I still want to live to see what my attempt at translation comes to. And also a whole set of other curiosities. And I still feel within me much to be articulated. An insistent murmur of language not yet ripened in that sweet, heavy, and mysterious fruit called "the word." Who knows? I did not even begin to live, and to philosophize, and all I just wrote is no more than an introduction and preface to the theme: in search of meaning.

(1969)

Notes by the Editor

1. Brazilian scholar, philosopher, and educator.

2. The Marburg School was named after the German town of Marburg. At its university, philosophers such as Hermann Cohen and Ernst Cassirer reinterpreted Immanuel Kant in a more radical and logistical manner. This was a very influential philosophical movement in the early twentieth century.

3. A character from Guimarães Rosa's novel *Grande Sertão: veredas* (The big Sertão: pathways).

4. Vicente Ferreira da Silva (1916–63), one of the most original Brazilian thinkers, taught that Western thinking is rooted in a deep hatred of nature. He was influenced by Heidegger, and was a close friend of Vilém Flusser during the last two years of his life.

5. Leonidas Hegenberg, professor of logic, cofounder of the Brazilian Society of Logic (Sociedade Brasileira de Lógica) in São Paulo, introduced Flusser to formal logic.

6. "A filosofia da linguagem" was never published, although ITA had planned to do so.

7. Milton Vargas was born around 1915 in Rio de Janeiro. Engineer of

the mechanics of soil, historian of science and technology, professor at the University of São Paulo, he was Vilém Flusser's best friend.

8. Max Bense (1910–90) was a German philosopher, mathematician, and theorist of science, semiotics, and aesthetics. In the 1950s, he first experimented with computer-generated poetry: "mathematically existentialist" visual and concrete poetry.

9. Haroldo de Campos, born in 1929, poet and literary critic, became famous as the main creator of Brazilian concretist poetry in the 1950s.

10. Miguel Reale, born in 1910 in the interior of the state of São Paulo, is a professor of law. Reale is one of the authors of the Brazilian constitution, and the founder of the Brazilian Institute of Philosophy (Instituto Brasileiro de Filosofia). He appointed Vilém Flusser a member of the institute. The manuscript of "Até a terceira e quarta geração" was given to him for safe-keeping, because it was never published. Flusser wrote the text in 1965 and revised it again in 1970 for a planned publication by Editoria Universitária that never happened. Later on, in the 1990s, Stefan Bollmann scheduled a German-language publication as volume 12 of the *Schriften*. However, only the first five volumes were published.

Selected Bibliography

Works by Vilém Flusser

In English

1972

"Bottle." *Main Currents in Modern Thought* 28(4).

1973

"Line and Surface." *Main Currents in Modern Thought* 29(3).

1977

"Two Approaches to the Phenomenon: Television." In *The New Television: A Public/Private Art,* ed. Douglas Davis and Allison Simmons. Cambridge and London: MIT Press.

1984

Towards a Philosophy of Photography. Ed. Derek Bennett. Göttingen: European Photography. Republished, with an Introduction by Hubertus von Amelunxen, by Reaktion Books, London, 2000.

1985

"Introduction." In Joan Fontcuberta, *Herbarium.* Göttingen: European Photography.

1986

"Comments on Gottfried Jäger's 'Generative Photography': A Systematic, Constructive Approach." *Leonardo* 19(4).

"The Photograph as Post-Industrial Object: An Essay on the Ontological Standing of Photography." *Leonardo* 19(4).

1986–92

"Curies' Children." Under this title, Flusser published a column in *Artforum*: 25(1) (1986); 26(1–2) (1987); 26(7, 8, 10), 27(2, 4) (1988); 27(7) (1989); 28(7, 9), 29(2, 4) (1990); 29(6, 9), 30(3) (1991); 30(7, 10) (1992).

1987

"On Edmund Husserl." Ed. Lewis Weiner. *Review of the Society for the History of Czechoslovak Jews* 1.

1989

"Environment: On Future Architecture." *Artforum* 27(8).

"Wondering about Science." *Artforum* 27(3).

1991

"Ecological and Anthropological Feedback between Tools and Their Users: Ethics in Industrial Design?" *Industrieel ontwerpen* 3.

"Habit: The True Aesthetic Criterium *[sic]*." *European Photography: The International Art Magazine for Contemporary Photography and New Media* 45. Ed. Andreas Müller-Pohle. Trans. Eleanor Mann.

"What Is the Literal Meaning of 'Photography'?" *European Photography: The International Art Magazine for Contemporary Photography and New Media* 47.

1992

The Philosopher of Photography. Video documentation of an interview with Flusser by Miklós Peternák. 45 min.

"Vilém Flusser Issue." *European Photography: The International Art Magazine for Contemporary Photography and New Media* 50. Ed. Andreas Müller-Pohle. Trans. Dorothy Bell.

1993

"Change of Paradigms," "Orders of Magnitude and Humanism," and "The Future of Writing." *Yale Journal of Criticism* 6(2). Ed. Esther Da Costa Meyer et al. Trans. Elizabeth Wilson and Andreas Ströhl.

1994

"To Photograph Is to Define." *European Photography: The International Art Magazine for Contemporary Photography and New Media* 55.

1997

"The Glory That Touches the Stars," "Introduction," and "Desks." *Wéber Studies: An Interdisciplinary Humanities Journal* 14. Ed. Michael Wutz. Trans. Elizabeth Wilson and Andreas Ströhl.

1999

The Shape of Things. Introd. Martin Pawley. London: Reaktion Books.

2000

From Subject to Project: Becoming Human. London: Free Association Books.
Towards a Philosophy of Photography. Introd. Hubertus von Amelunxen. London: Reaktion Books.

In Portuguese, French, or German

1963

Lingua e realidade. São Paulo: Herder.

1965

A história do diabo. São Paulo: Livraria Martins Editoria.

1967

Da religiosidade. São Paulo: Comissão Estadual de Cultura.

1972

La Force du quotidien. Paris: Mame.

1974

Le Monde codifié. Paris: Institut de l'Environnement.

1978

Natural:mente. São Paulo: Duas Cidades.

1983

Für eine Philosophie der Fotografie. Göttingen: European Photography.
Pós-história: Vinte instantâneos e um modo de usar. São Paulo: Duas Cidades.

1985

Ins Universum der technischen Bilder. Göttingen: European Photography.

1986

Schlagworte—Schlagbilder. Ein Gespräch mit Vilém Flusser. Video documentation by Harun Farocki. 13 min. Cologne: WDR.

1987

Die Schrift: Hat Schreiben Zukunft? Göttingen: European Photography. Republished: Frankfurt am Main: Fischer Taschenbuch Verlag, 1992.
With Louis Bec. *Vampyroteuthis infernalis: Eine Abhandlung samt Befund des Institut Scientifique de Recherche Paranaturaliste.* Göttingen: Immatrix Publications.

1988

Krise der Linearität. Bern: Benteli.

1989

Angenommen: Eine Szenenfolge. Göttingen: Immatrix Publications.

1990

Nachgeschichten: Essays, Vorträge, Glossen. Ed. Volker Rapsch. Düsseldorf: Bollmann.

1991

Die Informationsgesellschaft: Phantom oder Realität? Ed. Thomas Knöfel and Klaus Sander. An audio CD documentation of Flusser's lecture at the conference CULTEC–Culture and Technology in the Twenty-first Century in Essen. November 23. 45 min. Cologne: supposé.
Gesten: Versuch einer Phänomenologie. Düsseldorf and Bensheim: Bollmann.

1992

Bodenlos: Eine philosophische Autobiographie. Bensheim and Düsseldorf: Bollmann.
Ende der Geschichte, Ende der Stadt? Vienna: Pinkus.
Virtuelle Räume: Simultane Welten. Ed. Sabine Kraft. Special issue on Flusser by *ARCH+: Zeitschrift für Architektur und Städtebau* 111.

1993

Die Geschichte des Teufels. Ed. Andreas Müller-Pohle. Göttingen: European
Photography.

Dinge und Undinge: Phänomenologische Skizzen. Munich: Hanser.

Vom Stand der Dinge: Eine kleine Philosophie des Design. Ed. Fabian Wurm.
Göttingen: Steidl.

Lob der Oberflächlichkeit: Für eine Phänomenologie der Medien, Schriften 1.
Ed. Stefan Bollmann. Bensheim and Düsseldorf: Bollmann.

Nachgeschichte: Eine korrigierte Geschichtsschreibung, Schriften 2. Ed. Stefan
Bollmann and Edith Flusser. Bensheim and Düsseldorf: Bollmann.

1994

*Brasilien oder die Suche nach dem neuen Menschen: Für eine Phänomenologie
der Unterentwicklung, Schriften 5.* Ed. Stefan Bollmann and Edith
Flusser. Mannheim: Bollmann.

Vom Subjekt zum Projekt: Menschwerdung, Schriften 3. Ed. Stefan Bollmann.
Bensheim and Düsseldorf: Bollmann.

Vilém Flussers Fluß. A video documentation shot in August 1991 by Michael
Bielicky. 45 min. Cologne: 235 Media.

Von der Freiheit des Migranten: Einsprüche gegen den Nationalismus. Ed.
Stefan Bollmann. Bensheim: Bollmann.

1995

*Die Revolution der Bilder: Der Flusser-Reader zu Kommunikation, Medien
und Design.* Ed. Stefan Bollmann. Mannheim: Bollmann.

Jude sein: Essays, Briefe, Fiktionen. Ed. Stefan Bollmann and Edith Flusser.
Mannheim: Bollmann.

1996

Kommunikologie, Schriften 4. Ed. Vera Eckstein and Stefan Bollmann.
Mannheim: Bollmann.

Zwiegespräche: Interviews 1967–1991. Ed. Klaus Sander. Göttingen:
European Photography.

1997

Bilderbuch. Ed. Andreas Müller-Pohle. Göttingen: European Photography.

Medienkultur. Ed. Stefan Bollmann. Frankfurt am Main: Fischer Verlag.

1998

Ficções filosoficas. Ed. Milton Vargas and Maria Lília Leão. São Paulo: EDUSP.

Standpunkte: Texte zur Fotografie. Ed. Andreas Müller-Pohle. Göttingen: European Photography.

1999

A dúvida. Ed. Dilmo Milheiros. Rio de Janeiro: Relume Dumará.

Heimat und Heimatlosigkeit. Audio CD. Cologne: supposé.

2000

Briefe an Alex Bloch. Ed. Edith Flusser and Klaus Sander. Göttingen: European Photography.

Vogelflüge. German translation of *Natural:mente.* Munich: Hanser.

Secondary Literature

In English

Goldberg, Vicki. 1985. "Photography Takes Over: Two Works Probe the Chilling Attraction of the Camera." *American Photographer* (December): 34–36.

Ströhl, Andreas. 1996. "Flusser and Beyond." In *Orbis Fictus: New Media in Contemporary Arts,* Catalog of the Second Annual Exhibition of the Soros Center for Contemporary Arts–Prague. Trans. David Vaugh. 133–40.

Wilson, Elizabeth, and Andreas Ströhl. 1993. "Vilém Flusser." *Yale Journal of Criticism* 6(2): 285–88.

———. 1997. "On the Philosopher Vilém Flusser." *Wéber Studies: An Interdisciplinary Humanities Journal* 14(1): 29–31.

In German

Druckrey, Timothy. 2001. *Second International Flusser Lecture. Medien, Gedächtnis, Moderne.* Ed. Vilém Flusser Archiv an der Kunsthochschule für Medien Köln. Cologne: Walther König.

Farocki, Harun. 1986. "Das Universum ist leer: Zu Vilém Flussers Philosophie der technischen Bilder." *Der Falter* 12.

———. 2001. *Third International Flusser Lecture. Bilderschatz.* Ed. Vilém Flusser Archive an der Kunsthochschule für Medien Köln. Cologne: Walther König.

Imdahl, Georg. 1994. "Unser elektronisches Dorf soll schöner werden: Vilém

Flusser fordert eine Revolutionierung der menschlichen Denkstruktur." *Süddeutsche Zeitung,* March 15, 11.

Jäger, Gottfried, ed. 2001. *Fotografie denken. Über Vilém Flussers Philosophie der Medienmoderne.* Bielefeld: Kerber.

Kamper, Dietmar. 2000. *First International Flusser Lecture. Körper-Abstraktionen. Das anthropologische Viereck von Raum, Fläche, Linie und Punkt.* Ed. Vilém Flusser Archiv an der Kunsthochschule für Medien Köln. Cologne: Walther König.

Knöfel, Thomas. 1994. "Vilém Flusser: Die Geschichte des Teufels." *manuskripte* 124: 95–101.

———. 1994. "Vom Überfließen der Schrift zum Fließen der Bilder." *Ästhetik und Kommunikation* 84: 93–96.

Lovink, Geert. 1993. "Mediatheory Is Here to Go: Ein Kommentar zu Mark Terkessidis." *Symptome* 11: 45–46.

Lucht, Frank. 1993. "Eine neue Einbildungskraft? Über Vilém Flusser." *Merkur: Deutsche Zeitschrift für europäisches Denken* 47(9–10) (special issue *Medien. Neu? Über Macht, Ästhetik, Fernsehen,* ed. Karl Heinz Bohrer and Kurt Scheel): 893–97.

Moles, Abraham. 1988. "Zur Philosophiefiktion bei Vilém Flusser." *kultuRRevolution* 17–18: 109–12.

Müller, Hans-Joachim. 1991. "Der Philosoph als fröhlicher Wissenschaftler: Ein Portrait des unakademischen Denkers Vilém Flusser." *Die Zeit,* March 15, 71.

Neswald, Elizabeth. 1998. *Medien-Theologie: Das Werk Vilém Flussers.* Cologne, Weimar, and Vienna, Böhlau.

Rapsch, Volker, ed. 1990. *überflusser: Die Fest-schrift zum 70. von Vilém Flusser.* Düsseldorf: Bollmann.

Rötzer, Florian, ed. 1992. "Beiträge zum Tode von Vilém Flusser." *Kunst-forum International: Die aktuelle Zeitschrift für alle Bereiche der Bildenden Kunst* 117: 70–110.

Schmidt-Klingenberg, Michael. 1989. "'Die Macht geht auf blöde Apparate über': Über den Computer-Philosophen Vilém Flusser." *Der Spiegel* 19: 133–38.

Strasser, Peter. 1992. "Und der Himmel über uns: Flussers Auschwitz und Hoffnung." *manuskripte* 117: 111–13.

Ströhl, Andreas. 1994. "Golem, Robot, Kinetismus: Prag hat eine alte Leidenschaft wiederentdeckt: die Beschäftigung mit neuen Medien." *GI Prisma: Aus der Arbeit des Goethe-Instituts* 2: 40–47.

———. 1996. "Technische Apriori a posteriori: Kommunikationsphilosophie als Medienkunst, Technikgeschichte als Medientheorie." In *The Thing Between: Internationales Kunstprojekt,* ed. Roland Boden and Ulrike Gärtner. Catalog of an exhibition in the Technische Sammlungen Dresden, September 20–30: 14–19.

———. 2000. "Hommage an Vilém Flusser." *Bohemia. Zeitschrift für Geschichte und Kultur der böhmischen Länder. A Journal of History and Civilisation in East Central Europe* 41(1): 102–12.

———, ed. 2001. "Vilém Flusser" Special issue of *Der Schnitt, Das Filmmagazin,* 24 (November): 6–29.

Ströhl, Andreas, and Christoph Bartmann. 1992. "Heimkehr nach Prag: Zum Tod des Philosophen Vilém Flusser." *GI Prisma: Aus der Arbeit des Goethe-Instituts* 1: 88–91.

Terkessidis, Mark. 1993. "Medienphilophobie." *Symptome* 11: 38–45.

Theismann, Anja, and Klaus Sander. 1995. *Erfahrung und Unschuld.* A video documentation of the Flusser-Symposium at the steirischer herbst '94. 32 min.

Zill, Rüdiger. 1993. "Mit dem Hebel philosophieren: Die Bedingung der Möglichkeit der Erkenntnis der Suppe?" *die tageszeitung,* August 4.

English Texts by Flusser on the Internet

"The Technical Image" (translation of "Das technische Bild"): *http://fotoplus.com/flusser/.htm*

"Two Approaches to the Phenomenon, Television": *http://www.artcontext.org/crit/scrapbook/Flusser.html*

Vilém Flusser interviewed by Miklós Peternák: *http://www.c3.hu/events/97/flusser/participantstext/miklos-interview.html*

Web Sites

General Flusser Web Sites

http://equivalence.com/labor/glossary.htm
A very helpful glossary of the English translation of terms often used by Flusser.

http://www.hydra.umn.edu/flusser/
Informative, although slightly outdated, Flusser site—in German.

http://fotoplus.com/flusser
Comprehensive Web site on Flusser emphasizing Brazilian aspects—in Portuguese.

http://www.fh-fulda.de/iceus/flusser/Fussler1.htm
Nice-looking Web site with information—in English—on Flusser's biography and *Communicology.*

http://www.flusser.de/intro.htm
Beautiful, extensive Flusser Web site—in German.

http://www.khm.de/flusser/archiv.html
http://www.khm.de/flusser/logo.htm
Web sites of the Flusser Archives in Cologne.

http://www.c3.hu/events/97/flusser/englishinfosheet.html
English-language information on the 1997 Budapest Flusser Symposium (and earlier ones).

http://www.heise.de/tp/english/pop/event_1/4056/1.html
Report from the 1997 Flusser Symposium in Budapest—in English.

Introductions to Flusser

http://www.altx.com/ebr/w%28ebr%29/essays/flusser.html and *http://weberstudies.weber.edu/archive/Vol.%2014.1/14.1Wilson.htm*
English introduction to Flusser by Wilson/Ströhl published in *Wéber Studies.*

http://home.snafu.de/klinger/fluss.htm
An introduction in German.

http://home.snafu.de/~klinger/flusser1.htm
An introduction to Flusser's central ideas—in German.

http://netzspannung.org/journal/issue0/mediachange/index.xml?lang=en
English language article by Nils Röller on the Flusser Archives in Cologne.

http://www.schnitt.com/site/index/htm
Flusser in relation to film theory—in German.

http://www.stud.uni-hamburg.de/users/ben/flusser.html
A student's précis of Flusser's *Communicology* in German.

Bibliographies

http://www.fotoplus.com/fpg/gbib01.htm
Best online bibliography available.

http://equivalence.com/labor/flusser.htm
Flusser's books published by European Photography.

http://www.txt.de/bollmann/flusser/schrift.htm
Flusser's books published by Bollmann Verlag.

http://www.emaf.de/1994/flusse_e.html
English-language information on Michael Bielicky's video *Vilém Flussers Fluß.*

Link Lists to Flusser

http://home.snafu.de/~klinger/flusslinks.htm
"Flusser Surfboard"—excellent links list (to mostly German sites).

http://info.uibk.ac.at/c/c6/c601/edv/medien/projekte/huetter/flusser2/ index.html
A good link list—although not quite up to date, and in German.

Copyright and Original Publication Information

and was republished in Flusser, *Lob der Oberflächlichkeit*. Copyright European Photography; reprinted by permission of Andreas Müller-Pohle, www.equivalence.com.

"Habit: The True Aesthetic Criterion" was originally published in German and English as *Gewohnheit als ästhetisches Kriterium schlechthin*, in *European Photography* 45, ed. Andreas Müller-Pohle, trans. Eleanor Mann (January/February/March 1991). Copyright European Photography; reprinted by permission of Andreas Müller-Pohle, www.equivalence.com.

"Betrayal" was written in English and was formerly unpublished. Copyright Edith Flusser.

"The Future of Writing" was originally written in English in 1983–84 and published in the *Yale Journal of Criticism* 6(2), ed. Esther Da Costa Meyer et al. (fall 1993). Copyright Edith Flusser.

"Images in the New Media" was originally titled "Bilder in den neuen Medien" and was the manuscript of a lecture at the Museum of Design in Basel on May 12, 1989. It was published in 1993 in Flusser, *Lob der Oberflächlichkeit*. Copyright Edith Flusser.

"On the Crisis of Our Models" was written in English in the 1980s and was formerly unpublished. Copyright Edith Flusser.

"Change of Paradigms" was originally titled "Paradigmenwechsel" and was the manuscript of Flusser's last lecture, at the Goethe-Institut Prague on November 25, 1991. It was published in German in Andreas Steffens, ed., *Nach der Postmoderne: Ein Zeitmitschrift-Buch mit philosophischen Texten zur Gegenwart* (Düsseldorf and Bensheim: Bollmann, 1992), and in Roland Boden and Ulrike Gärtner, eds., *The Thing Between: Internationales Kunstprojekt*, catalog of an exhibition at Technische Sammlungen Dresden, September 20–30, 1996. This was also published in English in the *Yale Journal of Criticism* 6(2) (fall 1993). Copyright Edith Flusser.

"Taking Up Residence in Homelessness" was originally titled "Wohnung beziehen in der Heimatlosigkeit: Heimat und Heimatlosigkeit—Wohnung und Gewohnheit" and was the manuscript of a lecture at the Second International Kornhaus-Seminar on the topic "Home and Homelessness" in Weiler im Allgäu. It was written in 1984 or 1985 and first published in Christa Dericum and Philipp Wambolt, eds., *Heimat und Heimatlosigkeit* (Berlin: Karin Kramer, 1987), and was republished in

Vilém Flusser, *Bodenlos: Eine philosophische Autobiographie* (Düsseldorf and Bensheim: Bollmann, 1992). Copyright Edith Flusser.

"Exile and Creativity" was originally published as "Exil und Kreativität," in *Spuren*, no. 9 (December1984–January 1985). It was republished in Vilém Flusser, *Von der Freiheit des Migranten: Einsprüche gegen den Nationalismus*, ed. Stefan Bollmann (Bensheim: Bollmann, 1994). Copyright Edith Flusser.

"A New Imagination" was originally published as "Eine neue Einbildungskraft," in Volker Bohn, ed., *Bildlichkeit: Internationale Beiträge zur Poetik* (Frankfurt am Main: Suhrkamp, 1990). The English translation published here follows a slightly shortened version of the essay that was republished in Vilém Flusser, *Die Revolution der Bilder: Der Flusser-Reader zu Kommunikation, Medien und Design*, ed. Stefan Bollmann (Mannheim: Bollmann, 1995). Copyright Edith Flusser.

"Mythical, Historical, and Posthistorical Existence" was originally titled "Mythisches, geschichtliches und nachgeschichtliches Dasein: Macumba, Kirche und Technokratie" and was the manuscript of a lecture at the University of St. Gallen on December 1, 1981. It was published in Vilém Flusser, *Nachgeschichte: Eine korrigierte Geschichtsschreibung, Schriften* 2, ed. Stefan Bollmann (Bensheim and Düsseldorf: Bollmann, 1993). Copyright Edith Flusser.

"Photography and History" was originally titled "Fotografie und Geschichte" and was the manuscript of a lecture delivered at the colloquium on Document and Invention at the Obere Galerie im Haus am Lützowplatz, Berlin, on May 24, 1989. It was published as "Im Stausee der Bilder: Fotografie und Geschichte" (In the reservoir of images: Photography and history) in Jörg Boström, ed., *Dokument und Erfindung: Fotografien aus der Bundesrepublik Deutschland 1945 bis heute* (Berlin: edition q, 1989). It was republished in Vilém Flusser, *Standpunkte: Texte zur Fotografie*, ed. Andreas Müller-Pohle (Göttingen: European Photography, 1998). Copyright European Photography; reprinted by permission of Andreas Müller-Pohle, www.equivalence.com.

"A Historiography Revised" was originally titled "Eine korrigierte Geschichtsschreibung" and was written no later than 1982 (probably earlier). It was published in 1993 in Flusser, *Nachgeschichte*. Copyright Edith Flusser.

"The Vanity of History" was originally published as "Da futilidade da história," in *O Estado de São Paulo* (July 26, 1969). It was republished in German as "Die Nichtigkeit der Geschichte," in Flusser, *Nachgeschichte.* Copyright Edith Flusser.

"On the End of History" was originally titled "Vom Ende der Geschichte" and was a variation of a manuscript of a lecture given at the Vienna City Hall on March 13, 1991. It was first published in *Ende der Geschichte, Ende der Stadt?* (Vienna: Pinkus, 1992) and was republished in Flusser, *Nachgeschichte.* Copyright Edith Flusser.

A shorter version of "Waiting for Kafka" was originally published as "Esperando por Kafka," in *Cavalo Azul* (April–June 1963). The extended version that appears here was first published in Vilém Flusser, *Da religiosidade* (São Paulo: Comissão Estadual de Cultura, 1967), and later published in German as "Warten auf Kafka," in Vilém Flusser, *Jude sein: Essays, Briefe, Fiktionen,* ed. Stefan Bollmann and Edith Flusser (Mannheim: Bollmann, 1995). Copyright Edith Flusser.

"Orders of Magnitude and Humanism" was written in 1987 and originally published as "Größenordnung und Humanismus," in Flusser, *Nachgeschichte.* The English translation was first published in the *Yale Journal of Criticism* 6(2) (fall 1993). Copyright Edith Flusser.

"Celebrating" was originally published as "Feiern," chapter 18 of Vilém Flusser, *Ins Universum der technischen Bilder* (Göttingen: European Photography, 1985). Copyright European Photography; reprinted by permission of Andreas Müller-Pohle, www.equivalence.com.

"Designing Cities" was written in 1988 and originally published as "Städte entwerfen," in Vilém Flusser, *Vom Subjekt zum Projekt: Menschwerdung, Schriften* 3, ed. Stefan Bollmann (Bensheim and Düsseldorf: Bollmann, 1994). The English translation that appears here follows a shortened version published in Flusser, *Die Revolution der Bilder.* Copyright Edith Flusser.

"Humanizations" was written in 1990 and originally published as "Menschwerdungen," in Flusser, *Vom Subjekt zum Projekt,* in 1994. Copyright Edith Flusser.

"Essays" was originally published in Portuguese as "Ensaio," in *O Estado de São Paulo* (August 19, 1967). Copyright Edith Flusser.

"In Search of Meaning (Philosophical Self-portrait)" was originally written in English; there are also versions in Portuguese ("Em procura do sentido") and German ("Auf der Suche nach Bedeutung"). The Portuguese and the English versions were written in October–November 1969 in São Paulo; the Portuguese version was published under the title "Em busca do significado" in Stanislaus Ladusans, *Rumos da filosofia atual no Brasil em auto-retratos* (São Paulo: Edições Loyola, 1976), 493–506. Copyright Edith Flusser.

The estate of Vilém Flusser has been housed at the Academy of Media Arts Cologne since October 1998. Edith Flusser generously entrusted the estate to the Academy, where the contents are preserved and maintained.

The archive contains approximately 2,500 manuscripts of Flusser's publications as well as numerous correspondences. These texts are predominantly in German but also in Portuguese, French, and English. They can be accessed through a system of some 180 specific keywords—from Africa, cyberspace, and fuzzy logic to human relationships, Western civilization, and ZNS.

This multilingual and heterogeneous work is complemented by Flusser's own traveling library; by numerous audio and visual documents containing interviews, conversations, and lectures; by an ever-increasing body of secondary literature; and by a growing volume of M.A. and Ph.D. dissertations.

At present the archive is open only on Tuesdays and Thursdays. In the future it should be possible to access the archive via the Internet.

In encouraging use of the archive for current research purposes, we would also like to ask for assistance in continuing to supplement its contents. The donation of copies of relevant M.A. and Ph.D. dissertations and other publications would be appreciated.

Vilém Flusser Archiv
Academy of Media Arts Cologne
Peter-Welter-Platz 2
D-50676 Cologne
Germany
E-mail: flusser@khm.de

Index

Vilém Flusser was born in Prague in 1920. In 1940, he and his wife escaped from the Nazi occupation of Prague to Brazil, and he became a professor of philosophy at the University of São Paulo. He left Brazil in 1972 to settle in France, where he elaborated his theories on codes and cultural techniques, lecturing and writing on language, communication, and the media, but also on simple objects of everyday life. His many books include *Towards a Philosophy of Photography* and *The Shape of Things: A Philosophy of Design*. During the 1980s, he became famous in Europe for his startling analyses and predictions. He died in 1991.

Andreas Ströhl is the director of the film department of the Goethe-Institut Inter Nationes in Munich. He previously worked at the Goethe-Institut Prague, where he organized several annual symposia on Vilém Flusser.

Erik Eisel received his Ph.D. in comparative literature from the University of California, Los Angeles. He currently works for a software technology company in Southern California.